Lecture Notes in Computer

Commenced Publication in 1973
Founding and Former Series Editors:
Gerhard Goos, Juris Hartmanis, and Jan van

Danny Weyns   Marie-Pierre Gleizes (Eds.)

Agent-Oriented Software Engineering XI

11th International Workshop, AOSE 2010
Toronto, Canada, May 10-11, 2010
Revised Selected Papers

 Springer

Volume Editors

Danny Weyns
Linnæus University
School of Computer Science, Physics and Mathematics
Hus B 3009, 35195 Växjö, Sweden
E-mail: danny.weyns@lnu.se

Marie-Pierre Gleizes
Université Paul Sabatier
Institut de Recherche en Informatique de Toulouse
118 Route de Narbonne, 31062 Toulouse Cedex 9, France
E-mail: marie-pierre.gleizes@irit.fr

ISSN 0302-9743   e-ISSN 1611-3349
ISBN 978-3-642-22635-9   e-ISBN 978-3-642-22636-6
DOI 10.1007/978-3-642-22636-6
Springer Heidelberg Dordrecht London New York

Library of Congress Control Number: 2011937819

CR Subject Classification (1998): D.2, I.2.11, F.3, D.1, C.2.4, D.3

LNCS Sublibrary: SL 2 – Programming and Software Engineering

Typesetting: Camera-ready by author, data conversion by Scientific Publishing Services, Chennai, India

Printed on acid-free paper

Springer is part of Springer Science+Business Media (www.springer.com)

Preface

Since the mid-1980s, software agents and multi-agent systems have grown into a very active area of research and also commercial development activity. One of the limiting factors in industry take-up of agent technology, however, is the lack of adequate software engineering support and knowledge in this area. The Agent-Oriented Software Engineering (AOSE) workshop is focused on this problem and provides a forum for those who study the synergies between software engineering and agent research.

The concept of an agent as an autonomous system, capable of interacting with other agents in order to satisfy its design objectives, is a natural one for software designers. Just as we can understand many systems as being composed of essentially passive objects, which have state, and upon which we can perform operations, so we can understand many others as being made up of interacting, autonomous or semi-autonomous agents. This paradigm is especially suited to complex systems. Software architectures that contain many dynamically interacting components, each with their own thread of control, and engaging in complex coordination protocols, are typically orders of magnitude more complex to correctly and efficiently engineer than those that simply compute a function of some input through a single thread of control, or through a limited set of strictly synchronized threads of control. Agent-oriented modeling techniques are especially useful in such applications.

Many current and emerging real-world applications – spanning scenarios as diverse as business integration, intelligent traffic and transportation, ubiquitous computing, and sensor networks, just to mention a few examples – have exactly the above characteristics. As a consequence, agent-oriented software engineering has become an important area: both as a design-modeling means, and as an interface to platforms which include specialized infrastructure support for programming in terms of semi-autonomous interacting processes. The particular focus of this 11th edition of the workshop was on how to bridge the gap between AOSE and conventional software engineering.

The papers in this volume include both selected and thoroughly revised papers from the AOSE 2010 workshop and invited papers. The papers cover a broad range of topics related to software engineering of agent-based systems, with particular attention for integration of concepts and techniques from multi-agent systems with conventional engineering approaches on the one hand, and the integration of agent-oriented software engineering and methodologies with conventional engineering processes on the other hand. We hope that the papers of this volume stimulate further research in agent-oriented software engineering and its integration with conventional software engineering.

We are grateful to the AAMAS 2010 organizers for hosting AOSE. We thank the PC members for their critical review work. Finally, we thank the Springer staff for supporting the publication of this volume.

April 27, 2011   Danny Weyns
                                                              Marie-Pierre Gleizes

Organization

AOSE 2010 was organized in conjunction with the 9th International Conference on Autonomous Agents and Multiagent Systems (AAMAS), Toronto, Canada, May 10, 2010.

Program Co-chairs

Danny Weyns   Linnaeus University, Sweden
Marie-Pierre Gleizes   Université Paul Sabatier, France

Program Committee

Carole Bernon   University of Toulouse III, France
Juan Antonio Botia Blaya   Universidad de Murcia, Spain
Yuriy Brun   University of Washington, USA
Massimo Cossentino   ICAR-CNR, Italy
Scott DeLoach   Kansas State University, USA
Virginia Dignum   Delft University of Technology,
                                The Netherlands
Ruben Fuentes   Universidad Complutense de Madrid, Spain
Alessandro Garcia   PUC Rio, Brazil
Aditya Ghose   University of Wollongong, Australia
Holger Giese   Hasso Plattner Institute Postdam, Germany
Paolo Giorgini   University of Trento, Italy
Adriana Giret   Technical University of Valencia, Spain
Jorge J. Gómez Sanz   Universidad Complutense de Madrid, Spain
Laszlo Gulyas   AITIA International Inc., Hungary
Brian Henderson-Sellers   University of Technology, Australia
Vincent Hilaire   Belfort-Montbeliard Technology University,
                                France
Tom Holvoet   Katholieke Universiteit Leuven, Belgium
Vicente Julian Inglada   Universidad Politecnica de Valencia, Spain
Jeffrey Kephart   IBM T.J. Watson Research Center, USA
Mark Klein   Software Engineering Institute,
                                Carnegie Mellon, USA
Joao Leite   Universidade Nova de Lisboa, Portugal
Juergen Lind   Iteratec, Germany
Viviana Mascardi   Università di Genova, Italy
Philippe Mathieu   University of Lille, France
Frédéric Migeon   Paul Sabatier University, France
Simon Miles   King's College London, UK

Haralambos Mouratidis	University of East London, UK
Flavio Oquendo	Université de Bretagne-Sud, France
Michal Pechoucek	Czech Technical University in Prague, Czech Republic
Gauthier Picard	ENS Mines, Saint-Etienne, France
Anna Perini	Fondazione Bruno Kessler, Italy
Alessandro Ricci	Università di Bologna, Italy
Fariba Sadri	Imperial College, UK
Valeria Seidita	University of Palermo, Italy
Onn Shehory	Haifa University, Israel
H. Van Dyke Parunak	TechTeam Government Solutions, USA
Michael Winikoff	University of Otago, New Zealand
Eric Yu	University of Toronto, Canada
Michael Zapf	Universität Kassel, Germany

Website

http://www.irit.fr/AOSE2010/index.html

Table of Contents

Principles for Value-Sensitive Agent-Oriented Software Engineering

Christian Detweiler, Koen Hindriks, and Catholijn Jonker

Man-Machine Interaction Group, Delft University of Technology
{c.a.detweiler,k.v.hindriks,c.m.jonker}@tudelft.nl
http://mmi.tudelft.nl

Abstract. As software plays an increasingly important role in people's lives, the impact it has on their values frequently becomes apparent. Many software design methods address "soft issues", but very few address values explicitly. We present six principles that design methods should meet in order to properly deal with values. One area in which adherence to stakeholder values is important, is Agent-Oriented Software Engineering (AOSE). The Tropos AOSE method, with its concept of soft-goal, comes close to meeting our principles, but does not address values explicitly. Value-Sensitive Design is a methodology that does explicitly address value issues, but it offers little guidance in operationalizing them. We discuss a case study in which we attempt to capture values in Tropos' soft-goals after eliciting them using Value-Sensitive Design. Subsequently, we discuss to what extent Tropos adheres to our principles. Finally, we propose the introduction of values as a first-class entity in Tropos in order to meet our aims of dealing with values.

Keywords: Values, Value-Sensitive Design, Requirements Engineering, Non-Functional Requirements, Tropos.

1 Introduction

In 2009, the designers of the social networking website Facebook introduced a number of changes to the website. Due to these changes, users were no longer able to choose with whom they shared the list of people (their "friends") they were connected to on the website. Anyone logged in to Facebook could now see to whom any member of the website was connected. Further, Facebook decided users' profile pictures and the pages they "like"[1] were now publicly accessible information. That is, information users shared on the website regarding their interests would now be available to the Internet at large.

Facebook (partially) violated two values by introducing these changes. The changes violated users' value of autonomy by giving them diminished control over how their information is shared. Furthermore, the fact that certain personal information was now public impacted users' privacy. The violation of these values

---

[1] Web pages on Facebook about topics, people, places, books, etc. that people can "like".

D. Weyns and M.-P. Gleizes (Eds.): AOSE 2010, LNCS 6788, pp. 1–16, 2011.

led to user outrage and criticism by organizations such as Electronic Frontier Foundation [1]. Facebook responded that it tried to uphold the value of openness shared by their target audience [2].

This conflict of values and the way it became clear exemplifies the problem we seek to address in this paper. Designers necessarily impart social and moral values in making choices in the design of information systems [3]. That is, designers' values, such as openness, are "put into" software artifacts, albeit implicitly. Once a system has been put into use, it affects its stakeholders by supporting or hindering their values to various degrees. This ultimately affects the acceptability of information systems. Often, these values and value issues only become explicit after the software has been put into use, at which point the damage has been done. Therefore, we plead for dealing with values explicitly by treating them as separate "first-class entities" throughout the design process in software design methods.

This problem holds for software engineering in general, but is especially relevant in agent-oriented software engineering (AOSE), where we design agent-based systems. These systems are autonomous, reactive, pro-active, and have social ability [4]. Moreover, they act on stakeholders' behalf, so it is important that they meet stakeholders' requirements. Values can be considered requirements in that they are stakeholder needs that systems should uphold. The issue of meeting requirements is part of one of the areas of AOSE research identified in [5]. Weyns et al. conclude that we have to extend our research into goal-oriented design, verification and validation in order for agent-oriented software engineering to be adopted in industry. In particular, we should be able to provide guarantees with respect to stakeholder requirements.

In as far as design methodologies explicitly take values into account in the design process, it is in the form of non-functional requirements [6] or similar constructs. However, designers run the risk of leaving the impact values have on design implicit by representing values as non-functional requirements. Methods such as Quality Attribute Workshops and its notion of scenarios [7] and Attribute-Driven Design [8] deal with non-functional requirements formally, and have been applied to AOSE by Weyns [9]. However, AOSE methods typically neglect non-functional requirements. Values should be included explicitly as entities in themselves in order to be properly considered and to have an identifiable and justifiable effect on the design.

AOSE methodologies such as Tropos do focus on stakeholders' requirements (in the form of goals) throughout the design process, but do not explicitly take values into account. To address values in Tropos, they have to be represented as (soft)goals. Many important characteristics of values are lost in representing values as goals. Value-Sensitive Design [10] (VSD) provides a comprehensive framework for eliciting values, but provides little to make these values concrete. In this paper we propose to address this issue by combining elements of VSD with Tropos. This should form an AOSE approach that meets our aim of making the influence of values on the design explicit during all design phases.

This paper is organized as follows. In section 2 we briefly discuss the concept of values and discuss six value-related principles design methods should adhere to. We then discuss some common ways of dealing with such issues in requirements engineering. Then, in section 3 we discuss a case study to discover to which extent values can be dealt with in Tropos. In section 4, we analyze to what extent Tropos adheres to our principles and discuss important differences between values and the soft-goals we use to include values in Tropos, and propose introducing a value entity in Tropos. We draw conclusions and suggest directions for future work in section 5.

2   Values in Existing Software Engineering Methods

This section discusses to what extent values are already taken into account in existing software engineering approaches with an emphasis on agent-oriented software engineering methods, and in particular Tropos. Before this discussion, we present an overview of the concept of values and discuss the role of values in relation to the stakeholders and designers in the design of multi-agent systems. Finally, we provide a short introduction of the Value Sensitive Design method and discuss why VSD is not an answer in itself.

2.1   Values

The introduction describes a real world case of stakeholders' values (i.e., privacy, autonomy and openness) being hindered or supported by technology. Other values implicated in system design include human welfare, ownership and property, freedom from bias, and trust [10]. The general notions of norms and values are known to us all; norms and values are instilled into all of us during our childhood by our parents and social surroundings and continue to be throughout our lives.

Values are abstract (e.g., [11,12]), motivational constructs that apply across contexts and time [11]. They convey what is good (e.g., [13,14]) and important to us (e.g., [11,10]). For example, privacy was something good and important for users in the Facebook case. As a result, they were outraged when their privacy was not respected. They would have reacted similarly if another website, person or institution had failed to respect their privacy, as values hold across situations. As Hodges and Baron argue, values are convictions that some things ought to be and others not [15]. To make the concept of a value more precise it can be differentiated from similar concepts, such as laws, rules, goals, norms, standards, and so on (e.g., [12,13,16,14,17]).

Values have a special status due to their importance to their holders (violation of values is seen as deplorable or morally wrong) and the expectations they generate regarding the behavior of the holder and of others. Values create preference for behavior or action that supports them, which gives them a normative character. As Miceli and Castelfranchi point out regarding the normative character of values, "if something is good, it should be pursued" [13, p. 181]. For example, "honesty" is a value which gives rise to a norm "be honest". Moreover, if something is good, it should not only be pursued by the holder of the value; it should be pursued by others as well. However, others do not always hold the same values. This normative character of values is a ground for conflicts when people hold different values or different priorities among their values.

Our work is concerned with the design of multi-agent systems and systems that are expected to have a social impact. Considering that the systems we build can conflict with the values and norms of the stakeholders of these systems, it is especially important to explicitly recognize the role values play in design.

Returning to the Facebook example, we can say that the value openness of Facebook gave rise to a norm of the Facebook team, i.e., "everybody should share personal information", which conflicts with the value of privacy of the users. In retrospect, could we not say that the way out of this conflict lies in considering the shared value of autonomy, with an associated norm that everybody should be able to decide for herself? Based on this shared norm we can derive the more specific norm that everybody has to decide for herself whether to share information or not. It is a compromise between openness and privacy that is acceptable to both developers and users of Facebook.

This example illustrates the abstract and normative nature of values. Values can be instantiated according to the situation at hand. For example, the value of autonomy is instantiated to insisting on control over how to share personal information on Facebook. The dormant problem of two conflicting abstract values (openness and privacy) became acute at the instantiated level. This leveled approach, working with instantiations, can also be found in the work of Maio [12]. To discover possible conflicts at an early stage of system development, we advocate value elicitation at the start of the project to make people consciously aware of their values; this will reduce costs, effort, and frustration. Proynova et al. make a similar plea [18], focusing mainly on elicitation.

We recognize that, though conflicts between moral values are not dealt with as such in the approaches described here, many mainstream software engineering methods do deal with conflicts of a similar form. Certain design decisions may hinder one value while achieving another. Conflicts with this structure are dealt with in mainstream software engineering methods in the form of tradeoffs between quality requirements (see, for example, [9]).

In our opinion the process of value elicitation at the start of a design process should answer the following questions. Which people's values can be impacted by the system under design and which people's values can impact the design of the system? In our view, this question is essential for the design of system and its answer is both obvious as well as treacherous by its obviousness. The answer to the first part of the question is the stakeholders, and the answer to the second part is the stakeholders and the designers/developers. The last addition, that of the designers, is easy to overlook, as the designers might unconsciously assume that their values are shared by the stakeholders. The Facebook example is illustrative of this point. We conclude that to avoid the negative consequences of violating values and to promote the support of values as much as possible, the following principles should be satisfied by design methods.

1. The values of all stakeholders including designers/developers should be elicited in as far as relevant for the system under design.
2. Stakeholder values should be addressed during all phases of the design process.
3. Conflicts between values of the designers and those of the stakeholders need to be discussed with those who issued the order for the system.
4. To account for the relevant values, to the relevant values need to be instantiated explicitly throughout the design process.
5. Design decisions can and need to be justified and evaluated in terms of explicit (instantiations of) stakeholders' values.
6. Conflicts between values need to be made clear and addressed in cooperation with the stakeholders.

These principles are used in the next section to discuss how existing requirement engineering methods as part of design methods deal with values.

2.2   Requirements and Values

Requirements engineering is one of the first steps in the larger process of software development. It is the process of identifying stakeholders and their needs, and documenting these in a form that can be analyzed, communicated, and subsequently implemented [19]. Broadly speaking, there are two types of requirements: functional requirements and non-functional requirements [6]. The former are requirements that define a function of the system, or something that a system will do. The latter define not what a system will do, but how it will do it. Requirements engineering has attention for "soft issues" such as politics and people's values, although dealing with soft issues is problematic as there is little guidance on how to do so [20]. Concepts used to specify soft issues include *non-functional requirements*, *quality attributes*, *soft constraints*, and *soft-goals*.

Though there is no consensus in the requirements engineering community as to exactly what non-functional requirements are [21], broadly speaking a non-functional requirement is "a software requirement that describes not what the software will do, but how the software will do it" [6, p. 6]. Non-functional requirements are often refered to as "-ities" or "-ilities" [22]. Examples of non-functional requirements include usability, maintainability, adaptability, efficiency, and flexibility.

The concept of non-functional requirement appears to be broad enough to cover values. In fact, some values, namely security and privacy (as a feature of security), have been dealt with in an extension of the Tropos method [23]. However, not all non-functional requirements are values. Non-functional requirements such as maintainability or portability, while important, are conceptually far removed from the moral good worth pursuing that values such as autonomy, trust, and justice point to. The examples of non-functional requirements given here are closely related to the envisioned system, whereas the examples of values are more closely related to humans, culture, or society. Furthermore, as far as we know, no specific guidelines exist for dealing with moral values in design methods that use the concept of non-functional requirements.

The related concept of *quality attribute* can be defined as "[a] feature or characteristic that affects an item's quality" where quality is understood as "[t]he degree to which a system, component, or process meets specified requirements" or "[t]he degree to which a system, component, or process meets customer or user needs or expectations" [24, p. 60]. As with non-functional requirements, this term is so general that it provides no guidelines for dealing with values specifically.

Soft constraints are requirements for dealing with over-constrained problems, as well as for dealing with uncertainty, vagueness or imprecision [25]. As stated in [25]: "They can be seen as a preferential constraint whose satisfaction is not required, but preferred." Treating soft constraints as "preferred but not required" disqualifies soft constraints as the way to model values as the moral wrongness of violating a value is lost. Nonetheless, we can try dealing with values as soft constraints. Soft constraints are to be elicited during the requirements engineering process, however, if values are not specifically addressed chances are that no values will be made explicit (principle 1). Soft constraints of stakeholders are typically taken into account, and that way principle 2 can be said to hold in as far as principle 1 is upheld. Principle 3 is not treated using values. Principles 4, and 5 are treated accepting that values are part of the whole set of soft constraints. Principle 6 is not dealt with as such.

Soft-goals, as used in e.g., Tropos [26], are requirements that are not clearly defined and do not have clear criteria for satisfaction, drawing on the notion of satisficing instead [27]. They are a form of non-functional requirements that refer explicitly to goals, an important concept in agent technology.

As we are particularly interested in agent-oriented software engineering [28] we focus on Tropos and its soft-goals. Treating values as soft-goals, we can summarize that principles 1, 2, 4, and 5 are treated to some extent in Tropos, but principles 3 and 6 are in no way part of the Tropos method. With respect to principle 1, indirect stakeholders are not taken into account, although the method could be easily adapted to cover this. Principle 2 is covered in the sense that soft-goals can play a role during all phases of the design. Principle 5 is covered in the sense that decisions are related to soft-goals, but not in as far as one soft-goal is weighed more heavily than another to make a choice.

Section 3 describes our effort to see how far we can get with modeling values as soft-goals in Tropos and will explain our conclusions regarding the principles.

Before focusing on Tropos and the possibilities soft-goals offer to include values in the design, we would like to mention one more approach that might be useful with respect to values.

2.3   Value-Sensitive Design

VSD "is a theoretically grounded approach to the design of technology that account for human values in a principled and comprehensive manner throughout the design process" [29]. In VSD, emphasis is given to supporting moral values or values with ethical import, such as human welfare, ownership of property, privacy, and freedom from bias [10].

VSD provides an iterative and integrative three-part methodology consisting of conceptual, empirical, and technical investigations. Conceptual investigations focus on discovering affected stakeholders, their values, and analyzing these values and tensions between them [30]. The first step is to perform a stakeholder analysis to identify direct and indirect stakeholders, which are the people who interact directly with the technology, and those who are impacted by the technology without interacting with it, respectively.

For each group of stakeholders, potential harms and benefits are identified. The list of harms and benefits can be used to map harms and benefits onto associated values, especially human values with ethical import.

Once these key values have been identified, a conceptual investigation of the values is conducted supported by (philosophical) literature, resulting in clear definitions of those values. Potential value conflicts, which can constrain the design space, are examined. Stakeholders are involved if conflicting values hinder one another in the design, such as accountability versus privacy.

Conceptual investigations need to be informed by empirical investigations of the technology's context. VSD does not prescribe a specific method for this stage, stating that "the entire range of quantitative and qualitative methods used in social science research is potentially applicable" [10]. Friedman and colleagues do suggest that semi-structured interviews of stakeholders can be a useful method to understand stakeholders' judgments about a context of use, an existing technology, or a proposed design.

Technical investigations focus on the properties and mechanisms of existing technologies that support or hinder human values. Alternatively, technical investigation can consist of designing a system to support identified human values. Though technical investigations of the first form and empirical investigations seem similar, technical investigations focus on the technology itself, and not on the individuals affected by it, as empirical investigation does. During this stage, it can be helpful to make explicit how design trade-offs map onto value conflicts and affect different groups of stakeholders.

It could be argued that, individually, the steps taken in VSD are common sense. Common sense as they may be, these steps are rarely taken together in a structured manner. As a result values are often neglected in design and addressed after the fact, as cases of privacy issues with social networking websites, bias in search engines, and intellectual property issues with file-sharing software illustrate. VSD offers a structured approach to addressing values.

The strengths of VSD lie in its focus on direct and indirect stakeholders, how they are or will be affected by the technology, and what values are implicated. The focus on a broad range of stakeholders, along with the identification of potential value conflicts and the aim to deal with values throughout design, suggest that VSD adheres to our six principles. However, VSD would benefit from means to not just elicit values, but actually incorporate them in design and eventually implement them.

3   Case Study: Values in Tropos

To discover to which extent values can be dealt with in Tropos in adherence to the six principles of Section 2.1 we performed a case study. The chosen case study is that of designing a conference management system with an emphasis on the values involved. We picked this case study as it was used in [28] to illustrate the use of three agent-oriented software engineering methods, including Tropos, and was based on an earlier case study presented in [31]. Furthermore, conference management systems are at the core of the peer-reviewing established by researchers to protect the quality of research. The decisions made during peer-reviewing have a high impact on researchers. Therefore, the design of such a system must be done in such a way that the norms and values of the stakeholders are respected as much as possible.[2]

The rest of this section is organized as follows. We first identify Tropos, we then describe the general purpose of conference management systems and identify the stakeholders, after which we inject the process of value elicitation for use later on. We then proceed with the remaining value-related steps in the Tropos method with an emphasis on how values are addressed in these steps.

The Tropos software development methodology supports the agent-oriented paradigm and the associated concepts of actors, plans and goals throughout the software development process [26], [28], [32]. Its main value-related steps are stakeholder identification, goal identification, and goal decomposition.

The general purpose of a conference management system depends on the stakeholders involved and vice versa. Tropos identifies stakeholders early in the design process, in the Early Requirements phase. The main stakeholders involved are a paper authors, paper reviewers, program chairs, and publisher of the proceedings [31]. To this we add the general public / government and the researcher as indirect stakeholders. We assume that the fundamental choice for blind peer reviewing has already been made in the organization of the conference. The general purpose is to support paper submission, bidding for papers for review, distribution of papers to reviewers, collection of reports, supporting program committee meetings, communication of results, and submission of camera ready versions of papers. All these aspects are subservient to the underlying concern of publishing high quality research only and blocking substandard research reports. The general purpose and the underlying concern already implicitly refer to a number of values.

Value elicitation was performed with each stakeholder group and ourselves as system designers. We used semi-structured interviews as suggested in the

---

[2] Note that the design of a conference management system in terms of the roles involved is primarily determined by the organization structure of the conference. In this case we chose for a conference management system that adheres to that of smaller conferences or workshops and ignored the more recent use of a Senior Programme Committee as is used in the AAMAS conference. It would be good practice to design the organization structure of the conference before designing the conference management system. However, for our purpose of showing how to deal with values, it is enough to start with some conference organization structure.

VSD method of [10]. In the interviews we explained the intention of designing
a conference management system and described the basic activities it would
support. We asked stakeholders to identify potential harms and benefits of such
a system, and together with them identified the values underlying these harms
and benefits. It is important to note that most interviewees had experience with
existing systems and due to that it is likely they were reflecting on the systems
they were familiar with. Also, most interviewees had experience with multiple
stakeholder roles, making it difficult to rule out that they projected values they
hold in one role to another role.

The authors mention anonymity of reviewers and conflicts of interests as potential harms and anonymity of authors as a benefit. They stated that anonymity
removes context, which makes it difficult to assess reviewers' expertise and dam-
ages the quality of the discussion. Also, it allows reviewers to "ride their hobby
horse", posing a threat to their objectivity. On the other hand anonymity of authors removes hierarchical considerations, leading to judgments based on quality
and not on academic position. This is a potential benefit. The authors warned for
conflict of interests arising from users occupying multiple roles within the same
system. This could lead to reviewers who are also authors seeing the ranking of
their own paper or reviewers reviewing papers of friends. The authors concluded
that the harms are based on their values of transparency, fairness, and accountability, while the benefits are based on their values of fairness and privacy and
would improve the quality of publications.

Reviewers mentioned anonymity of reviewers as a benefit. It also allows reviewers to be as critical as (they feel) they need to be. Together, we concluded
that the underlying values are privacy and quality of publications. PC chairs considered reuse of the system across conferences to be a potential benefit, which
contributes to the trustworthiness of the system. Trust is the underlying value
here. A potential harm that one PC Chair identified was the potential for bias
in seeing authors' names. This could lead to bias based on gender and ethnicity.

Publishers benefit from the peer review process the system supports. By publishing high-quality research and barring substandard research, the reputation of
the publication and that of the publisher potentially increase, as do sales. This
supports publishers' values of quality, profit and trust.

Researchers in general consider it a potential harm that poor quality research
is disseminated. Poor quality research is damaging to the reputation of the research community with the general public and with government. Also, if researchers' own work is disseminated and of poor quality, it is damaging to their
reputation with peers. Both senses of reputation, and the related value of scientific integrity, are values held by researchers.

The general public and government see the publication of high quality research
and the barring of sub-standard level publications as potential benefits. These
ultimately support the value of knowledge.

As system designers in this case, we discovered that we were influenced by
our identification with the roles of author, reviewer, and PC chair, and as such
shared many of the values of those stakeholders groups.

All stakeholders identified use of the conference management system for multiple conferences as a benefit. Reuse enhances the trustworthiness of the system and the process it supports. Also, the record of interactions with the system supports transparency and accountability.

In summary, we can see a range of values at stake here, among which potential or real conflicts exist, for example between transparency and privacy. This example conflict leads to opposing views on whether the system should provide anonymity. A compromise between such values must be found, that is, a feature that supports both or at least hinders neither.

Stakeholders' goals are identified next, and for every goal the developer decides whether the actor itself can achieve it or whether it needs to be delegated to another actor. Goals represent strategic interests of actors. A distinction can be made between (hard) goals and soft-goals. Hard goals have clear criteria for satisfaction. Soft-goals do not have clear criteria for satisfaction, drawing on the notion of satisficing instead [27].

The only option that Tropos has for representing the values identified in the previous stage are soft-goals. Due to space limitations, we will only discuss how the potential harm/benefit of anonymity, the potential harm of conflicts of interest and the underlying values at stake could be addressed in Tropos. Tropos actors are written in italicized bold. Goals and soft-goals are written in bold.

Authors saw the anonymity of reviewers as a potential harm as it prevents them from assessing the expertise of the reviewer. So, we could say the *Author* has a goal, **know reviewer identity**, which contributes positively to the values of **transparency** and **accountability**. The **know author identity** goal is why-linked to a goal dependency between the *Author* and the *PC Chair*, **disclose reviewer identity**. We will discuss how this conflicts with *Reviewers'* goals shortly.

Authors saw their own anonymity as a potential benefit. So, we introduce the goal **anonymity from reviewers**. This goal contributes positively to the *Author*'s values of **privacy** and **fairness**, which we represent as soft-goals. The goal is why-linked to the goal dependency **protect author anonymity** between the *Author* and the *PC Chair*.

Authors also saw conflicts of interest as a potential harm. So, the *Author* actor depends on the *PC Chair* to **avoid conflicts of interest**. This goal contributes positively to the value of **fairness**, represented as a soft-goal. However, since **avoid conflicts of interest** is a goal dependency and hence becomes the *PC Chair*'s goal, the only option we have to link it to the *Author*'s value of **fairness** in Tropos is the why-link.

Reviewers saw anonymity as a potential benefit. Therefore, we say that the *Reviewer* actor has a goal dependency, **protect reviewer anonymity**, on the *PC Chair* actor. This contributes positively to the *Reviewer*'s values of **scientific integrity** and **privacy**, represented as soft-goals. Since the **protect reviewer anonymity** is a goal dependency, the only option we have to indicate the link between it and the values it contributes to is the why-link. However, the why-link is also a type of dependency, and only one link can be constructed for a

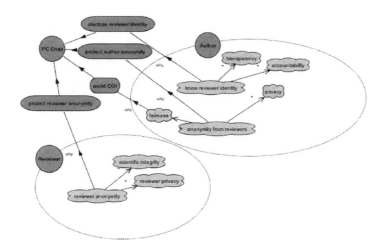

Fig. 1. Early requirements model of conference management system in Tropos with values as represented as softgoals

dependency. So, we have to define an intermediate goal, **reviewer anonymity**, which contributes positively to **scientific integrity** and **privacy** and is why-linked to **protect reviewer anonymity**.

Reviewers' goal **protect reviewer anonymity** obviously conflicts with authors' goal to **know reviewer identity**. Reviewers' value of **privacy** conflicts with authors' value of **transparency** here.

We attempted to model values in Tropos as soft-goals in order to meet the aims expressed in our six principles. However, there are a number of issues with this that we will discuss in the next section.

4 Discussion

4.1 Six Principles

We will now discuss the results of the case study described in section 3 in light of the six principles described in section 2.

The first principle states that the values of all stakeholders and designers or developers should be elicited as far as relevant to the system under design. While stakeholders are considered in Tropos, the group of stakeholders considered is limited to actors that will eventually use the system in some way. Indirect stakeholders, such as the general public in the case study above, are not considered, though they may be affected by the (output of the) system. Also, designers and developers are not considered in Tropos.

The second principle states that stakeholder values should be addressed throughout the design process. As the case study demonstrates, if we represent values as soft-goals in Tropos, then they can be said to be addressed throughout the design process. However, as we discuss below, values are not (soft) goals.

The third principle states that conflicts between the values of the designers and those of the stakeholders need to be discussed with those who issued the order for the system. Since Tropos does not consider the designers as such, conflicts between their values and those of the stakeholders do not become apparent.

The fourth principle states that values have to be instantiated explicitly throughout the design process. If we represent values as soft-goals, we can say that values are instantiated throughout the design process through the process of goal decomposition. However, there are problems with treating values as goals, which we discuss below.

The fifth principle is that design decisions need to be justified and evaluated in terms of explicit instantiations of stakeholders' values. We can say that goals and decompositions of goals into lower-level goals are design decisions. By drawing contribution links between these goals and soft-goals representing values, we can in a sense evaluate and justify these design decisions by seeing which design option (alternative subgoal) contributes best to the soft-goal (value) in question. It should be noted that the extent to which contribution can be expressed is limited. The metrics + and ++ indicate partial and sufficient positive contribution, respectively, and the metrics − and −− indicate partial and sufficient negative contribution, respectively [26].

The sixth principle states that conflicts between values need to be made clear and addressed in cooperation with the stakeholders. In Tropos, the only links between (soft) goals are varieties of decomposition links, namely AND or OR decompositions, means-end links, or contribution links. Also, only one link can exist between these (soft) goals. That is, we cannot have a goal 1 contribute to a goal 2, and have that goal 2 contribute to goal 1. Therefore, we cannot express conflict between (equally abstract) values as such, for example openness and privacy. We could define a higher level soft-goal (value) and say that one lower-level soft-goal contributes positively to it, while another contributes negatively. These soft-goals would then be in conflict, in terms of how they contribute to the higher-level soft-goal, but this is not an option for intrinsic values (or ends) in conflict.

In summary, we can say that the first, fifth and sixth are satisfied to some extent; the second and fourth are satisfied if we consider values to be goals; the third cannot be said to be satisfied. However, this is the very reason why Tropos does not adhere to our principles. To adhere to the principles we would have to represent values as soft-goals, but values should not be treated as soft-goals.

4.2   Differences between Values and Goals

Values are not the same thing as goals. Miceli and Castelfranchi provide a useful distinction between these concepts. "Values are not goals, they are assumptions (more precisely, evaluations). A value is a judgment, though very general and vague. It says of something that it is good or bad. A goal is a regulatory state in someone's mind" [13, p.179]. They illustrate a further important feature of values in discussing the difference between values and norms: "Values in fact offer grounds for, or give rise to norms. Hence the normative' facet of values: If something is good, it should be pursued" [13, p. 181]. If we represent values as soft-goals, the evaluative aspect ("X is good") and the normative aspect ("X should be pursued") are lost. Represented as a soft-goal, a value becomes something that can be satisficed (i.e., sufficiently satisfied). Not achieving a goal is not morally wrong as such. Violating a value is seen as morally wrong. This distinction is important. Not taking these aspects into account could lead to problems once the design has been implemented and put into practice, as we saw in the example of Facebook.

4.3   Dealing with Values in Tropos

Considering the issues with representing values as soft-goals, we propose some additions to the Tropos approach. First of all, in line with our first principle, we propose that the notion of stakeholder in Tropos be extended beyond those groups that delegate their goals to a system to all who will be affected by the system (i.e., direct and indirect stakeholders) and those who shape the system. These groups of stakeholders need to be approached as a source of requirements (values and otherwise) early in the requirements engineering process.

Second, since values should not be represented as goals, we propose the addition of a first-class value entity to Tropos. Since values are held by stakeholders, the value entity needs to be connected to the stakeholders that hold it. As we discussed above, values are general and abstract evaluations. They are conceptions of what is good and are important to their holder. We need to be able to indicate the goodness and importance of each value to its holder in some way, so we can prioritize values and assess the importance of addressing each one. Further, since what is good should be pursued, values can give rise to goals and norms. Hence, we need to be able to represent links between values and the norms and goals they generate. Norms should also be represented, but this is beyond the scope of this paper. Values eventually need to be implemented in some way. Antunes and Coelho's Belief, Values, Goals (BVG) architecture uses values as central motivational mechanisms in their agents' minds [33]. We see this as even more of a motivation to address values early on in design. Also, designers could make use of such an architecture to implement the values elicited and represented during the requirements phase.

Third, values and their instantiations can conflict. The conflict between Facebook's value of openness and users' value of privacy is a case in point. We need to be able to identify such conflicts in order to deal with them early on. To this end, we propose the addition of a conflict relationship between entities, specifically values, in Tropos.

Including indirect stakeholders as a source of (value) requirements, treating values as separate entities in models, explicitly representing conflicts between values, and dealing with values throughout design, as implementing our proposals will allow us to do, will provide us with an approach that adheres to the six principles described in section 2.1.

5   Conclusions

In summary, software impacts human values. In light of this fact and the special status values have, we proposed six principles designers should adhere to. Some requirements and software engineering concepts seem similar to values. However, there are some important differences between values and these concepts. VSD is a methodology that aims to account for (moral) values in design. VSD is a useful methodology for eliciting and defining stakeholders' values. However, VSD as-is does not provide a means for implementing such values. This makes it difficult to assess the extent to which values are incorporated in actual designs.

In our case study in we attempted to capture values in Tropos soft-goals and showed that Tropos as-is cannot fully handle our six principles. We argued that Tropos' soft-goals are fundamentally different from human values as described here. Representing values as soft-goals does not make values sufficiently explicit.

To address these problems, we propose complementing Tropos with a separate, first-class entity to capture values. This entity will allow the designer to explicitly represent values throughout the design process, and to make values concrete enough to operationalize them and to expose and address conflicts between them.

Future work should address the issue of representing values. Also, future work should deal with representing and addressing value conflicts, as these are an important source of many of the issues with values in design. To this end, a formal framework of values is needed. Further, the issue of dealing with different stakeholders' views on specific values should be addressed.

Acknowledgments. We would like to thank Danny Weyns, Marie-Pierre Gleizes, and the participants of the AOSE 2010 workshop for the suggestions they gave during a fruitful discussion there. Also, we would like to thank the anonymous reviewers for their helpful comments.

References

1. Bankston, K.: Facebook's new privacy changes: The good, the bad, and the ugly (2009)
2. Kirkpatrick, M.: Facebook's zuckerberg says the age of privacy is over (2010)
3. Friedman, B.: Human Values and the Design of Computer Technology. Cambridge University Press, CSLI, New York, Stanford, CA (1997)
4. Wooldridge, M., Ciancarini, P.: Agent-oriented software engineering: the state of the art. In: Agent Oriented Software Engineering III, pp. 55–82. Springer, Heidelberg (2001)
5. Weyns, D., Parunak, H., Shehory, O.: The future of software engineering and multi-agent systems. International Journal of Agent-Oriented Software Engineering 3(4) (2009)
6. Chung, L., Nixon, B., Yu, E., Mylopoulos, J.: Non-functional requirements in software engineering (2000)
7. Barbacci, M., Ellison, R., Lattanze, A., Stafford, J., WeinStock, C., Wood, W.: Quality attribute workshops (qaw) (cmu/sei-2003-tr-016). Technical report, Software Engineering Institute, Carnegie Mellon University, Pittsburgh, PA (2003)

8. Wojcik, R.: Attribute-driven design (add), version 2.0 cmu/sei-2006-tr-023. Technical report, Software Engineering Institute, Carnegie-Mellon University, Pittsburgh, PA (2006)
9. Weyns, D.: Architecture-Based Design of Multi-Agent Systems. Springer, New York (2010)
10. Friedman, B., Kahn, P., Borning, A.: Value sensitive design and information systems. In: Human-Computer Interaction and Management Information Systems: Foundations, pp. 348–372. ME Sharpe, New York (2006)
11. Bardi, A., Schwartz, S.: Values and behavior: Strength and structure of relations. Personality and Social Psychology Bulletin 29(10), 1207 (2003)
12. Maio, G.R.: Mental representations of social values. Advances in Experimental Social Psychology 42, 1–43 (2010)
13. Miceli, M., Castelfranchi, C.: A cognitive approach to values. Journal for the Theory of Social Behaviour 19(2), 169–193 (1989)
14. Schroeder, M.: Value theory. In: Zalta, E.N., ed.: The Stanford Encyclopedia of Philosophy. Fall 2008 edn. (2008)
15. Hodges, B.H., Baron, R.M.: Values as constraints on affordances - perceiving and acting properly. Journal for the Theory of Social Behaviour 22(3), 263–294 (1992)
16. Rokeach, M.: Beliefs, attitudes and values: A theory of organization and change (1968)
17. Spates, J.: The sociology of values. Annual Review of Sociology 9(1), 27–49 (1983)
18. Proynova, R., Paech, B., Wicht, A., Wetter, T.: Use of personal values in requirements engineering–a research preview. Requirements Engineering: Foundation for Software Quality, 17–22 (2010)
19. Nuseibeh, B., Easterbrook, S.: Requirements engineering: a roadmap, pp. 35–46. ACM, New York (2000)
20. Thew, S., Sutcliffe, A.: Investigating the role of'soft issues' in the re process. In: 16th IEEE International Requirements Engineering, RE 2008, pp. 63–66 (2008)
21. Glinz, M.: On non-functional requirements. In: 15th IEEE International Conference on Requirements Engineering, RE 2007, pp. 21–26. IEEE, Los Alamitos (2007)
22. Chung, L., do Prado Leite, J.: On non-functional requirements in software engineering. In: Conceptual Modeling: Foundations and Applications, pp. 363–379 (2009)
23. Mouratidis, H., Giorgini, P.: Secure tropos: A security-oriented extension of the tropos methodology. International Journal of Software Engineering and Knowledge Engineering 17(2), 285–309 (2007)
24. Ieee standard glossary of software engineering terminology. IEEE Std 610.12-1990 (1000)
25. Bartak, R.: Modelling soft constraints: a survey. Neural Network World 12(5), 421–432 (2002)
26. Bresciani, P., Perini, A., Giorgini, P., Giunchiglia, F., Mylopoulos, J.: Tropos: An agent-oriented software development methodology. Autonomous Agents and Multi-Agent Systems 8(3), 203–236 (2004)
27. Yu, E.S.K.: Towards modelling and reasoning support for early-phase requirements engineering. In: Proceedings of the Third IEEE International Symposium on Requirements Engineering, RE 1997, pp. 226–235 (1997)
28. DeLoach, S., Padgham, L., Perini, A., Susi, A., Thangarajah, J.: Using three aose toolkits to develop a sample design. International Journal of Agent-Oriented Software Engineering 3(4), 416–476 (2009)

29. Friedman, B., Kahn, P., Borning, A.: Value sensitive design: Theory and methods. University of Washington Technical Report (2002)
30. Miller, J., Friedman, B., Jancke, G.: Value tensions in design: the value sensitive design, development, and appropriation of a corporation's groupware system, pp. 281–290. ACM, New York (2007)
31. Ciancarini, P., Nierstrasz, O., Tolksdorf, R.: A case study in coordination. In: Conference Management on the Internet (1998)
32. Giunchiglia, F., Mylopoulos, J., Perini, A.: The tropos software development methodology: processes, models and diagrams. LNCS, pp. 162–173 (2003)
33. Antunes, L., Coelho, H.: Redesigning the agents' decision machinery. Affective Interactions, 121–137 (2000)

Analyzing Contract Robustness
through a Model of Commitments

Amit K. Chopra[1], Nir Oren[2], Sanjay Modgil[3], Nirmit Desai[4],
Simon Miles[3], Michael Luck[3], and Munindar P. Singh[5]

[1] University of Trento
chopra@disi.unitn.it
[2] University of Aberdeen
n.oren@abdn.ac.uk
[3] King's College London
{sanjay.modgil,simon.miles,michael.luck}@kcl.ac.uk
[4] IBM Research – India
nirmit.desai@in.ibm.com
[5] North Carolina State University
singh@ncsu.edu

Abstract. We address one of the challenges in developing solutions based on multiagent systems for the problems of cross-organizational business processes and commerce generally. Specifically, we study how to gather and analyze requirements embodied within business contracts using the abstractions from multiagent systems.

Commerce is driven by business contracts. Each party to a business contract must be assured that the contract is *robust*, in the sense that it fulfills its goals and avoids undesirable outcomes. However, real-life business contracts tend to be complex and unamenable both to manual scrutiny and domain-independent scientific methods, making it difficult to provide automated support for determining or improving their robustness. As a result, establishing a contract is nontrivial and adds significantly to the transaction costs of conducting business. If the adoption of multiagent systems approaches in supporting business interactions is to be viable, we need to develop appropriate techniques to enable tools to reason about contracts in relation to their robustness.

To this end, we propose a powerful approach to assessing the robustness of contracts, and make two main contributions. First, we demonstrate a novel conceptual model for contracts that is based on *commitments*. Second, we offer a methodology for (i) creating commitment-based models of contracts from textual descriptions, and (ii) evaluating the contract models for robustness. We validate these contributions via a study of real-world contracts.

1   Introduction

When agent-oriented software engineering (AOSE) first emerged, it developed a rich panoply of concepts, abstractions, and techniques based on the notion of agents and allied notions such as roles, protocols, organizations, and commitments. These notions address the inherently interactive nature of multiagent system and provide the key basis

D. Weyns and M.-P. Gleizes (Eds.): AOSE 2010, LNCS 6788, pp. 17–36, 2011.

both for developing business applications that involve autonomous and heterogeneous participants and for distinguishing AOSE as a technical discipline from the rest of software engineering. The applications that AOSE is geared to addressing include cross-organizational business processes and commerce in general. These have clearly gained social importance in the last decade or so since AOSE has been practiced. The needs that they bring up, especially of flexible modeling and enactment, and of managing complexity continue to speak to the importance of AOSE as a discipline.

However, as both traditional software engineering and AOSE have grown, it has become more and more important to bridge the gap between the two. In some cases, researchers have sought to use the tools and techniques of traditional software engineering to enhance AOSE, including efforts in programming tools and methodologies and in formal methods. Examples of the former include several works such as those surveyed by Nunes et al. [14], and examples of the latter include works by Meneguzzi et al. [13] and Telang and Singh [19,20]. In other cases, researchers have sought to formalize concepts that originate in AOSE in ways that might influence traditional software engineering. Examples of this are works by Bordini et al. [2,3] and by Weyns et al. [21]. The above works demonstrate the expanding overlaps between agent-oriented and traditional software engineering. However, they also demonstrate an interesting limitation in that generally the forays of AOSE into traditional practice so far take place in the later stages of design and development: either in the formalization of system specifications or in the development of executable or nearly executable software artifacts and in their verification and validation.

The present work addresses one of the least understood and hence riskiest phases of the software engineering life cycle, namely, the determination and analysis of system requirements in the first place. Not only is the requirements phase the riskiest, it is also one where (for problems involving commerce, in particular) multiagent systems concepts can apply naturally and potentially facilitate the later phases.

Another novelty of the present work is that it takes what one might understand as a hybrid approach. It adopts the idea of commitments from AOSE as its key organizing principle and uses it to present a generalized model of business contracts in terms of a variety of commitments. This model sustains both (1) a methodology for identifying various types of commitments from traditional text-based contracts and (2) an approach for assessing the robustness of such contracts from the perspective of any of the parties involved. In other words, the present work seeks to incorporate AOSE concepts into the heart of traditional software engineering practice, seeking neither to replace traditional practice with AOSE concepts and technique nor merely to place AOSE concepts in a thin veneer on top while leaving the rest unchanged.

A business contract specifies the terms under which the contracting parties exchange services. In this context, a contract is *robust* for a party if it satisfies that party's goals and preferences even in the face of unexpected circumstances. In general, practical contracts can be quite complex, usually because each party inserts clauses to protect its own individual interests. The question of whether such a contract is robust is an important one that is not trivial to answer. In fact, the robustness of a contract may be assessed in different ways. For example, whereas a contract may specify that a particular service will be provided, it need not specify *how* the specified service will be provided, leaving open the possibility that the method may be inappropriate in the eyes of some party. Alternatively, a contract may specify exactly what and how a service should be provided, but make no provision for rectifying problems when the service fails to be delivered due to accident or malice.

Two aspects of the complexity of contracts makes ensuring robustness difficult. First, traditional contracts are not explicitly structured according to a suitable high-level model. Second, the free text form of today's contracts complicates analyzing their content in any automated way. Multiagent systems offer promising solutions to help manage business relationships and enact business processes; however, without first assessing the robustness of contracts, agents cannot be relied upon to adopt or execute contracts of real significance.

In this paper, we provide an approach to modeling contracts specifically in order to address the problem of unambiguously analyzing their robustness. We treat a contract as a set of interrelated *commitments* among those parties, that is, the agents, who have signed it. These commitments play differing, interconnected roles in the overall contract and support analysis to determine potential threats to the robustness of the given contract. For example, robustness is enhanced when a commitment to provide a service occurs with a concomitant commitment to resolve problems in cases where that service could not be delivered.

We make the following contributions.

- We provide a structured commitment-based model for expressing contracts. The structure of the model captures relationships among the commitments in the contract.
- We outline a *methodology* which helps contract designers in two ways. One, it helps identify the various kinds of commitments that occur in textual contracts and helps create structured commitment-based contract models. Two, it specifies *rules* that can be applied to the models in order to determine the robustness of the underlying contracts.

We motivate our approach using examples from a real services contract between Advanced Semiconductor Engineering (ASE) and Motorola.[1] The contract is for the assembly and testing of semiconductor chips, and the provisioning of related services. To save space, we describe only its relevant snippets. The preamble identifies the parties and their motivations for entering into the contract, as the following snippet shows.

Preamble: MANUFACTURING SERVICES AGREEMENT... WHEREAS, Motorola and ASE desire to establish a strategic supplier relationship in which ASE will utilize the capacity at its final semiconductor manufacturing operation and facilities of ASE Korea located at Paju, Korea (the "PAJU FACILITY") on a priority basis to perform the assembly, test, and associated services on certain semiconductor products for Motorola.

The contract includes distinct sections, each grouping clauses that impose interrelated demands on the contracting parties. ASE will use its facility in Korea to assemble

---

[1] http://contracts.onecle.com/ase/motorola.mfg-korea.1999.07.03.shtml

and test semiconductor products (the *contract products*) for Motorola. Motorola will provide the requisite specifications and equipment to enable ASE to carry out its task. Motorola will also provide monthly forecasts to aid ASE in capacity planning. Motorola will place purchase orders with ASE for the contract products, upon which ASE will ship the products to destinations specified by Motorola. ASE will then invoice Motorola for payment according to the prices agreed upon in the contract. Clauses in the contract also cover concerns such as insurance, indemnity, liability, and so on.

We validate our approach against another real contract, which we introduce later.

This paper is meant to be expository in that it outlines the conceptual underpinnings of contact robustness and presents compelling examples to motivate these concepts as well as to validate them. However, the formalization of the commitment-based model of contracts, the robustness rules, and properties thereof are defered to future work.

The rest of the paper is organized as follows. Section 2 describes our structured, commitment-oriented model of contracts. Section 3 outlines our methodology for translating free text contracts into our model. Section 4 introduces the definition of contract robustness and specifies the rules for determining robustness. Section 5 provides an evaluation using a second case study, and Section 6 discusses related work. Section 7 concludes with discussion of future directions for research.

2 A Commitment-Based Model for Contracts

In this section, we first give the relevant background on commitments and then describe our commitment-based model for contracts.

2.1 Background: Commitments

The expression C(DEBTOR, CREDITOR, CONTEXT, *antecedent, consequent*) means that the debtor commits to the creditor for bringing about the consequent provided the antecedent holds. In contractual terms, a commitment represents a proposed business exchange: the antecedent and consequent represent the considerations of the creditor and debtor, respectively.

Importantly, a commitment arises within a context, which captures the legal, social, or community setting in which the commitment is enforced. A subtle feature of our approach is that here the context can correspond to either a real-life institution or organization, such as eBay or the European Union or the famous fish market of Blanes [16]. A context is an active entity and can be modeled as an agent in its own right: a context in this sense imposes regulations on the participants, and it might penalize or eject noncompliant participants. The context itself may or may not have any consideration in the business exchange; its primary function is regulation. Often, the context plays the role of an arbiter in disputes. Within a contractual setting, the context typically consists of the legal framework under which the contract is signed, together with the domain ontology and the contract document itself. In other words, given a certain legal system, an understanding of the world, and a contract (all of which make up the context), certain commitments between the contracting parties arise and are manipulated in a natural manner.

More specifically, a contract is a set of commitments, each of which has the same context. As an example, an ordering process may involve two commitments: $c_1 = $ C(SELLER, BUYER, ORG, *pay*, *shipGoods*) and $c_2 = $ C(BUYER, SELLER, ORG, *buyGoods*, *pay*). Here we use ORG as the context within whose scope the contract takes place. The first commitment requires the seller to ship the goods to the buyer once payment has been made, whereas the second commits the buyer to pay for goods it has purchased. Notice that the BUYER and the SELLER may themselves be organizations, each with its own internal structure.

A key benefit of the commitments representation is that commitments can be manipulated in a perspicuous and principled manner, thus yielding the flexibility needed in automated contractual interactions. A commitment may be *created*. When its antecedent holds, it is *detached* meaning that it reduces to a commitment to bring about the consequent unconditionally. When its consequent holds, it is *discharged*—this could even happen before the commitment is detached. The creditor may *assign* a commitment to another agent. Conversely, a debtor may *delegate* a commitment to another agent. A debtor may *cancel* a commitment and a creditor may *release* the debtor from the commitment.

Note that the debtor and creditor of a commitment need not be its direct performer or beneficiary [17]. Often, each party would play a role in a participating organization, and would represent the interest of the organization for the purposes of the commitment. For example, a manufacturer may commit to repairing some piece of machinery for a factory, but the repairer may be a subcontractor of the manufacturer.

2.2 Enhanced Commitment Structure

From our examination of real-life contracts, we observe that the commitments occurring within them exhibit a particular structure.

At the heart of this structure is the idea of a *service*. A service is the creation of some *product* by a *process* under the *assumed circumstances*, as shown in Figure 1. The product is what an agent actually wants, whereas the process is the means by which the product is brought about. The product may be an artifact or an activity taking place or something holding true about the world. Significantly, it is often the case that a product can be evaluated by its consumer whereas the process is usually hidden. The *assumed circumstances* constitute normal, expected operation: a contract sets up expectations about what each party will do and does so assuming the rest of the world works in a particular way. Considering these assumed circumstances enables us also to consider what should happen when they do not hold in some situations.

We view contracts as inherently symmetric among the parties. Thus each party potentially provides one or more services to the others. A *service commitment* is, then, a commitment whose debtor plays a role in which it provides a service to the creditor of the commitment. A service commitment states what is to be produced by the service and under what assumed circumstances, without further describing the product or process. In terms of the overall structure of a commitment described in Section 2.1, the service product is the consequent of the commitment.

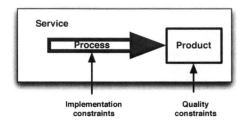

Fig. 1. Control flow for the reasoning process

A contract contains a set of service commitments. For each service, there are then a number of other constraints and commitments that are meaningful when understood in context of the service.

- *Quality constraints*, with regard to a service, are restrictions on the debtor to ensure that the service product is of a minimum acceptable quality.
- *Implementation constraints*, with regard to a service, are restrictions on the debtor to ensure that the process used for production meets certain requirements.
- A *contingency commitment*, with regard to a service, is a commitment on the debtor or a third party to provide an *alternative service* when the assumed circumstances do not hold (and stated *contingency circumstances* hold instead).
- A *resolution commitment*, with regard to a service, is a commitment on the debtor or a third party to provide an *alternative service* when the service commitment is violated.
- An *audit commitment*, with regard to a service, is a commitment on the debtor or a third party to perform an audit of the service, the product of which is the record of the service having been conducted.

Using the above enhanced structure, we model a contract as a set of such commitments. The structure for documenting a commitment C is shown in Table 1. As explained in Section 2.1, each contract has a CREDITOR and a DEBTOR agent. The *antecedent* is divided into an *Activation* condition, which states what triggers the commitment to apply, and *Assumed* circumstances, which states what is assumed to hold when the commitment applies. Both must be true for the commitment to apply, but they are dealt with in different ways. If the *Activation* condition does not hold at some time, then the commitment simply does not apply at that time. Conversely, if the *Activation* condition holds but the *Assumed* circumstances do not, then the *Contingency* commitment applies instead (if one is given).

The *consequent* is similarly divided into parts: for the *consequent* to be true, the *Product* must have been produced such that the *Quality* properties hold true of the service product and the *Implementation* properties hold true of the service process.

Each commitment C additionally has related commitments. A *Resolution* commitment is applicable when the original commitment C is violated, that is, the antecedent of the resolution commitment is the violation of the original commitment. An *Audit*

Table 1. Enhanced commitment structure

Enhanced commitment	
Reference	*An identifier to refer to the commitment*
Creditor	*The beneficiary of the service*
Debtor	*The party responsible for providing the service*
Antecedent	
Activation	*Under what circumstances this commitment applies*
Assumed	*Circumstances assumed in providing service*
Consequent	
Product	*The product of the service*
Quality	*The properties that should hold for the product*
Implementation	*The properties that should have held for the service process*
Related	
Contingency	*A commitment regarding what should be done when the assumed circumstances do not hold (referred to by identifier)*
Resolution	*A commitment regarding what should be done when this commitment is violated (referred to by identifier)*
Audit	*A commitment to produce data about how this service is performed (referred to by identifier)*

commitment is applicable whenever commitment C's process is enacted (and thus has as antecedent the same or a more general antecedent than C) and produces documentation regarding the service process.

A contract, then, is a set of enhanced commitments, EC(CREDITOR, DEBTOR, *activation, assumed, product, quality, implementation*), together with functions that map from enhanced commitments to resolution, contingency, and audit commitments (each of which themselves is an enhanced commitment).

3   Modeling Contracts

Our proposed methodology has two phases: first, it involves mapping the contract text to the commitments model introduced in Table 1; and, second, it involves applying rules to this mapping to check for robustness.

The first phase of our methodology consists of a number of steps, with each step identifying certain artifacts within the contract, and verifying whether these artifacts meet some *prerequisites* to ensure the contract is correct and robust in basic ways. For example, verifying might mean ensuring that no commitment has the same creditor as debtor, and that it is clear when the contract begins and ceases to have force. In the next section (Section 4), we introduce the more rigorous robustness rules, which may not hold even for apparently well-drafted contracts.

Our methodology consists of the following steps. For each step, we give the number of the section in this paper in which that step is explained.

1. Identify the critical entities involved in the commitments (Section 3.1)
   (a) Identify the contracting parties (Section 3.1)

    (b) Identify each contracting party's goals (Section 3.1)
    (c) Identify domain concepts (Section 3.1)
    (d) Identify contract scope (Section 3.1)
2. Map the above entities into the commitment model (Section 3.2)
    (a) Model services, processes, and products (Section 3.2)
    (b) Model commitments regarding services (Section 3.2)
3. Check the robustness of the commitments (Section 4)
    (a) Check that the contract meets each party's goals (Section 4.1)
    (b) Check that it is well specified how services should be provided and how to handle circumstances in which the services are not provided as specified (Section 4.2)
    (c) Check that the contract does not place conflicting demands on the parties (Section 4.3)

We illustrate the methodology via clauses selected from the ASE-Motorola contract, especially an abbreviated form of Clause 11.

> **Clause 11:** ASE shall ship the Contract Products to the destinations identified by Motorola. Motorola shall acknowledge to ASE the receipt of each shipment of Contract Products, stating the quantity and type of, and any damages existing at delivery to, such Contract Products within [X days] of receipt at Motorola's ultimate destination ... ASE shall certify to Motorola with each shipment that the Contract Products contained therein have successfully passed applicable testing and meet all specifications ... If Motorola rejects any Contract Products, Motorola and ASE shall confer to determine the reason for the rejection. ASE shall immediately exercise commercially reasonable efforts to develop and implement a corrective action plan for any errors, including manufacturing errors or defects, identified in its systems.

3.1   Entity Identification

It is crucial to identify the various artifacts referred to in the contract. These artifacts may then be used within commitments in some structured or unstructured manner. In the former case, rules may be created identifying how they may, or should, be used in order to lead to a robust contract. The following entities are of interest.

Contracting Parties. A contracting party named by the contract is an entity whose commitments and responsibilities are described by the contract, and who is a signatory to the contract. In Clause 11, ASE and Motorola are the contracting parties.

A contract may identify specific roles within a contracting party, when it is an organization. For example, ASE is committed to providing *Motorola Employees* with office facilities according to Clause 5 (not shown). Other roles mentioned in the contract include those of a *coordinator* and the *ASE account team*, which then includes additional roles such as *manager* and *executive*.

Contract Goals. Business parties adopt a contract if it is conducive to achieving their goals—if the contract is robust, then these goals will be achieved. The preamble specifies the overarching goal; here, this is the successful production and delivery of semiconductor products from ASE to Motorola. This leads to other identifiable subgoals regarding high-level concepts such as the goal of having ASE deliver the product in a timely manner, the defect rate falling below some threshold, and so on. As we discuss below, each of these goals must be satisfied by some combination of commitments specified in the contract.

Domain Concepts. Contracts specify what the contracting parties are committed to do within some domain, specifying the relevant states of domain artifacts and how to manipulate them. Domain concepts in Clause 11 include *products, rejection, receipt, destination, damage*, among others. Although it is beyond the scope of this paper, we assume a suitable ontology for each domain.

Scoping. A robust contract should specify when it is in effect, and when it expires, for example, via a termination clause that specifies the conditions under which the contract ends. Clause 3 (not shown) within the Motorola-ASE contract states that the contract is effective from the signing date, and is in force for five years. It also provides alternative ways of terminating the contract early. A prerequisite of robustness is clarity of the scope.

Prerequisite 1. *A robust contract specifies the conditions when the contract begins and ends.*

3.2 Mapping to Commitment Model

Once we have identified the critical entities, we map them into our commitment-based model.

Services, Processes, and Products. Clearly, it is necessary to identify the services to which the contractual commitments apply. For each service, its product—that is, its desired outcome—must also be identified. Each service is expressed, or sometimes implied, in contract clauses using the identified domain concepts, and each party's goals are expressed in terms of the services.

The *Preamble* in our example contract describes the primary services under consideration, as follows: "the assembly, test and associated services on high quality semiconductor products in volume." This hints at a service whose product is assembled semiconductor products and a service whose product is tested semiconductor products. Later clauses identify other "associated" services. For example, Clause 11 includes "ASE shall ship the Contract Products to the destinations identified by Motorola," the product of which is the delivery of goods, and goes on to make statements about how this service should be provided.

Service Commitments. Because we view a contract as an aggregation of the commitments it imposes upon the contracting parties, determining whether a contract is robust involves identifying the commitments found in the contract. The remainder of the methodology focuses on these commitments, and the relationships between them.

Each service identified in the contract has a corresponding commitment, with one identified party as debtor, and another as creditor. It is a prerequisite for robust execution that any commitment *must* have some contracting party (and sometimes a specific role within it) as the commitment's debtor and creditor, implying the following rule.

Prerequisite 2. *A robust contract must ensure that every commitment within the contract will have a contracting party as a debtor and a creditor.*

For the primary shipment service referred to in Clause 11, the creditor is Motorola and the debtor is ASE. Further, a valid commitment must have distinct parties as debtor and creditor.

Prerequisite 3. *The same entity may not be named a debtor and a creditor within a single commitment.*

Finally, the given contract must translate unambiguously to our model, and so the following prerequisite applies.

Prerequisite 4. *A commitment must only refer to concepts that have been defined within the domain ontology.*

Example. We apply the above to the initial modeling of Clause 11. Table 2 expresses the commitment to perform the primary service of the clause, that is, shipment of products to specified destinations. This commitment is given an identifier, C11-Shipment, and refers to three other commitments extracted from the clause: C11-Rejection, C11-Receipt, and C11-Quality. For brevity, we omit the models for the latter two audit commitments; those refer to Motorola's commitment to provide a timely receipt for

Table 2. Service commitment for shipping

Commitment for shipment service	
Reference	C11-Shipment
Creditor	Motorola
Debtor	ASE
Antecedent	
Activation	When products ready to ship
Assumed	
Consequent	
Product	Products arrived at specified Motorola site
Quality	No damage to products
Implementation	Perform applicable tests to certify products
Related	
Contingency	
Resolution	C11-Rejection
Audit	C11-Receipt
Audit	C11-Quality

Table 3. Commitment to rectify problems (rejected products)

Commitment for acting in case of rejection	
Reference	C11-Rejection
Creditor	Motorola
Debtor	ASE
Antecedent	
Activation	Motorola rejects delivered products
Assumed	Within X days of delivery
Consequent	
Product Quality Implementation	Corrective plan of action developed and implemented by ASE
Related	
Contingency Resolution Audit	

products received, and ASE's commitment to provide a statement of quality, respectively. The resolution commitment, C11-Rejection, is invoked when the service product is not achieved, the commitment to quality (no damage) is violated, or the commitment to implementation (tests performed) is not fulfilled.

Table 3 shows the model for C11-Rejection. Here, the service performed is the correction of the cause of rejection. No further commitment is involved, as the clause does not specify what should be done to audit the commitment or in contingency situations.

4 Robustness of a Contract

The robustness of a contract depends on how its commitments relate to the goals of the contracting parties. Definition 1 relates each of a party's goals to commitments in the contract. It says that the fulfillment of a subset of commitments—in any manner—must lead to the satisfaction of the goal, that is, the goal must be *supported*. The set of commitments leading to fulfillment of the goals may represent either the normal way to fulfill the goals where all services are delivered successfully, or a *compensating* way to fulfill the goals where some commitments are violated but compensating commitments are fulfilled.

Definition 1. *A contracting party's goal is* supported *by a contract if and only if the fulfillment of the subset of contract commitments, in which the party is the creditor, entails the goal.*

Given the above definition, we can then define what it would mean for a contract to be robust for a contracting party.

Definition 2. *A contract is* robust *for a contracting party if all of the contract party's goals are supported by the contract. A contract is* robust *overall if it is robust for all its contracting parties.*

In order to specify how to assess robustness, we must define what it means for (1) a contracting party's goals be *entailed* by the contract and (2) a commitment to *compensate* the failure of another commitment. Both of the above relate to the different types of behavior a contractual commitment can address. Therefore, it is important to model the kinds of commitments depending on the purpose they serve in the contract. Below, we enhance our basic commitment model to include the specification of commitments based on their purpose.

Given the model of contracts in the preceding section, we now specify *rules* for determining the robustness of contracts expressed in that model. We divide such rules into the following main categories:

1. those that determine whether the contract contains the content required by each party;
2. those that determine whether each contract commitment is handled robustly; and
3. those that apply to consistency between commitments.

4.1 Necessity Robustness Rules

A robust contract must ensure that each contracting party's goals are satisfied when the contract executes correctly. The consequent of a service commitment may be used to capture the creditor's goals (when the commitment's antecedent holds). Therefore, the desired outcome of a contract may be captured by some subset of the contract's service commitments. A robust contract must thus satisfy the following rule.

Robustness Rule 1. *Each goal expected to be satisfied by the contracting parties should be (a necessary implication of) the consequent of a service commitment.*

Applying this rule to our example, the commitments shown in Tables 2 and 3 are judged robust with regard to this rule: on the former's completion, Motorola will have the components it desires; on the latter's completion, any problems will have been appropriately addressed.

4.2 Coverage Robustness Rules

A service commitment can often be fulfilled in multiple ways, and not all are of equal value to the contracting parties. In order to be robust, the contract must ensure that a commitment is met appropriately.

Robustness Rule 2. *Each service commitment must have corresponding quality constraints that specify what it means for the service product to achieve an adequate standard.*

Table 2 shows a simple statement of the quality required of the product: no damage should have occurred. In the commitment in Table 3, no quality constraints are given. Whereas this omission may be deemed appropriate by the contracting parties, the above rule highlights the fact that the contract is less robust if Motorola places no criterion on what an acceptable corrective plan can be.

Whereas the quality constraints concern the service product, we may also apply criteria for judging the process by which the service is conducted, leading to the following rule.

Robustness Rule 3. *If a service commitment may be met in a number of ways, a proper subset of which capture the creditor's goals, then the service commitment should have corresponding implementation constraints that specify what it means for the service commitment to have been achieved in a satisfactory manner.*

Table 2 shows a commitment by ASE to apply tests for damage and to ensure specifications are met prior to delivery (and therefore part of the service process). In contrast, Table 3 gives no implementation commitment. The above rule highlights the fact that the contract is less robust if Motorola places no criterion on what process is acceptable in developing a corrective plan, for example, the factors that ASE should take into account.

The fulfillment of service commitments and quality constraints is usually publicly observable. For example, whether ASE has manufactured the semiconductor chips up to the requisite standard is verifiable by Motorola once Motorola has received the chips. However, implementation constraints restrict the internal processes a contract party employs; compliance with such commitments is not visible outside the company. For example, Motorola cannot ascertain from outside ASE whether ASE has met the ISO 9000 standards in manufacturing the chips. Hence, implementation constraints call for audit commitments.

Robustness Rule 4. *Each service's implementation constraints must have a corresponding audit commitment that ensures that the satisfaction or violation of the constraints is detected.*

If a commitment has been violated (for example, if the product is not available, or if quality or implementation constraints haven't been followed), then the creditors' goals may not be achieved. In order to be robust, therefore, the creditor in the commitment requires that some compensating commitment comes into force.

Robustness Rule 5. *Each commitment must have a corresponding resolution commitment that ensures that the violation of the former commitment results in a suitable sanction on the debtor.*

Table 2 shows two commitments to ensure correct auditing by both parties involved. It is only by auditing that any violations of the implementation constraints are detected. There is also a resolution commitment, to specify what should be done when the product or process is inadequate according to the quality and implementation constraints. Table 3 shows no audit or resolution commitments are given. The above rules highlight the fact that the contract is less robust if there is no record of ASE having produced and implemented such a corrective plan, or what action to take if ASE fails to produce such a plan.

Further, for the debtors of a contract commitment, the contract is robust only if it adequately accounts for exceptional circumstances, beyond those assumed in normal operation. We ensure the robustness of the contracts in relation to these aspects, with the following rule.

Robustness Rule 6. *Each commitment may have corresponding contingency commitments that ensure that, in each exceptional circumstance envisaged, the violation of the former commitment does not result in an inappropriate sanction on the debtor.*

Table 2 shows no contingency commitments because the contract fails to specify assumed circumstances. The absence of assumptions should draw the modelers' attention, but may merely indicate that there is no contingency to consider. Table 3 also states no contingency commitment, but does have assumed circumstances. The above rule highlights the fact that the contract is less robust if it is not specified what should be done if Motorola only rejects a product long after (more than X days) it has been delivered.

It might seem that, if applied recursively, the above rules could lead to an infinitely large contract; for example, each commitment requires another commitment for resolution. However, our use of the context of a contract—as in a business contract within a wider legal system—provides a natural solution. Not all of the associated commitments mentioned in the rules above need to be in the contract document itself; many may be present in the wider context. Ultimately, the audit, resolution, or contingencies of contextual commitments may be captured via general approaches, such as "file a lawsuit."

4.3   Consistency Robustness Rules

The above rules consider the requirements of robustness on each commitment. The robustness of a contract as a whole depends in addition on whether its commitments are realizable.

It should always be clear to a contracting party what to do to fulfill the contract, even in the case of multiple failures. Further, if success in one commitment prevents success in another, then the contract cannot be robust. A particular example of this is where two commitments require the same party in the same system state to do two conflicting things. A robust contract does not have such conflicts between its commitments, and the following rule expresses this constraint.

Robustness Rule 7. *For any given contracting party and applicable system state, by performing an action necessary to avoid violating one commitment, the action should not violate any otherwise nonviolated commitment.*

Taken together, the rules specified above provide us with a means of ensuring that a contract is robust at the point of specification. The full set of rules is summarized in Table 4, indicating which aspects of the contract each rule applies to.

5   Evaluation

We used the Motorola-ASE contract as primary inspiration for our approach to modeling and assessing contract robustness (along with our prior experience with case studies as part of electronic contracting projects). To evaluate our proposed approach, we took an entirely independent contract and applied our methodology to it. Figure 2 shows an excerpt from a short contract[2] between a juggling society and an event organizer. We now show how our methodology applies to determine whether this contract is robust.

---

[2] http://users.ox.ac.uk/~juggsoc/contract.shtml

Table 4. Contract rules

Rule	Target
PREREQUISITE 1	Scope of contract
PREREQUISITES 2 & 3	Services and contracting parties
PREREQUISITE 4	Well-defined contract
ROBUSTNESS RULE 1	Product
ROBUSTNESS RULE 2	Quality constraints
ROBUSTNESS RULE 3	Implementation constraints
ROBUSTNESS RULE 4	Audit commitments
ROBUSTNESS RULE 5	Resolution commitments
ROBUSTNESS RULE 6	Contingency commitments

Table 5. Domain concepts for the *Juggler* contract, grouped according to the commitments that they most closely relate to

Service	performance, breaks, guests, venue, equipment
Contingency	deposit, damage, injury, guarding, poor weather, cancellation
Implementation	alcohol consumption, cloakroom, performance area, indoors, height, outside
Resolution	compensation, liability, refund

5.1 Entity Identification

The two contracting parties involved in this contract are the JUGGLING CLUB (UJC), and the CANTERBURY CENTRE DINNER (CCD). Additional roles include PERFORMER and JUGGLER. As we see below, this contract obeys Prerequisites 2 and 3.

The CCD's goal from the contract is to obtain performers for their dinner. The UJC's goal is to get paid.

Apart from temporal concepts (relating to dates and times), and general concepts such as money, we may identify the domain concepts listed in Table 5. Since only these concepts are referred to within the contract, Prerequisite 4 is satisfied.

The contract initiates as soon as it is signed and it is *implied* that it expires at the end of the performance. Note that the lack of an explicit expiration condition suggests one problem with the robustness of the contract. One may envision a situation where some equipment is damaged, and a disagreement arises as to whether this damage falls under the contract or not (for example, when the jugglers and guests are on their way home from the dinner). Thus, Prerequisite 1 is not satisfied within this contract.

5.2 Mapping to Commitment Model

We now map clauses from the contract to the commitment model. Clauses 3 to 7 imply a service to be provided: the provision of jugglers and equipment by UJC, modeled in Table 6. UJC is the debtor, CCD is the creditor and the eventual product of the service is that the jugglers perform at the event. Implementation constraints are specified: that the jugglers remain sober (Clause 12). Where the service cannot be provided due to poor weather conditions (assumed circumstances not holding, Clause 11) or the performance

Contract For: Canterbury Centre Dinner 2003 ("CCD"),
Friday 6 June 2003, 24 High Street, Canterbury.

This agreement is entered into between the University Juggling Club ("UJC") and
the Canterbury Center Dinner 2003 on the following terms:

1. Service Provider: University Juggling Club.
2. Employer: Canterbury Center Dinner.
3. To be provided by UJC: Performers: J Woods (juggler); one other juggler; all
   equipment necessary for performance.
4. To be provided by CCD: Cloakroom.
5. Venue address: 24 High Street, Canterbury.
6. CCD understands that performances are restricted in venues with ceilings of
   insufficient height. The ideal height is 5 meters. Outside performances are restricted in rain or strong winds.
7. Date of Performance: Friday 6 June 2003, starting at 6:30PM.
8. Duration of Performance: 1.5 hours. Short (less than one minute) breaks are
   part of the performance.
9. Fee: £30 per juggler + £10 expenses + £90 insurance (total £160).
10. If UJC is forced to cancel, all monies (including £90 deposit) will be refunded
    in full. If the Employer cancels with at least 24 hours notice, UJC will retain
    £90 and return any other monies.
11. Should poor weather mean that the Event takes place indoors, UJC will refund
    £10 expenses.
12. Performers will not consume any alcohol until after completion of services as
    agreed.
13. CCD will be responsible for compensation to UJC for damage to equipment
    caused by those attending the Event unless damage is caused when (if) Per-
    formers have left equipment unguarded.
14. UJC will be liable for any injury sustained by a guest at the Event if such
    injury results from provision of services as agreed upon in this contract unless
    the Event fails to provide a suitable area for performance.

Fig. 2. An extract from a contract to provide juggling services

is canceled by UJC (violation of commitment under assumed circumstances, Clause 10),
contingency and resolution commitments apply, respectively. Clause 9 is a commitment
for a separate payment-for-juggling service, and so is not modeled here.

5.3 Assessing Robustness

Having identified the commitments, we may check whether they meet the appropriate
robustness rules. Clearly, each desired outcome of the contract meets the commitments
specified in Clauses 3, 4, 7, 8 and 9, as a performance will take place, and UJC will be
paid. Thus, Rule 1 is satisfied.

According to Rule 2, each service commitment must have associated quality constraints. Whereas one assessment of quality is given for the service in Table 6, and so

Table 6. Service commitment: provide jugglers, equipment (the numbers refer to clauses in the textual description)

Commitment for providing resources	
Reference	C-ProvisionOfResources
Creditor	CCD (2)
Debtor	UJC (1)
Antecedent	
Activation	Agreement to contract
Assumed	Venue is indoor and of adequate height or outdoor and there is no rain or strong winds (6)
Consequent	
Product	C-JugglerPerform (3,4,5,7)
Quality	C-PerformanceFor1.5Hours (8)
Implementation	C-JugglersWillNotConsumeAlcohol (12)
Related	
Contingency	C-PoorWeather (11)
Contingency	C-Cancellation (10)
Resolution	C-CompensationResponsibility (13)
Resolution	C-Injury-Liability (14)

the clause can be judged somewhat robust, other quality measures may also be considered (for example, specifying how capable the juggler should be).

UJC agrees to implementation constraints: that the jugglers do not consume alcohol while performing. Note that although there is no corresponding audit commitment, this is only because the contracted performance is slated to happen in a public venue and CCD would easily be able to detect noncompliance on part of the juggler. Thus Rule 4 is satisfied. The parties may consider additional implementation constraints, for example if there are any stipulations that should be made about how the product is reached, such as whether the organizers are given prior warning about when the jugglers will arrive.

There are some commitments for contingency and resolution in Table 6. Therefore, there is some robustness in this regard according to Rules 5 and 6. However, the contract can be even more robust if consideration is made of the other ways in which the assumed circumstances may not come about or the service is not provided. For example, the assumed circumstances are a conjunction of criteria and the contract does not say how to handle jugglers arriving at a venue with too low a ceiling. Similarly, the quality constraints require jugglers to remain sober, but there is no means of redress specified if this commitment is violated.

The juggling contract's inability to deal with such unexpected situations, together with its vagueness, means that it lacks robustness in several ways, and that in unexpected situations, disagreements between the parties may occur that the contract may be unable to resolve.

6 Related Work

Tropos is one of the leading AOSE methodologies with a substantial emphasis on early-stage requirements [4]. Tropos is centered on the notion of goals (along with dependencies among goals), and generally works best where the system-to-be is built to accommodate the goals of the stakeholders, modeled as actors. Tropos does not naturally apply to cross-organizational settings, where there is no unique system-to-be but rather one per stakeholder and where often the challenge is to specify the interaction *protocol* or rules of encounter rather than a complete implementation of a system. Mallya and Singh [12] relate protocols with Tropos using dependencies as bases for inducing protocols. Telang and Singh [18] have sought to incorporate commitments into Tropos as first-class modeling concepts. However, the existing works on Tropos have a general bias toward greenfield system designs whereas the approach we propose above begins from existing contracts and thus potentially can apply when a functioning (though potentially inadequately functioning) cross-organizational system is already in place.

Much work has been done on using automated contracts within computer science, and particularly within the area of multiagent systems. It is possible to categorize this work based on the contract life cycle. Our work in this paper concerns itself with the first stage of the contract life cycle, namely contract drafting. In this phase, themes such as the precise language used to represent the contract are important, as well as challenges such as contract negotiation (for example, as studied by Carbogim and Robertson [5]) and contract validation. Once a contract is drafted, it comes into effect, and further challenges such as contract monitoring and enforcement become important, but are not further discussed here. Daskalopulu et al. [7] describe logic-based tools for this end.

Our use of commitments to model contracts represent a significant departure from existing works on modeling contracts. Both contracts and commitments are social constructs in that they are both grounded in communication among the participants. By contrast, constructs such as business rules and obligations (as studied in deontic logic) are not social. Many contract languages that have been proposed, including those by Abrahams and Bacon [1], Grosof and Poon [11], and Governatori [10]. However, none of them represent contracts as a set of commitments as we do.

We do not study how a contract comes into being, concentrating instead only on whether it is robust or not. Thus, our work falls into the area of contract validation. However, most work on contract validation concerns itself with either ensuring that contract clauses are consistent, for example, by Daskalopulu [6], or ensuring that a sound legal basis exists, for example, by Gisler et al. [9]. The notion of robustness adds to, rather than replaces these concerns.

The only other large-scale analysis of contractual requirements that we are aware of is the work of Daskalopulu et al. [6], who investigate how to support large engineering contracts. However, their work was focused on identifying language requirements for such contracts, not on a software engineering methodology as here.

The work of Desai et al. [8] is relevant in this regard. Desai et al. study contracts from the perspective of utility theory as a basis for determining from the perspective of a contracting party whether a particular contract is *safe* (never produces negative utility) or *beneficial* (produces positive utility) for it. It would be useful to incorporate Desai et al.'s representation and reasoning approach into our methodology, although a practical challenge that such economic approaches face is determining the relevant utilities and probabilities in domains of sufficient complexity to be practically valuable.

7 Conclusions and Directions

In this paper, we have sought to develop a model, a methodology, and heuristic rules by which we can capture and analyze requirements from business contracts as a potential basis for developing robust multiagent implementations of software systems in open environments.

We identified the notion of *robustness* as critical to a contract. Informally, a robust contract is one that meets the contracting parties' goals for the contract, and handles unexpected situations gracefully. We proposed a methodology for determining whether a contract is robust, and evaluated portions of this methodology on portions of two real contracts. Our approach models contracts such that their robustness is assessed in a structured manner. However, many open questions remain.

First, it would be interesting to map the notions of robustness into an existing contract language, such as the one proposed by Oren et al. [15], and to automate the rules for robustness, creating an algorithm that may identify whether a contract is robust or not. It would also be useful to study a large number of additional contracts, and see whether our rules for robustness are exhaustive, or should be altered in some way. Further, it may be possible to identify additional commonly occurring classes of commitments, together with associated robustness rules.

The notion of robustness becomes increasingly important as agents autonomously negotiate and create contracts between themselves. By creating a robust contract, able to state what should occur in all situations (within the context of the contract), an agent's cognitive load is reduced, as it does not need to reason about whether the contract was adhered to or not. Further, robust contracts minimize the situations in which humans need to intervene in order to handle agent disagreements. While many open problems remain, this paper provides an initial approach to identifying and creating robust contracts.

Acknowledgments. Amit Chopra was supported by a Marie Curie Trentino award.

References

1. Abrahams, A.S., Bacon, J.M.: A software implementation of Kimbrough's disquotation theory for representing and enforcing electronic commerce contracts. Group Decision and Negotiation 11(6), 487–524 (2002)
2. Bordini, R.H., Dastani, M., Dix, J., Fallah-Seghrouchni, A.E.: Multi-Agent Programming: Languages, Platforms and Applications, Multiagent Systems, Artificial Societies, and Simulated Organizations, vol. 15. Springer, Heidelberg (2005)
3. Bordini, R.H., Hübner, J.F., Wooldridge, M.J.: Programming Multi-Agent Systems in AgentSpeak using Jason. John Wiley & Sons, Chichester (2007)
4. Bresciani, P., Perini, A., Giorgini, P., Giunchiglia, F., Mylopoulos, J.: Tropos: An agent-oriented software development methodology. Journal of Autonomous Agents and Multi-Agent Systems 8(3), 203–236 (2004)
5. Carbogim, D., Robertson, D.: Contract-based negotiation via argumentation (a preliminary report). In: Proceedings of the Workshop on Multi-Agent Systems in Logic Programming: Theory, Application, and Issues (MAS) held at the International Conference on Logic Programming (ICLP), Las Cruces, New Mexico (1999)

6. Daskalopulu, A.: Logic-based tools for legal contract drafting: Prospects and problems. In: Proceedings of the First Logic Symposium, pp. 213–222. University of Cyprus Press (1997)
7. Daskalopulu, A., Dimitrakos, T., Maibaum, T.: Evidence-based electronic contract performance monitoring. Group Decision and Negotiation 11(6), 469–485 (2002)
8. Desai, N., Narendra, N.C., Singh, M.P.: Checking correctness of business contracts via commitments. In: Proceedings of the 7th International Joint Conference on Autonomous Agents and MultiAgent Systems (AAMAS), pp. 787–794. IFAAMAS, Columbia (2008)
9. Gisler, M., Stanoevska-Slabeva, K., Greunz, M.: Legal aspects of electronic contracts. In: Proceedings of the CAiSE Workshop on Infrastructure for Dynamic Business-to-Business Service Outsourcing (IDSO), Stockholm. CEUR Workshop Proceedings, vol. 30, CEUR-WS.org (2000)
10. Governatori, G.: Representing business contracts in RuleML. International Journal of Cooperative Information Systems 14(2-3), 181–216 (2005)
11. Grosof, B., Poon, T.C.: SweetDeal: Representing agent contracts with exceptions using semantic web rules, ontologies, and process descriptions. International Journal of Electronic Commerce 8(4), 61–98 (2004)
12. Mallya, A.U., Singh, M.P.: Incorporating commitment protocols into Tropos. In: Müller, J.P., Zambonelli, F. (eds.) AOSE 2005. LNCS, vol. 3950, pp. 69–80. Springer, Heidelberg (2006)
13. Meneguzzi, F., Miles, S., Holt, C., Luck, M., Oren, N., Faci, N., Kollingbaum, M.: Electronic contracting in aircraft aftercare: A case study. In: Proceedings of the 7th International Conference on Autonomous Agents and Multiagent Systems, pp. 63–70 (2008)
14. Nunes, I., Cirillo, E., de Lucena, C.J.P., Sudeikat, J., Hahn, C., Gomez-Sanz, J.J.: A survey on the implementation of agent oriented specifications. In: Gomez-Sanz, J.J. (ed.) AOSE 2009. LNCS, vol. 6038, pp. 169–179. Springer, Heidelberg (2011)
15. Oren, N., Panagiotidi, S., Vázquez-Salceda, J., Modgil, S., Luck, M., Miles, S.: Towards a formalisation of electronic contracting environments. In: Proceedings of the International Workshop on Coordination, Organization, Institutions and Norms in Agent Systems (COIN) held at AAAI, Chicago, pp. 61–68 (2008)
16. Rodríguez-Aguilar, J.A., Martín, F.J., Noriega, P., Garcia, P., Sierra, C.: Towards a test-bed for trading agents in electronic auction markets. AI Communications 11(1), 5–19 (1998)
17. Singh, M.P.: An ontology for commitments in multiagent systems: Toward a unification of normative concepts. Artificial Intelligence and Law 7, 97–113 (1999)
18. Telang, P.R., Singh, M.P.: Enhancing Tropos with commitments. In: Borgida, A.T., Chaudhri, V.K., Giorgini, P., Yu, E.S. (eds.) Conceptual Modeling: Foundations and Applications. LNCS, vol. 5600, pp. 417–435. Springer, Heidelberg (2009)
19. Telang, P.R., Singh, M.P.: Abstracting and applying business modeling patterns from RosettaNet. In: Proceedings of the 8th International Conference on Service-Oriented Computing (ICSOC), pp. 426–440. ACM, San Francisco (2010)
20. Telang, P.R., Singh, M.P.: Specifying and verifying cross-organizational business models: An agent-oriented approach. IEEE Transactions on Services Computing 4 (in press, 2011)
21. Weyns, D., Haesevoets, R., Helleboogh, A.: The MACODO organization model for context-driven dynamic agent organizations. ACM Transactions on Autonomous and Adaptive Systems (TAAS) 5(4), 16:1–16:29 (2010)

A Case for New Directions
in Agent-Oriented Software Engineering

Ingrid Nunes[1,2], Donald Cowan[3], Elder Cirilo[1], and Carlos J.P. de Lucena[1]

[1] PUC-Rio, Department of Informatics, LES - Rio de Janeiro, Brazil
{ionunes,ecirilo,lucena}@inf.puc-rio.br
[2] King's College London, Strand, London, WC2R 2LS, United Kingdom
[3] University of Waterloo, David R. Cheriton School of Computer Science - Waterloo,
N2L 3G1, Canada
dcowan@uwaterloo.ca

Abstract. The state-of-the-art of Agent-oriented Software Engineering (AOSE) is insufficiently reflected in the state-of-practice in developing complex distributed systems. This paper discusses software engineering (SE) areas that have not been widely addressed in the context of AOSE, leading to a lack of mechanisms that support the development of Multi-agent Systems (MASs) based on traditional SE principles, such as modularity, reusability and maintainability. This discussion is based on an exploratory study of the development of a family of buyer agents following the belief-desire-intention model and using a Software Product Line architecture. Based on the discussion presented in this paper, we hope to encourage the AOSE community to address particular SE issues on the development of MAS that have not yet been (widely) considered.

Keywords: agent-oriented software engineering, multi-agent systems, software reuse, software product lines, software architectures.

1 Introduction

Multi-agent Systems (MASs) synthesize contributions from different areas, including artificial intelligence, software engineering (SE) and distributed computing. In the context of SE, MASs are viewed as a paradigm, whose main idea is to decompose complex and distributed systems into autonomous, pro-active and reactive agents with social ability. Such properties are particularly appropriate in the development of modern software systems, which tend to be open, distributed and situated in dynamic environments. However, the state-of-the-art of Agent-oriented Software Engineering (AOSE) is rarely seen in the state-of-practice in developing complex distributed systems [1]. One of the reasons for this is the poor connection between agent research and mainstream SE. While the SE community cares about modularity, stability, reusability and maintainability when developing applications, the MAS community has shown little research effort in building systems following these SE principles.

D. Weyns and M.-P. Gleizes (Eds.): AOSE 2010, LNCS 6788, pp. 37–61, 2011.

AOSE has emerged as a means of investigating SE issues related to the development of MAS. In the last few years, there appears to be a significant effort devoted to agent-oriented methodologies, processes and modeling languages. This can be seen, for instance, by analyzing the post-proceedings of the AOSE workshop (2000 to 2008), and verifying that there are a total of 154 papers of which 88 (more than 50%) are related to modeling approaches. It is important to address these kinds of approaches, but as a consequence other important issues have received little attention in the context of MAS development. In this paper we identify and discuss some of these issues, based on a case study that involves Software Product Lines (SPLs) of agents.

In previous work [2], we have proposed building customized service-oriented agents using a SPL approach. SPL [3] aims at systematically deriving families of applications based on a reusable infrastructure with the intention of achieving both reduced costs and reduced time-to-market. This work has evolved from previous research [4], which aimed at documenting and modeling multi-agent SPLs with a focus on coarse-grained variability. Current research that aims at integrating MASs and SPLs has not dealt with fine-grained variability, i.e. variability within an agent architecture, such as optional and alternative beliefs, goals and plans. Fine-grained variability is essential when extracting features from legacy applications. Furthermore, some existing SPLs could benefit from fine-grained variability to reduce code replication or improve readability [5].

Given that an SPL architecture must address variability within a domain, it is essential to adopt techniques to modularize variable portions of the architecture, thus enabling the reuse of these assets in different product configurations. This modularization is particularly challenging when dealing with fine-grained variability. It is important to rely on implementation techniques that support modular configuration of the variable parts. Otherwise, the stability of an agent SPL architecture will naturally decay over time and this instability will be perpetuated through all future generations of product architectures. During the development of our case study of [2], we have identified several issues in the state-of-the-art AOSE to allow building modularized agent SPL architectures with reusable assets.

The focus of this paper is to report and discuss lessons learned during the development of our case study, mainly related to the lack of techniques that support building agent architectures that take SE principles into account. We present an exploratory study of the development of a family of software agents, in which we aim at adopting appropriate techniques to build agents using reusable assets. The main objective of this study is to explore how parts of an agent architecture can be modularized and be made sufficiently generic for reuse. In particular, our study focuses on agents that follow the BDI architecture [6], which is widely used for developing cognitive agents. In addition, we focus on web-based systems with some components that are software agents. Many software systems are not operating in isolation, but are in a distributed and dynamic environment like the web, where new problems such as trust and coordination between components become important. Even though MASs have characteristics that may be appropriate to solve these problems, alternative technologies such as service-oriented computing (SOC) are being chosen, because of a lack of reusable agent assets [7]. Based on our case study, we discuss issues that arose during its development, which are: modularization techniques of different variability types, architecture models, generative programming and large scale software reuse. In addition, we also discuss the relevance and the need for empirical studies involving MASs. With the discussion presented in this paper, we aim at encouraging the AOSE community to address particular SE issues on the development of MAS that have not yet been (widely) considered.

The paper is organized as follows. Section 2 presents a background on SPLs. Section 3 describes our case study, the family of buyer agents. Section 4 discusses problems identified during the development of our study, followed by Section 5, which provides further considerations on SE research areas not widely explored in the context of MASs. Section 6 concludes the paper.

2   Background: Software Product Lines

The Software Product Line (SPL) approach is a new trend in the context of software reuse that provides a systematic method for integrating the design and implementation of several closely related systems. The term family of programs was first introduced by Parnas in [8], defining it as a set of programs with so many common properties that it is an advantage to study these common properties before analyzing individual members. The concept of SPL is similar to this definition: "*a set of software intensive systems that share a common, managed set of features satisfying the specific needs of a particular market segment or mission and that are developed from a common set of core assets in a prescribed way [3].*" A feature is a system property that is relevant to some stakeholder and is used to capture common aspects of the software or discriminate among products in a product line [9]. The features are organized into a coherent model referred to as a feature model (originally proposed in [10]), which specifies the features of a product line as a tree, indicating *mandatory, optional* and *alternative* features. Mandatory features are part of the SPL core and are present in all products derived from it. Optional features are present just in some members of the SPL and alternative features are the ones that vary from one member to another. Features are essential abstractions that both customers and developers understand.

The main aim of Software Product Line Engineering (SPLE) is to analyze the common and variable features of applications from a specific domain, and to develop a reusable infrastructure that supports the software development. Variability management is the major unique product-line discipline that must be established within non-product-line organizations. It is responsible for systematically managing the scope itself, and ensuring its traceability with genericity of product line artifacts. There are several motivations for the adoption of a SPL approach, the three main ones being the reduction of development costs, enhancement of quality and reduction of time-to-market. The costs are reduced by reusing artifacts to derive products from the SPL. This is the same reason for a reduced time-to-market. The enhancement of quality is achieved by reviewing and testing the SPL artifacts in many products. However, although the development of reusable artifacts requires an up-front investment and a higher time-to-market in the initial phases of the SPL development, but this extra effort is usually regained after the third derived product [11].

To enable SPLE, a well-accepted convention is to divide the engineering process into two different processes: domain engineering and application engineering. Domain Engineering is the process in SPLE in which the common and variable aspects of the SPL are defined and realized. It is responsible for scoping the SPL, and ensuring that the core assets have the variability that is needed to support the desired scope of products. Domain engineering approaches aim at collecting, organizing, and storing past experience in building systems or parts of systems in a particular domain in the form of reusable assets, as well as providing an adequate means for reusing these assets when building new systems [9]. Application Engineering, in turn, is the process of SPLE in which applications of the SPL are built by reusing domain artifacts and exploiting the SPL variability. It takes the common assets of the SPL and uses them to create products. Domain engineering and application engineering can be called *engineering-for-reuse* and *engineering-with-reuse*, respectively.

2.1   Existing Agent-Based Product Line Approaches

Recent approaches have focused on the integration of SPLs and MASs [4,12,13], which has been called Multi-agent Systems Product Lines (MAS-PLs). In [12] an approach is proposed to build the core architecture of a MAS-PL based on the composition of role models. However, the approach deals with model composition and not implementation composition. Therefore, it is not clear how reusable implementation assets can be combined to form customized products. There are two other approaches proposed in the context of MAS-PLs, which are an extensible agent-oriented requirements specification template for distributed systems that supports safe reuse [13], and a domain engineering process for MAS-PLs [4]. But both approaches deal only with coarse-grained variability, such as optional and alternative agents, roles and capabilities, i.e. self-contained software entities. This is also the case in [14], in which empirical studies of MAS-PL implementation techniques were performed. Therefore, there are still many challenges in the integration of MAS and SPL, and more generically supporting large scale software reuse.

3   The Buyer Agent Family Case Study

As described in the introduction, our exploratory study consists of the development of a family of agents in the domain of electronic commerce. This family is composed of buyer agents referred to as buyer agent SPL in the remainder of the paper. The idea is to develop an agent architecture that supports domain variability. When a user makes a request to buy a product with a specific config-uration, a customized buyer agent is derived from this architecture according to the configuration and it buys, or tries to buy, the requested product. A configu-ration is a selection of a valid set of features. For instance, in a car product line, there may be two variable features: optional air conditioning and the alternative between a manual or automatic transmission. In this case, a configuration could be air conditioning and automatic transmission.

In this section, we describe our case study. As buyer agents are situated in an environment composed of other agents, first we present a macro-level view of this MAS, named e-Marketplace (Section 3.1). Next, we detail the buyer agent architecture (Section 3.2) and the implementation techniques to support the variability (Section 3.3). Finally, we describe how customized buyer agents are derived from this architecture (Section 3.4).

3.1 E-Marketplace Overview

The domain of electronic commerce is a typical application domain of MASs, as some commercial decision-making can be delegated to agents. Our exploratory study focuses on the internal structure of a customizable buyer agent that enters into the MAS and interacts with other agents to achieve its goals. In this section, we present the MAS to which this buyer agent belongs, which captures the typical characteristics of virtual electronic commerce environments and was built to support the development and execution of this customizable buyer agent.

The e-Marketplace MAS is composed of four main organizations. The *e-Marketplace* organization contains buyers and sellers that interact in order for a seller to sell a product to a buyer. In the *Payment Services* organization, there are two agents, the `PayPal` and `CreditCardCompany`, which provide the neces-sary services for paying for a product. The *Geographic Services* organization is composed of the `Map` agent that calculates the distance between two locations. It is used by the buyer agent to find stores that are near the buyer. The fourth or-ganization is the *Ipagent*. This organization is composed of agents of the *Ipagent* system. The system structure is based on the Web-MAS architectural pattern [15] that has the aim of integrating agents into web-based systems. This architec-tural pattern is an extension of the layered pattern [16] typically structured with three layers for web systems: (i) *presentation* – responsible for processing web requests and generating dynamic pages; (ii) *business* – responsible for executing business processes and handling business rules; and (iii) *data* – responsible for the data persistence. The `User` agent acts on behalf of users, and is composed of services provided for them, including the buy service, which is responsible for deriving customized `Buyer` agents. These organizations and layers are presented in Figure 1, which depicts the overall structure of the e-Marketplace MAS.

Our focus is not to address the development of the entire MAS. Organiza-tions representing stores and other companies are already deployed in the system and ready to interact and provide services to other agents. This existing MAS

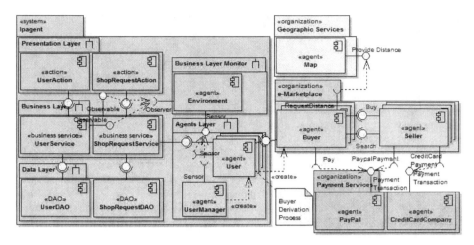

Fig. 1. E-Marketplace MAS

provides an ontology giving a formal representation for a set of concepts, which includes the messages exchanged by agents within the domain and protocols related to the exchange of messages.

3.2   Buyer Agent SPL Architecture

The buyer agent represents a user in the *e-Marketplace* organization. Given that users are individuals, their preferences should be part of the buyer agent so this agent can act appropriately on their behalf. Thus, we have analyzed the domain related to buying products and we have identified the variable aspects of this domain, and the goals and subgoals of the buyer agent SPL. These points of variability (variable features) are taken into account while designing and implementing the agent SPL architecture making it possible to derive customized buyer agents based on a configuration provided by the user.

It is important to highlight that the issue we are addressing is not only presenting customized behavior, which in simple cases can be achieved by making settings (i.e. customizing data) in software systems. Our goal is to investigate changes in software agent structures, and therefore parts that can be changed must be modularized so they can be (un)plugged from the agent architecture. One could say that in our exploratory study it is not necessary to derive specific agents to present customized behavior, and introducing parameters, i.e. changing "data," into the architecture is enough. This is not a good solution because these parameters are control variables, which is a program variable that is used to regulate the flow of control of the program. They introduce a control coupling in the system and, if we are dealing with large scale software, it is hard to understand and maintain the code. This is the principle of separation of concerns [17] in architectures and modularizing them as much as possible, and as introduced in Section 2 it is essential to manage variability in SPLs. We agree that this case study is not sufficiently large enough to illustrate adequately the problem of introducing control variables and the need for adopting more sophisticated techniques to handle variability, but it provides the necessary variable features that create scenarios to be modularized, which is our main interest.

One of the most popular agent architectures is based on the belief-desire-intention (BDI) model [18], which is inspired by human reasoning. The BDI architecture [6] states that an agent has a set of beliefs, desires and intentions. Desires are the goals that the agent wants to achieve. When an agent is committed to achieve a desire, this goal is an intention, which is typically associated with a plan defining a course of action necessary to achieve the desire. All this reasoning process is based on the agent's view of the world, which are its beliefs. The buyer agent SPL was structured using this architecture, as the agents are proactive and have goals. In addition, this architecture has been thoroughly analyzed, and implemented on several agent platforms. Based on these considerations, we designed our agents based on the concepts of goals, beliefs and plans.

The variable features with their alternatives that we identified and considered in the buyer agent SPL are: (i) *Payment Type*, with alternatives: Credit Card, Pay Pal and Pay upon Pick up; (ii) *Shipping Type* with alternatives: Ground Shipping and Pick up at Store; and (iii) *Store Selection Strategy*, with alternatives: cheaper and faster. In addition, constraints were defined in order to allow only the selection of valid sets of features, e.g. the Pay upon Pick up feature can only be selected if the Pick up at Store feature is also selected.

In order to build an agent that supports these variable features, we adopted techniques since the beginning of development (the analysis phase), in which we identified the goals and subgoals of the buyer agent, which are depicted at the top of Figure 2. A set of subgoals must be achieved in order to reach the parent goal. As domain variability was also considered, we decomposed goals in such a way that leaf subgoals are only related to one alternative feature. For instance, the goal *Verify If Product in Stock* can be achieved either by a set of actions that verifies the online stock of a seller (*Consult Online Stock* plan), in the case where "Ground Shipping" is chosen, or by achieving two subgoals (*Find Near Stores* and *Check Store Stock*) to verify the stock of a store of the seller, in the case where "Pick up at Store" is chosen. A (sub)goal may be optional, meaning that it will be part of the agent only if the feature related to the goal is selected for the agent being derived, such as the *Execute PayPal Transaction* goal.

The plans for the buyer agent that achieve its goals are shown at the bottom of Figure 2. Note that some goals can be achieved by different plans that support the different alternative features. Based on a buyer agent configuration, the plans related to the selected features will be chosen to be part of the derived agent. The complete agent architecture design and implementation is presented in Figure 3.

In Figure 3, we represent the buyer agent using the structure of our target agent platform, Jadex.[1] The buyer agent (stereotyped with ≪agent≫) is composed of capabilities (stereotyped with ≪capability≫), which support the modularization of a set of BDI concepts according to a chosen criterion such as cohesion. The capabilities aggregate beliefs, goals and plans, and the latter also

---

[1] http://jadex-agents.informatik.uni-hamburg.de/

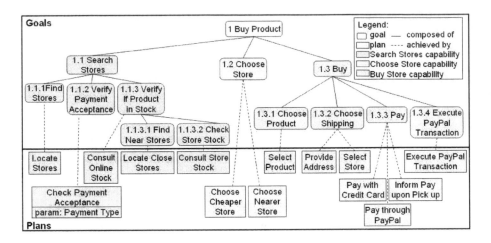

Fig. 2. Buyer Agent SPL – Goals and Plans

have an implemented body (stereotyped with ≪plan≫). It can be seen that plans match the ones identified in the analysis phase and presented in Figure 2. Colors in Figure 3 indicate where the variability is present in the buyer agent architecture, each color is associated with one feature.

3.3   Techniques for Supporting Variability

Modularization is one essential property of software development, because it promotes benefits such as reusability and maintainability. In the context of SPLs, it is even more important, as it must be possible to (un)plug features from the SPL architecture to customize products. This customization can occur at different binding time in the software development, depending on the techniques adopted to support variability. For instance, at design time, design patterns can be used to modularize variable features in coarse-grained entities so each can be more easily (un)plugged from the code. At compilation time, conditional compilation can be adopted.

In order to support the variability of the buyer agent SPL, we have adopted different modularization techniques, which involve different phases of the software development process (analysis, design and implementation). Some of these modularization approaches are related to the agent platform used to implement our SPL. As stated previously, the buyer agent SPL was implemented with the Jadex agent platform, which is an implementation of the BDI architecture. Jadex supports programming software agents in XML and the Java programming language. An agent is defined in an XML file, named Agent Definition File (ADF), which specifies the agent's beliefs, goals and plans. An ADF can also contain the definition of other concepts that help with the agent implementation such as messages that can be sent and received. Although plans are declared in the ADF, their body is implemented in Java classes, which extend the `Plan` class of the platform.

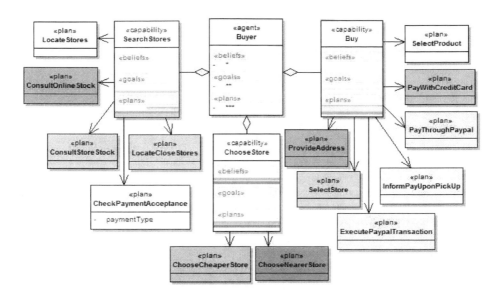

Fig. 3. Buyer Agent SPL Architecture and its Variabilities

Next, we describe the four variability techniques adopted in our exploratory study. The binding time of the first three is during the SPL analysis and design, and the last is performed at compilation time. We aimed to modularize all variable parts of the buyer agent SPL using design techniques, which can be used with any BDI platform. However, even though some entities are modularized in design models (such as a plan), as Jadex requires the plan declaration inside an ADF file, we had to use conditional compilation to manage this type of variability.

Goal Decomposition and Plan Modularization. The variability modularization starts in the analysis phase, while identifying goals and decomposing them into subgoals. When this decomposition is performed, some goals may be alternatives or optional, such as the *Find Near Stores* and *Check Store Stock*, which are related to the Ground Shipping feature. In addition, plans are modularized in such a way that each of them is either mandatory or corresponds to one single feature. The goal decomposition helps with this modularization because the finer-grained the goals, the more specific the plans.

Plan Parametrization. Passing parameters to plans allows reusing them in different contexts. The goal *Verify Payment Acceptance* could be achieved by three different plans, each corresponding to one payment type. However, the only difference in these plans would be a parameter passed in a message. Therefore, we adopted the technique of passing parameters to plans to reuse the same plan for the different payment types where there were three different parameters. It is important to notice that this technique was used at the design level, but we were able to implement plans in this way because Jadex supports plan parametrization.

Capabilities. A capability [19] is essentially a set of plans, a fragment of the knowledge base that is manipulated by those plans and a specification of the interface to the capability. This concept is implemented by JACK and Jadex agent platforms. Capabilities have been introduced into some MASs as a SE mechanism to support modularity and reusability while still allowing meta-level reasoning. We used the capability concept in order to encapsulate beliefs, goals and plans related to a certain concern, such as searching stores. Therefore, we have modularized related concepts into a component, the capability, which can be easily (un)plugged from the agent and reused in other agents.

Conditional Compilation. The last implementation technique we adopted is conditional compilation. The buyer agent SPL architecture has optional and alternative parts that were not modularized in specific code assets, mainly because all beliefs, goals and plans must be declared in ADFs. For instance, even though the *Pay* goal is achieved by three different plans, i.e. Java classes, the plan must be declared in the ADF. Therefore, the three different plans are declared in the ADF with tags surrounding them indicating the feature related to this XML code fragment. With this information, it is possible to remove the fragments that are related to unselected features before compiling the code. This technique is also adopted in Java class files. When a goal is decomposed into subgoals, a plan is created to dispatch the set of subgoals, but some of these subgoals may be optional. In this case, tags surrounding the dispatch of the subgoal are introduced in the code in order to make conditional compilation possible.

3.4   Automatically Deriving Buyer Agents

Customized instances of buyer agents are automatically and dynamically derived from the buyer agent SPL during the execution of the *Ipagent* web-system. This process differs from the traditional application engineering process of SPLE because it is typically performed statically, but essentially the process is the same: a set of features is selected to be part of the customized product, and appropriate software assets are selected and customized to be combined and form the desired product. This task becomes more complicated without modularizing features, and additional techniques, such as conditional compilation that was adopted in our exploratory study, are required. Tools, e.g. pure::variants[2] and GenArch,[3] support the product derivation process of product lines, but because we needed to perform product derivation dynamically, we have developed a mechanism to support the process, which is described next.

When users want to buy a certain product, they must configure, through the web interface of the system, a buy request by choosing the alternatives of the SPL

---

[2] http://www.pure-systems.com
[3] http://www.inf.puc-rio.br/~ecirilo/genarch/

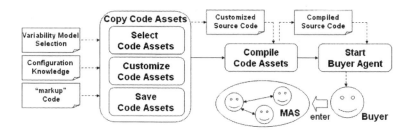

Fig. 4. Buyer Agent Derivation process

features and the desired product. This selection must respect the constraints that define valid sets of features. After doing that, the `Environment` agent detects that this business operation was executed, and propagates it to the `User` agent. This agent is responsible for deriving the customized `Buyer` agent and starting it. Figure 4 depicts the process performed by the `User` agent in order to derive `Buyer` agents. We now describe this process.

The first step of the derivation process is to produce customized source code. Three inputs are necessary for this task: (i) configuration knowledge – it is part of the `User` agent's belief base and stores the knowledge of which code assets are related to which features; (ii) "markup" code – the tags described in the last section indicate which code fragments are related to which features; and (iii) the user configuration – the set of selected features. With these inputs, the `User` agent first loads code assets that have been selected based on the configuration knowledge and the user configuration, then removes the code fragments related to the unselected features and finally saves the customized source code. The code is then compiled and the `Buyer` agent is started. When the derived `Buyer` agent is operational, it sends a message to the `User` agent indicating its operational status. The `User` agent then requests the `Buyer` agent to buy the product that the user wants. After finishing buying the product or realizing that the purchase is not possible, the `Buyer` agent informs the user about the success or lack of success while pursuing the buy request, and then dies.

4   Discussion

In this section, we present and discuss issues identified while developing the buyer agent SPL. In order to build our study, we adopted techniques that support domain variability, and as a consequence, we had to design and implement the SPL architecture, in such a way that variable parts are modularized and SPL assets can be reused to derive different buyer agent configurations. The issues are related mainly to the following: modularization of different types of variability (Section 4.1), representation of MAS architectures (Section 4.2), and large scale software reuse (Section 4.3).

4.1   Intra-agent Modularization

Each agent of a MAS may be classified in two different ways [20]: (i) internally as a software system with its own purpose (*intra-agent viewpoint*); and (ii) externally as part of a society interacting with other individuals (*inter-agent viewpoint*). Figure 1 shows the inter-agent view of our study, presenting the agents and organizations that are part of the MAS and how they interact. Figures 2 and 3 depict the internal structure of the buyer agent SPL. In this section, we discuss modularization techniques for MAS architectures, mainly related to an intra-agent viewpoint.

A modularized software architecture is one that has been decomposed into a set of modules that are cohesive and loosely coupled. From an inter-agent viewpoint, agents have a lower coupling than objects, which is achieved by a higher degree of encapsulation. A main difference between an agent and an object [21] is that the former encapsulates not only data (its state), but also the behavior selection process and when such behaviors are necessary. In addition, agents are not aware of method signatures that must be known to be invoked, but have to understand message exchange protocols. Nevertheless, the principles of low coupling and high cohesion of an agent's internal architecture have received little attention from the research community.

In our study, we focus on exploring fine-grained variable structures of the intra-agent viewpoint and not coarse-grained structures. The latter involves self-contained software entities, such as agents and capabilities, and the first refers to entities that are part of coarser-grained ones, e.g. beliefs, goals and plans. Variability on these structures means that they are optional or alternative across different products. While developing the buyer agent SPL, we have identified the following variable structures:

- *Capabilities:* we used the capability concept provided by Jadex to aggregate beliefs, goals and plans that are related to a specific concern, such as search stores and buy product. Another capability that could be part of the buyer agent SPL is a negotiation capability, which would aggregate concepts to provide means for the agent to negotiate prices with sellers. Thus, capabilities can be optional or alternative in an agent SPL architecture.
- *Beliefs:* An agent's beliefs, in the BDI architecture, influences the two activities of practical reasoning: (i) deliberation – the activity of deciding what goals the agent wants to achieve; and (ii) means-ends reasoning – the activity of deciding how to achieve these goals. Therefore, a belief must be part of the agent knowledge base if it participates in at least one of these activities. In our study, the knowledge about the product store varies according to the shipping type and the choose store strategy. If the product is to be shipped and the strategy is to choose the cheaper store, the agent must know the sellers that have the product in online stock, while if the user is to pick the product up at a store and the strategy is to choose the nearer store, the agent must know the different stores that have the product in stock and their location. Consequently, the beliefs of an agent may also vary.

- *Goals:* As our study illustrates, subgoals for achieving a goal may be different when dealing with different features. An example is the *Verify If Product in Stock* goal, which can be achieved either by a plan or decomposed into two subgoals. Therefore, there are two optional subgoals. In the buyer agent SPL there are no alternative goals, however it is also a possible point of variation, given that alternative goals are optional goals with the restriction that they are mutually exclusive or have a specific cardinality.
- *Plans:* In the same way that a goal may be decomposed into different sets of subgoals, the goal can be achieved by different plans. Thus, these different plans are alternative descriptions. In addition, there are optional plans – if a goal is optional, the plan that achieves the goal is also optional.
- *Plan parameters:* As discussed in Section 3.3, we used the plan parametrization provided by Jadex. In the *Check Payment Acceptance* plan, there are alternative parameters that are given as input to a plan. Thus, Jadex allowed us to reuse the actions of the plan to implement three different features.

Figure 3 shows how these variable structures are present in the buyer agent SPL. We have adopted UML notation with stereotypes to represent agents, beliefs, goals, plans and capabilities. Each color in the figure represents a different feature and the white color indicates that the element (or fragment of an element) is present in all agent configurations, i.e. they are part of the SPL core. It should be noticed that each plan can be related to only one feature because, by means of goal decomposition, we have made plans very specific. However, other variability types are tangled and spread throughout the capabilities.

Most agent architectures are generic structures and domain independent. This is the case of the one we adopted, the BDI architecture, which provides modularization in terms of three mental attitudes – beliefs, goals and plans. However, other concerns (e.g. a system requirements) typically are associated with and implemented by a subset of an agent's beliefs, goals and plans, and the architecture lacks mechanisms to modularize these other concerns. We refer to a concern as anything that might be interesting to modularize in the architecture.

This situation happens in agents with more than one responsibility, i.e. agents that have goals related to different purposes. The concepts related to each of them will be mixed into the agent architecture, leading to code that is harder to understand and maintain. In our case study, for instance, if the Buyer agent were a User agent with different services, e.g. buy product and search the web, the beliefs, goals and plans associated with both services would be part of the agent, and there is no way of telling which service requires a certain belief. This scenario is also illustrated in Figure 3. In addition, each capability, concept introduced by the JACK platform and used in our study where all goals, beliefs and plans associated with buying a product are encapsulated into a capability, is associated with a set of plans that are related to different features (each color represents a different feature). However, some of these plans are related to the same feature, but this semantic relationship among them is not represented in the buyer agent SPL.

Moreover, with goal decomposition and plan modularization features of the buyer agent SPL could be modularized into single plans. This can be seen in Figure 3, in which all plans have only one color. However, given that all beliefs, goals and plans are part of an agent (or capability), and must be defined into ADFs, the code related to features are tangled and spread throughout the ADFs. Even though conditional compilation solved the problem of managing variable structures, this technique is not a good practice because it leads to code and configuration knowledge that is hard to understand and maintain. Conditional compilation increases the complexity of the code, because a developer has to understand the logic of conditional compilation tags, as well as the logic that is already present in the code. The configuration knowledge, i.e. the relationship between features and implementation elements, is buried in the code and there is no way of discovering the impact of a feature on the SPL architecture.

An alternative solution to this problem is an extensive use of the capability concept. In our case study, the Buy capability aggregates the concepts needed for buying a product and can be reused in other agents that need to buy a product in the e-Marketplace MAS. New capabilities could be created to encapsulate components related to specific features. Figure 5 illustrates this scenario generically. On the left side, we can see an agent modularized into three different mental attitudes, which have two different concerns that have an orthogonal decomposition. On the right side the use of capabilities to modularize such concerns is shown.

However, even though conditional compilation has the presented drawbacks, we have adopted this technique because, using capabilities, each variable part is modularized into a separate capability. Nevertheless, this technique would significantly increase the number of components of the agent's architecture thus increasing its complexity and the difficulty of understanding and management [22].

Consequently, we claim that there is a need to explore existing techniques or proposing new ones to provide mechanisms that allow the modularization of agent architectures, thus increasing the reusability and maintainability of systems. One example is the use of Aspect-oriented Programming (AOP) to modularize agent architectures [23]. AOP has been investigated in the context of SE as a technique to modularize cross-cutting concerns.

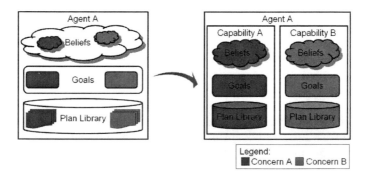

Fig. 5. Modularization by means of capabilities

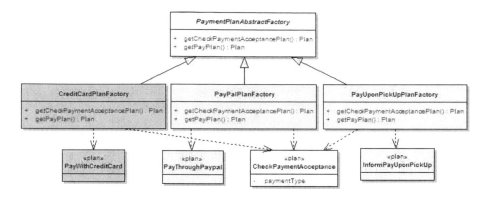

Fig. 6. Abstract Factory Design Pattern

Besides AOP, several other approaches in SE have been proposed to improve software architectures, following principles such as information hiding, encapsulation, reusability, maintainability, high cohesion and low coupling. An example of an approach that could be applied in the buyer agent SPL is the use of a design pattern, namely the Abstract Factory [24]. The intent of this pattern is to provide an interface for creating families of related or dependent objects without specifying their concrete classes. In our SPL, we have alternative sets of plans for achieving a given set of goals. Alternative plans have the same interface as specified by the pre- and post-conditions. This is exactly the problem that the Abstract Factory pattern solves where our goal is to instantiate a family of plans according to a selected feature. By means of the Abstract Factory pattern it is possible to show the semantic relationship between plans and features explicitly. Figure 6 shows this idea of applying the Abstract Factory pattern to show the semantic relationship between plans and features explicitly. In addition, this helps to manage the variable structure because using an abstract factory in the client code allows an interchange of concrete factories without impacting the client code. In addition, the inclusion of a new feature, i.e. a new payment method, would be easier because it only requires a new concrete factory and its associated plans. In this buyer SPL example, there are only two plans associated with the factories, but the pattern would bring more benefits if there were more plans.

MASs are inspired by different aspects of human nature, such as organizational and cognitive functions, which support promising approaches to developing systems with capabilities such as reasoning and learning. But several agent architectures and other AOSE approaches have addressed particular challenging MAS problems, such as openness, proactive behavior and reasoning, and have looked at "traditional" SE in a disconnected way. With the example described previously, we aim to show that AOSE could learn from research work that has been done in state-of-the-art SE to design and implement better software architectures.

4.2   Architectural Models

The definition of the software architecture is a crucial step in the realization of large scale software systems. The architecture provides a well conceived understanding of the large scale structures of the future system, and provides a means for predicting problems that may arise during the early stages of software development. Moreover, it is the software architecture that addresses quality attributes defined in the system requirements, such as availability, modifiability and other "ilities." Designing high quality architectures with properties such as modularity, and stability, are essential to reduce the impact of the software evolution. Otherwise, software architectures may degenerate over time, making their maintenance a nightmare, resulting in the need for refactoring, which increases costs.

The software architecture of a computing system is the structure of the system, which comprise software components, the externally visible properties of those components, and the relationships among them [25]. According to Szyperski et al. [26], a software component is a unit of composition with contractually specified interfaces and explicit context dependencies. An interface is a set of named operations that can be invoked by clients. Context dependencies are specifications of what the deployment environment needs to provide, such that components can function.

Agents are software components with some different properties. As opposed to "typical" components that are defined by provided and required named operations, agents are characterized by their behavior, mainly because of the proactive property of agents. From an external point of view, agents are defined by: (i) goals that they are willing to achieve; (ii) goals they may achieve for other agents; and (iii) goals they need other agents to achieve for them. In addition, protocols that regulate agent communication have an important role in the architecture, being seen as connectors among agent components. In this sense, using an agent-based approach can be seen as an architectural style.

Because of the limited expression of architecture models for MASs, architectures of agent-based applications are typically expressed by *ad hoc* notations (e.g. using specific symbols for agents and stereotypes in arrows to indicate a communication) or lack of information if common models are used. This can be seen in Figure 1, in which we used a typical UML diagram to show the architecture of the e-Marketplace MAS. No further information is provided in these models, such as described in the previous paragraph. As a consequence, all powerful agent abstractions to model complex domains disappear owing to a lack of appropriate architectural models.

Therefore, we identify a need for languages to represent agent components at an architectural level. Weyns [27] provided an important step in this direction by considering the environment as a first-class entity in agent architectures – besides providing a reference architecture for a specific class of MAS. Furthermore, Architecture Description Languagess (ADLs) are a recent approach for expressing software architectures. They describe systems in a formal way as a collection of components that interact with each other using connectors. Nevertheless, ADLs have received little attention in agent-oriented research. A potential first step to exploit ADLs in the context of MASs is to verify if proposed ADLs, such as ACME,[4] are able to express agent components.

4.3   Large Scale Software Reuse

Software reuse has been practiced since the development of computational systems began. It is the process of building software systems using existing software assets. These assets can be any artifact of software development, such as analysis/design models, objects and software components. The main benefits offered by reusing software are higher quality and reliability in a relatively short time. These factors reduce the costs of software development and maintenance. The computer industry has demonstrated that software reuse generates a significant return on investment by reducing cost, time, and effort while increasing the quality, productivity, and maintainability of software systems throughout the software life cycle.

The first initiatives on exploiting software reuse in MASs were the proposals of pattern reuse [28]. These existing approaches mainly focus either on protocol definitions or overall organizational structures [29], which leaves a gap between the textual description of the pattern and its implementation. This final step is highly dependent on the experience of the designer. Therefore, even though these approaches provide a solid basis for improving MAS development from a SE perspective, pattern reuse can be exploited in other directions. For instance, pattern reuse can provide structures for recurring design problems of MAS applications (similar to object-oriented (OO) design patterns). Similarly architectural patterns may also provide for reuse of general structures for MAS architectures that have been successfully adopted in existing systems.

Even though there are these approaches for reuse in MASs, most of MAS approaches do not adopt extensive reuse practices [30], and in particular SPLs, which are explored in our case study and were introduced in Section 2.1. As SPLs imply variability management, the exploratory study presented in this paper explores different levels of granularity in variability, e.g. belief and plan parameters, and is concerned with adopting new strategies to improve the agent architecture not just strategies using available platforms. We have adopted reuse techniques at different phases in the software development process, and some of these techniques are:

Goal reuse. Plenty of MAS approaches adopt the goal concept. Some of them associate agents with a list of goals and others represent goals as a tree, meaning that children of a goal are the subgoals that must be achieved in order to realize the goal. This relationship is represented in Figure 2. However, subgoals may be necessary to achieve more than one goal. Therefore, goals have an n:n relationship, and not 1:n as expressed in a tree structure. One methodology that models this n:n relationship is Tropos [31], which is based on the i* framework. In addition, Tropos models are powerful in the

---

[4] http://www.cs.cmu.edu/~acme/

sense that they provide lots of information, such as goals and plans that are part of an actor (agent) and relationships among goals and plans, which are aspects typically not captured by other existing agent-oriented models. Nevertheless, despite these advantages, Tropos has some limitations. We believe it has scalability issues, because each concept in a Tropos model is represented by a node and each node may have several arrows connecting it to other nodes, and as a consequence these models may become unreadable in complex system scenarios. Moreover, when a single model provides so much information, it may also compromise its readability and management. One solution for this problem is to define modules of the system in separate models, and provide different system views, which capture different aspects of the system (or a product line). We aimed to address these issues in our informal models presented in Figures 2 and 3, however we are aware that Tropos models are able to capture many other aspects, such as agent organizations and relationships among agents.

Capabilities. Capabilities are a mechanism that enables the modularization and reuse of a specific agent behavior. They are basically composed of the same concepts as agents, i.e. beliefs, goals and plans, however they must be incorporated into an agent in order to be part of a MAS. This concept was introduced by the JACK platform, but only a few approaches adopted capabilities as a first-class element. In MAS methodologies that do not present the capability concept, the only way of modularizing related concepts is to associate them with two or more different agents. Nevertheless, it may not be a good solution for two reasons: (i) semantically, the concepts must be part of the same agent. For instance, if in a MAS an agent A represents a person and this person plays the role of a mother and a teacher, agent A must aggregate the concepts related to both roles; and (ii) one must not forget that MASs are multi-threaded systems, and each agent has its own thread of execution. Therefore, creating new agents in the system for modularity reasons may cause unnecessary overhead.

Plan parameterization. Jadex allows inputs to plans and this provides for the instantiation of plans in different contexts. This idea can also be considered in human behavior, because people usually have a pre-defined course of actions to accomplish some goals (plans) that are instantiated according to a context. For instance, when going to the movies, a plan can be buy the ticket, enter the theatre, and watch the movie. In this situation, the input parameters may be the cinema and the film. Even though plan parameterization is a mechanism that can be adopted at the implementation level, few MAS design approaches provide such parametrization. In Figure 3, we represent the plan parameter as a class attribute.

These techniques used at the implementation level are supported by some agent platforms, in our case Jadex, however they cannot be expressed in design models of current MAS methodologies and modeling languages. Therefore, there is a lack of mechanisms to design reusable elements.

Finally, as agents are software components, it is interesting to think about agent repositories, or catalogs of agents for reuse. To produce a repository structure, it is essential to define agent metadata such as goals and protocols. This metadata provides the necessary information to reuse an agent. This need for metadata is consistent with the idea of exposing the agent "interface" (i.e. external behavior) in architecture models.

5   Further Considerations

In addition to the previously presented issues that are lessons learned from our exploratory study, we discuss in this section two important relevant SE areas, generative approaches (Section 5.1) and empirical studies (Section 5.2), that have not been widely explored in the context of MAS. We present a qualitative argument why these areas are relevant in AOSE and how research on it can improve the development of MAS. These arguments arose from our experience while developing different MASs and MAS-PLs [2,4,15,32].

5.1   Generative Approaches

High-level agent abstractions are based on human models and organizations. The vocabulary provided by these abstractions matches the proactive and autonomous behavior present in modern software systems. As a consequence, in the development of such systems, agents can facilitate communication between analysts and stakeholders, since they can speak a similar language [32]. Moreover, one major advantage of agent abstractions is that they are present in both analysis and design phases, thus reducing the gap between analysis and design. In contrast consider using OO approaches to model and design complex and distributed systems with agent-like properties. The analysts typically have to understand the domain by interacting with the stakeholders, and then model this domain using use cases and other analysis models, which are then used to produce a design model that uses classes, and objects.

On the other hand, the gap between design and implementation can be increased by the use of an agent-oriented approach. The first common option for implementing MASs is by the means of general purpose programming languages (typically OO). Consequently design models have to be translated to the abstractions provided by the programming language. The second option is implementing MASs with the aid of agent platforms, which usually either provide an application program interface (API) (e.g. JADE and Jadex) or a specific language that is translated to a general purpose language (e.g. Jason and JACK). In this case, the gap is reduced, but there is no assurance that the abstractions used at the design level are maintained by the implementation platform. Intuitively it seems better to choose a platform that provides abstractions that match with the ones used at the design phase. However this is not always the case because of other aspects that have to be taken into account such as runtime performance and integration with other technologies.

When it is the case that the chosen design approach is based on concepts that do not have counterparts in the implementation platform, the effort spent developing good design models, using principles such as modularity and reusability, may not be worthwhile, because these principles may not be reflected in the code. This gap between design and implementation models makes code understanding harder because elements in the implementation do not correspond directly to elements in the design. Consequently, it also makes it difficult to maintain and evolve the code, and creates the need for traceability models that show how design elements are implemented in the code.

In the past few years, the AOSE community has been proposing approaches that take advantage of Model-driven Development (MDD) and Model-driven Architectures (MDA) in order to bridge the gap between the design and implementation of MASs [33]. In a nutshell, the MDA approach defines system functionality using a platform-independent model (PIM) and appropriate domain-specific language. Then, given a platform definition model (PDM) corresponding to a specific platform, the PIM is translated to one or more platform-specific models (PSMs) that computers can run. Therefore, models designed with abstractions defined in a meta-model of a specific methodology can be automatically translated to a model that describes the same system in terms of platform-specific abstractions. The AOSE literature has shown substantial advances in use of MDA for generating code for MAS based on design models. However most of the work was devoted in creating translation of models of existing methodologies to specific platforms. Models are used to abstract lower-level details, and most of the models of existing MAS approaches contain all the information needed to generate code (programming in a graphical manner). Recent studies about MDD[5] have shown that this approach tends to be successful when the domain is specific enough, thus allowing the creation of high-level models where code is generated in combination with domain-specific knowledge. As MAS research addresses different classes of systems, such as electronic commerce applications and automated guided vehicles, it is interesting to look into more specific model-driven approaches. In our case study, for instance, we have created a set of assets that allows the creation of a family of agents of a specific domain, related to electronic commerce. When a user chooses a configuration for an agent, a specific instance of the code is generated based on a very high-level specification.

Another promising solution for the gap problem is the use of Generative Programming (GP) techniques, which have been barely explored for MAS. GP is about designing and implementing software modules which can be customized and combined to generate specialized and highly optimized systems fulfilling specific requirements [9]. Instead of focusing on the development of specific systems from scratch, GP focuses on designing and implementing reusable software for generating these systems. Consequently, the scope of GP is families of systems and not single systems. MASs can be seen as a family of systems, which shares several common features such as communication, reasoning, learning and mobility, and GP techniques are a potential solution for automating the related code generation.

---

[5] Information available at: `http://www.comp.lancs.ac.uk/~eamde/`

5.2   Empirical Studies

Experimentation has gained popularity in the context of SE in order to evaluate new approaches and compare existing ones. Empirical SE provides techniques to evaluate if proposed approaches bring the benefits they say they provide. Experimentation provides a systematic, disciplined, quantifiable, and controlled way to evaluate new theories and has been used in many fields such as physics, medicine and manufacturing. However, this idea started to be explored in the SE field, in the 70s. According to Basili [34], like other disciplines, SE requires the same high-level approach for evolving the knowledge of the discipline: the cycle of model building, experimentation and teaming, since we cannot rely solely on observation followed by logical thought. It involves an experimental component in order to test or disprove theories, to explore new domains. Therefore, there must be experiments with proposed methodologies to see how and when they really work, to understand their limits and how to improve them. However this approach of evaluation and validation has been barely explored in the context of AOSE. Only few empirical studies have been performed on agent-oriented systems, such as reported in [14]. Therefore, there is little evidence of the real benefits of agent-oriented approaches.

MASs are essentially inspired by different aspects of human nature, such as organizational and cognitive functions. Since MAS has been exploited as a new SE paradigm, there have been several research proposals but they rely on qualitative arguments that state the benefits of using an agent-oriented approach [35] rather than on experimental evidence. As an area matures this type of evidence is important to assess the real advantages of the approaches being proposed. A growing level of maturity can be seen in the AOP community as a large number of experiments have been performed to asses aspect-oriented approaches to identify situations in which aspects are an appropriate technique to solve a problem. Not only the benefits of aspects are identified but also the scenarios in which these benefits appear and the limitations of the approach. As a consequence, aspects are progressively being adopted in scenarios where they bring proven advantages, such as in transaction management and logging and in widely used frameworks.[6]

Several agent-oriented methodologies, languages and processes are proposed with the aim of representing the different aspects of MASs, including communication and coordination. However, the number of approaches (see Figure 7) makes the decision of choosing one of them to develop a MAS very difficult. In addition, their validation is usually performed by means of a set of case studies, showing that the methodology is expressive enough to model them. Recent research work [36] analyzed most of these approaches and proposed a generic metamodel for MAS development. Even though this research is a huge step for dealing with the large number of MAS methodologies, there is still little evidence how these approaches can improve software development in terms of quality, costs and time-to-market, as they are usually evaluated with a single and typically not industrial-size case studies.

---

[6] http://www.springsource.org/

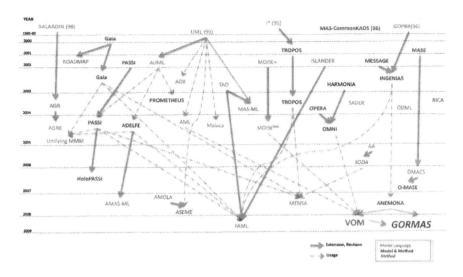

Fig. 7. Evolution of Agent-oriented Methodologies [37]

Because of the lack of empirical studies in the context of AOSE, we believe in doing experiments in SE to show real evidence of the advantages of agent-oriented approaches compared to other approaches such as OO. Moreover, experiments can provide quantitative comparative studies of agent-oriented methodologies.

Finally, empirical studies typically involve measuring case studies with metrics. There are several metrics adopted for evaluating different aspects of software systems, including their architectures. The AOP community has proposed new concern-driven metrics [38] in order to assess better the use of aspect-oriented techniques for modularizing crosscutting concerns. As there are only a few empirical studies performed in AOSE, it has not been investigated if existing metrics are appropriate to evaluate MAS architectures. Therefore, research should be performed on verifying existing metrics to determine if they are enough to measure MAS properties. As far as we know, only recent research has addressed a metrics suite for evaluation of agent-oriented architectures [39].

6   Conclusion

MASs aim at developing complex, distributed systems in terms of high-level abstractions in order to reduce the gap between the problem and solution spaces. The adoption of human-inspired abstractions, such as autonomous agents, mental attitudes, organizations and roles, helps in understanding and modeling complex problems owing to the reduced gap between these abstractions and real world situations. This fact also facilitates the communication between developers and stakeholders, who are able to communicate in a common language. In addition, multi-agent research has also contributed to reasoning, learning and other models, which become powerful tools for developing intelligent systems.

However, it is essential to rely on principles and guidelines to develop large scale software systems in a disciplined manner, which provides a solid basis for the success of large scale software projects. In this context, SE is the application of a systematic, disciplined, quantifiable approach to the development, operation, and maintenance of software. AOSE aims at adopting these techniques and mechanisms in the development of MASs, as well as tailoring them and proposing new ones that address particular aspects of MASs and related architectures. Nevertheless, promising SE techniques have not yet been (widely) explored. As a consequence, we claim that AOSE can profit from existing research in state-of-the-art SE to analyze, design and implement high-quality software systems, which are easier to manage, evolve and maintain.

In this paper, we presented an exploratory study of the development of a family of buyer agents following the BDI model and using a SPL architecture. This architecture allows the derivation of customized agents from an existing MAS which is configured according to a user specification. Within the buyer agent SPL, we have explored different levels of granularity in variability, including capabilities and fine-grained variable structures, such as beliefs, goals, plans and plan parameters. Based on our study, we presented and discussed important issues mainly related to the lack of techniques, both at the design and implementation levels, to develop MASs based on traditional SE principles, such as modularity, reusability and maintainability. These issues were categorized in five different research areas: modularization, software architectures, reuse, generative programming and empirical studies.

Finally, although the AOSE community provides qualitative arguments for the appropriateness of agent abstractions to model systems with autonomous and proactive characteristics, these models will not likely be adopted in industry if we do not show that they promote reduced time-to-market, lower costs and higher quality. Therefore, it is essential to address these issues quantitatively in order to promote industrial exploitation of the agent technology.

References

1. Weyns, D., Parunak, H.V.D., Shehory, O.: The future of software engineering and multi-agent systems (editorial, special issue). IJAOSE 3(4), 369–377 (2009)
2. Nunes, I., Lucena, C.J., Cowan, D., Alencar, P.: Building service-oriented user agents using a software product line approach. In: Edwards, S.H., Kulczycki, G. (eds.) ICSR 2009. LNCS, vol. 5791, pp. 236–245. Springer, Heidelberg (2009)
3. Clements, P., Northrop, L.: Software Product Lines: Practices and Patterns. Addison-Wesley, Reading (2002)
4. Nunes, I., Lucena, C.: On the development of multi-agent systems product lines: A domain engineering process. In: Luck, M., Gomez-Sanz, J.J. (eds.) AOSE 2008. LNCS, vol. 5386, pp. 109–120. Springer, Heidelberg (2009)
5. Kästner, C., Apel, S., Kuhlemann, M.: Granularity in software product lines. In: ICSE 2008, pp. 311–320. ACM, USA (2008)

6. Rao, A., Georgeff, M.: BDI-agents: from theory to practice. In: ICMAS 1995 (1995)
7. Brazier, F.M.T., Kephart, J.O., Parunak, H.V.D., Huhns, M.N.: Agents and service-oriented computing for autonomic computing: A research agenda. IEEE Internet Computing 13(3), 82–87 (2009)
8. Parnas, D.L.: On the design and development of program families. IEEE Trans. Software Eng. 2(1), 1–9 (1976)
9. Czarnecki, K., Eisenecker, U.W.: Generative programming: methods, tools, and applications. ACM Press/Addison-Wesley Publishing Co., New York (2000)
10. Kang, K., Cohen, S., Hess, J., Novak, W., Peterson: Feature-oriented domain analysis (foda) feasibility study. Technical Report CMU/SEI-90-TR-021, Software Engineering Institute, Carnegie-Mellon University (November 1990)
11. Pohl, K., Bckle, G., van der Linden, F.J.: Software Product Line Engineering: Foundations, Principles and Techniques. Springer, New York (2005)
12. Pena, J., Hinchey, M.G., Ruiz-Corts, A., Trinidad, P.: Building the core architecture of a multiagent system product line: with an example from a future nasa mission. In: Padgham, L., Zambonelli, F. (eds.) AOSE VII / AOSE 2006. LNCS, vol. 4405, pp. 208–224. Springer, Heidelberg (2007)
13. Dehlinger, J., Lutz, R.R.: Supporting requirements reuse in multi-agent system product line design and evolution. In: ICSM, pp. 207–216 (2008)
14. Nunes, C., Kulesza, U., Sant'Anna, C., Nunes, I., Garcia, A., Lucena, C.: Assessment of the design modularity and stability of multi-agent system product lines. J. UCS 15(11), 2254–2283 (2009)
15. Nunes, I., Kulesza, U., Nunes, C., Cirilo, E., de Lucena, C.J.: Extending web-based applications to incorporate autonomous behavior. In: WebMedia 2008 (2008)
16. Buschmann, F., Meunier, R., Rohnert, H., Sommerlad, P., Stal, M.: Pattern-oriented software architecture: a system of patterns. John Wiley & Sons, Inc., New York (1996)
17. Dijkstra, E.W.: EWD 447: On the role of scientific thought. Selected Writings on Computing: A Personal Perspective, 60–66 (1982)
18. Bratman, M.E.: Intention, Plans, and Practical Reason. Cambridge, MA (1987)
19. Busetta, P., Howden, N., Rönnquist, R., Hodgson, A.: Structuring bdi agents in functional clusters. In: Jennings, N.R. (ed.) ATAL 1999. LNCS, vol. 1757, pp. 277–289. Springer, Heidelberg (2000)
20. Zambonelli, F., Jennings, N.R., Omicini, A., Wooldridge, M.: Agent-oriented software engineering for internet applications (2001)
21. Odell, J.: Objects and agents compared. Journal of Object Technology (JOT) 1(1), 41–53 (2002)
22. Figueiredo, E., et al.: Evolving software product lines with aspects: an empirical study on design stability. In: ICSE 2008, pp. 261–270 (2008)
23. Garcia, A., Lucena, C.: Taming heterogeneous agent architectures. Commun. ACM 51(5), 75–81 (2008)
24. Gamma, E., Helm, R., Johnson, R., Vlissides, J.: Design Patterns: Elements of Reusable Object-oriented Software. Addison-Wesley, Reading (1995)
25. Bass, L., Clements, P., Kazman, R.: Software architecture in practice. Addison-Wesley Longman Publishing Co., Inc., Boston (1998)
26. Szyperski, C.: Component Software: Beyond Object-Oriented Programming. Addison-Wesley Longman Publishing Co., Inc., Boston (2002)
27. Weyns, D., Haesevoets, R., Helleboogh, A., Holvoet, T., Joosen, W.: The macodo middleware for context-driven dynamic agent organizations. ACM Trans. Auton. Adapt. Syst. 5, 3:1–3:28 (2010)

28. Lind, J.: Patterns in agent-oriented software engineering. In: Giunchiglia, F., Odell, J.J., Weiss, G. (eds.) AOSE 2002. LNCS, vol. 2585, pp. 47–58. Springer, Heidelberg (2003)
29. Gonzalez-Palacios, J., Luck, M.: A framework for patterns in gaia: A case-study with organisations. In: Odell, J.J., Giorgini, P., Müller, J.P. (eds.) AOSE 2004. LNCS, vol. 3382, pp. 174–188. Springer, Heidelberg (2005)
30. Girardi, R.: Reuse in agent-based application development. In: SELMAS 2002 (2002)
31. Bresciani, P., Perini, A., Giorgini, P., Giunchiglia, F., Mylopoulos, J.: Tropos: An agent-oriented software development methodology. JAAMAS 8(3), 203–236 (2004)
32. Nunes, I., Choren, R., Nunes, C., Fábri, B., Silva, F., Carvalho, G., de Lucena, C.J.P.: Supporting prenatal care in the public healthcare system in a newly industrialized country. In: 9th International Conference on Autonomous Agents and Multiagent Systems: Industry Track, AAMAS 2010, pp. 1723–1730. IFAAMS (2010)
33. Fischer, K., Hahn, C., Madrigal-Mora, C.: Agent-oriented software engineering: a model-driven approach. IJAOSE 1(3/4), 334–369 (2007)
34. Basili, V.R., Selby, R.W., Hutchens, D.H.: Experimentation in software engineering. IEEE Trans. Softw. Eng. 12(7), 733–743 (1986)
35. Zambonelli, F., Jennings, N.R., Wooldridge, M.: Organisational Abstractions for the Analysis and Design of Multi-agent Systems, pp. 235–251. Springer, Heidelberg (2001)
36. Beydoun, G., Low, G., Henderson-Sellers, B., Mouratidis, H., Gomez-Sanz, J.J., Pavon, J., Gonzalez-Perez, C.: Faml: A generic metamodel for mas development. IEEE Transactions on Software Engineering 99(RapidPosts), 841–863 (2009)
37. Argente, E., Garcia, M.E., Giret, A., Esparcia, S., Criado, N., Julian, V., Botti, V.: Vom: a service-oriented open mas meta-model (2009),
http://www.agreement-technologies.eu/wp-content/uploads/2009/12/cost-wg3-argente1.pdf
38. Sant'Anna, C., Figueiredo, E., Garcia, A., Lucena, C.: On the modularity of software architectures: A concern-driven measurement framework. In: Oquendo, F. (ed.) ECSA 2007. LNCS, vol. 4758, pp. 207–224. Springer, Heidelberg (2007)
39. García-Magariño, I., Massimo, C., Valeria, S.: A metrics suite for evaluating agent-oriented architectures. In: SAC 2010: Proceedings of the 2010 ACM Symposium on Applied Computing, pp. 912–919. ACM, New York (2010)

Engaging Stakeholders with Agent-Oriented Requirements Modelling

Tim Miller[1], Sonja Pedell[2], Leon Sterling[1], and Bin Lu[1]

[1] Department of Computer Science and Software Engineering
[2] Department of Information Systems,
University of Melbourne, Parkville, 3010, VIC, Australia

Abstract. One advantage of using the agent paradigm for software engineering is that the concepts used for high-level modelling, such as roles, goals, organisations, and interactions, are accessible to many different stakeholders. Existing research demonstrates that including the stakeholders in the modelling of systems for as long as possible improves the quality of the development and final system because inconsistencies and incorrect behaviour are more likely to be detected early in the development process. In this paper, we propose three changes to the typical requirements engineering process found in AOSE methodologies, with the aim of including stakeholders over the requirements engineering process, effectively using stakeholders as modellers. These changes are: withholding design commitment, delaying the definition of the system boundary, and delaying the stakeholder "sign-off" of the requirements specification. We discuss our application of these changes to a project with an industry partner, and present anecdotal evidence to suggest that these changes can be effective in maintaining stakeholder involvement.

1 Introduction

In software engineering, product and project stakeholders are a valuable resource for eliciting and validating requirements. Stakeholders are especially important for socio-technical systems, in which the interaction between people and technical systems can form behaviour outside of the control of the technology itself.

The agent paradigm recognises that most stakeholders are non-technical, so by using concepts such as roles and goals, which are palatable for most people, stakeholders can provide feedback on models early in the development process. As a result, artifacts in agent-oriented software engineering play a somewhat different role to other types of artifacts. As well as documenting the requirements engineers' understanding of the domain, which requirements specifications typically do, they can also be used to encourage rich discussion between stakeholders, including requirements engineers.

Many requirements engineering processes, including those in agent-oriented software engineering methodologies, aim to define the interface and product features, and to precisely specify and validate these as early as possible in the development lifecycle. Our view is that, while making these decisions early has

D. Weyns and M.-P. Gleizes (Eds.): AOSE 2010, LNCS 6788, pp. 62–78, 2011.
© Springer-Verlag Berlin Heidelberg 2011

benefits, premature commitment to certain solutions and definitions may discourage stakeholders that do not agree with or understand these decisions from participating in conversations with system developers. We advocate involving stakeholders in the development process for as long as possible, to continue engaging them in rich conversations that can help understand and define the system.

For engineering socio-technical systems, we propose small changes in the typical requirements engineering process found in software engineering (including AOSE) methodologies, with the aim of promoting conversation between stakeholders. The changes are based on results from existing research, which is discussed in Section 3. The proposed changes are:

1. Withholding design commitment by allowing inconsistencies and ambiguities early in the requirements engineering process. This allows different viewpoints of stakeholders to be represented, encouraging them into conversations for longer than they otherwise may. We are not the first authors to take this stance. For example, Easterbrook and Nuseibeh [7] discuss a framework with the purpose of allowing and dealing with different stakeholders' viewpoints. Paay et al. [19] suggest that withholding design commitment encouraged conversations between different stakeholders.
2. Delaying the definition of the system boundary. By defining the system boundary early in the process, some solutions may be eliminated before they can be discussed by the stakeholders, even though they may be more suitable than the remaining solutions.
3. Delaying the "sign-off" of requirements (or the end of the requirements engineering process) until the high-level agent design. That is, the requirements are considered only complete once we identify which agents are to be built and what their behaviour is to be. This is related to the second point, as it also helps to define the system boundary.

It is our view that these changes can be used in any agent-oriented development methodology, and are useful for breaking down barriers between stakeholders and software engineers, especially for social-technical systems. In Section 4, we present the application of these changes to an industry case study, and discuss the advantages and disadvantages that resulted from these changes. The goals of the paper are to present these processes to researchers and practitioners in agent-oriented software engineering in order to promote discussion and receive feedback on these ideas.

2   Agent-Oriented Requirements Engineering

With the agent paradigm increasingly becoming a popular and successful way for modelling complex systems [18], methodologies for agent-oriented software engineering have become an important research field. Several such methodologies have been proposed, such as Tropos [3], Prometheus [20], Gaia [30], INGENIAS [21], and ROADMAP [13].

The typical requirements engineering process in these methodologies involves the following steps[1]:

1. elicit requirements from the stakeholders on the project;
2. derive scenarios that specify typical usage of the system;
3. define the system boundary;
4. define the environment;
5. derive a goal model outlining the major goals of the system;
6. define the role descriptors for the roles that will help to achieve the system goals;
7. define the interaction model, which specifies how roles in the system will interact; and
8. iterate over steps 1-7 with stakeholders until a shared understanding of the system is reached.

Although agent methodologies do not discuss requirements sign off, they define the *software requirements specification* (SRS) as the combination of the system boundary, goal models, role, and interaction models. From this, we infer that the major stakeholders would sign off on these documents after step 8. This would form the basis of a contract for the system development to proceed.

Variations of these steps are possible; for example, the Gaia methodology defines preliminary version of the role and interaction models as requirements, and more detailed definitions as architectural design; and Prometheus defines interaction models as architectural design.

From this point in the development process, agent-oriented methodologies typically treat subsequent tasks as design-level, so stakeholder input would not be required. The tasks include defining the agent types in the system, which agent types will play which roles, the activities that the agents will perform (these activities will both fulfill the agent's role and the goals related to that role), and implementing and testing the agents.

2.1   Modelling with Roles and Goals

The work in this paper builds mainly on the work of Sterling and Taveter [23]. Their work has focused on how to make high-level agent-oriented models palatable to non-technical stakeholders. This is achieved using role and goal models with a straightforward and minimal syntax and semantics.

Goal models are useful at early stages of requirements analysis to arrive at a shared understanding [12, 14]; and the agent metaphor is useful as it is able to represent human behaviour. Agents can take on roles associated with goals. These goals include quality attributes that are represented in a high-level pictorial view used to inform and gather input from stakeholders. For example, a role may contribute to achieving the goal "Release pressure", with the quality goal "Safely". We include such quality goals as part of the design discussion and

---

[1] Some methodologies do not strictly follow this process, but this is a good approximation of all methodologies.

maintain them as high-level concepts while eliciting the requirements for a system. For this purpose the AOSE goal models have to be simple yet meaningful enough to represent the goals of social interactions.

Figure 1 shows the syntax employed by Sterling and Taveter, which we have used in our work. Goals are represented as parallelograms, quality goals are clouds, and roles are stick figures. These constructs can be connected using arcs, which indicate relationships between them. Figure 1 shows a high-level role and goal model from our industry project of an aircraft turnaround simulator. This system simulates the process of multiple aircraft landing at a single airport, allowing one to experiment with resource allocation. The goal *Aircraft Turnaround* is the highest-level goal, and the sub-goals below this contribute to fulfill the higher-level goal. The quality goal *Efficient* specifies that goal *Aircraft Turnaround* must be satisfied with the quality attribute *Efficient*. The roles play some part in bringing about the goal *Aircraft Turnaround.*

It is important here to note that the semantics described above is a complete definition of Sterling and Taveter's goal models, leaving space for interpretation of the model. This helps to engage stakeholders who have no experience in agent modelling, and encourages round-table discussion between stakeholders and requirements engineers.

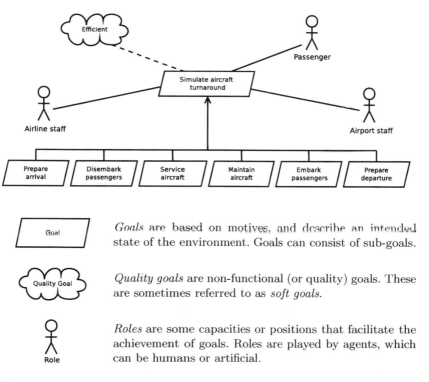

Fig. 1. An excerpt for the high-level goal on the aircraft turnaround project

3 Changing the Agent-Oriented Requirement Engineering Process

The changes presented in this paper are based on existing research in software engineering and interaction design, however, it is our view that the agent paradigm offers certain unique capabilities to the requirements engineering process that other paradigms to not. In this section, we motivate and justify our reasons for modifying the requirements engineering process, link this to existing literature that provides evidence to confirm our hypothesis, and discuss why the agent paradigm is particularly suited to these changes.

At first sight, delaying clear definitions seems antithetical or uncommon to the routines of software engineering, which is typically a structured process aimed at removing ambiguity and deriving clear definitions as early as possible in the development process. However, a body of literature that looks at software engineering from a social science perspective recognises that models and other documentation in software engineering have been used as a way to think through problems, to reach agreements, and to elaborate the needs of stakeholders in a different way than simply feeding into a formal process of modelling for system design [4, 16, 22]. For example, a goal and role model serves a different purpose for a designer than for a domain expert.

3.1 Withholding Design Commitment

The first change to the requirements engineering process is to withhold the commitment of system designs. By this, we mean holding off any particularly functional details of the system that fulfill the user requirements. At the early stages of requirements elicitation, we may not be able to clarify social concepts sufficiently to resolve uncertainty. For example, in a business domain, roles such as manager, researcher, and team leader can be well defined. However, in a social domain, roles may not be so straightforward to define. Consider trying to define the role of a grandparent, and the goals that role may want to achieve. As a result, we advocate that the social goals related to these concepts should be modelled ambiguously, even to the point where formal documents are written.

Quality requirements at the early stages of elicitation tend to be imprecise, subjective, idealistic and context-specific, as discussed by Jureta and Faulkner [14]. Garcia and Medinilla [9] describe high-level quality goals as a specific form of uncertainty that can be used as a descriptive complexity reduction mechanism and to model and discuss uncertainties in the environment. In our requirements elicitation process, we seek complexity reduction without losing the richness of the concepts themselves. Instead of eliminating uncertainty early in the process, we embrace it and withhold design commitment, at least until there is clarity and understanding between stakeholders of what it may mean to disambiguate [10].

High-level goals associated with activities can act as a point of reference for discussing the usefulness of design alternatives to achieve these goals instead of a decomposition into single requirements. The multi-agent paradigm offers benefits over other paradigms because the concepts used in modelling, such as roles, goals, and interactions, are part of every day language. Real organisations consist of roles, and specific people fill these roles each day, including stakeholders in a software engineering project. As such, stakeholders are familiar with these concepts, and are comfortable talking about them.

3.2   Delaying the Definition of the System Boundary

In many software engineering processes, the system boundary is defined before requirements analysis takes place. Often, this is one of the first agreements made between clients and software engineers.

Gause and Weinberg [11] found that natural subconscious disambiguation is one of the most common sources of requirements failure. In this situation, unrecognized or unconsciously assumed, incorrect meaning finds its way into the specification [2]. The problem is compounded by the fact that not only do software engineers consciously try to resolve uncertainty early in the process, before its impact on design is completely understood, they may also do this subconsciously. More importantly, checking the absence of requirements once we have a formal specification document is likely to be more difficult, because these documents are typically highly technical, and there less accessible to the stakeholders [15].

Once the boundaries of a system are defined, the focus of attention is within these boundaries; solutions beyond this boundary are no longer considered. Such a restriction discounts solutions that may be more suitable, and is more likely to result in some stakeholders losing interest in the project if their desired solution falls outside of these boundaries.

This does not imply that one should not be thinking about the system boundary. Specifically, all stakeholders should be aware of any other systems that may be used as part of the solution to the domain problem.

The multi-agent paradigm is well suited for such models, because high-level role and goal models can be discussed and modified without defining the system boundary, while still allowing all stakeholders to come to a shared agreement of what the entire socio-technical system will comprise.

3.3   Delaying the "Sign-off" of Requirements

The sign-off of the SRS often forms part of a contractual agreement between clients and developers. The SRS defines the external interfaces to a software system and provides a complete description of the extended behaviour of the software.

In the process of software engineering, the sign-off of a requirements specification is generally performed before any high-level design takes place. If left until after design commences, developers may unnecessarily waste time on design tasks, only to find the requirements have changed.

In the multi-agent domain, we advocate delaying the sign-off of the SRS by stakeholders until as late as possible before it impacts architectural design. This allows discussions to continue between stakeholders for a longer period. Further-more, it also helps stakeholders to understand the proposed behaviour of the system, because role and goal models define motivation, not behaviour.

3.4   Discussion

The first two changes proposed in this section are not new in the social domain. Our work is consistent with results from researchers cited in the previous sections. As far as the authors are aware, the third change, delaying the sign-off, has not been investigated before.

While we present these three proposed changes as being separate changes, they are in fact, closely related. By not defining the system boundary, we are in fact withholding design commitment. Similarly, by not signing off on the SRS early, we are leaving open design decisions, thereby withholding design commitment.

These changes are presented separately because we view them as different tasks. Withholding design commitment is a general approach in which we do not take design decisions too early, but in general, the requirements elicitation process will run in the same order. However, the definition of the system boundary is a specific task that we aim to put later in the requirements engineering process. Typically, defining the system boundary is one of the first tasks performed in requirements engineering, and this is suitable for most business applications. However, for socio-technical systems, we see that a benefit in delaying the definition of the system boundary until after we fully understand the behaviour of the *entire* socio-technical system, including humans and external systems, not just the software system being built.

These changes will clearly have a legal impact, because the requirements may be signed off later in the project. For projects in which requirements must be complete before a contract can be formalised, this will delay the contract signing. The trade off is that, at the end of the requirements, the stakeholders have a clearer shared understanding of the final outcome. Overall, this should result in shorter project durations. In fact, a better shared understanding is likley to make contract negotiations more efficient.

In practice, the legal issue has not been a problem for our industry partner, because arriving at a shared understanding is more difficult than negotiating the contract.

4   Experience

In this section, we present our experience on a project involving an industry partner. We discuss how the changes were achieved in an industry project, what effect they had on the project, and how other stakeholders responded to them.

4.1   The Project

The project is a joint project between the University of Melbourne and Jeppesen, a company that specialises in aeronautical services. The goal of the project is to construct simulation software for air traffic management using the agent paradigm as the modelling tool. The particular project on which we applied the modified requirements engineering process was a simulation of aircraft turnaround. This system simulates the process of multiple aircraft landing at a single airport, and how resources (including staff) could be allocated to efficiently turn around the aircraft, including re-stocking supplies, as well as cleaning, repairing, and maintaining the aircraft.

The major stakeholders of the project were our research team and a group of software engineers at Jeppesen who had no significant exposure to agent-oriented modelling in the past.

Figure 1 (in Section 2) shows part of the high-level role-goal model for the aircraft turnaround project. In this figure, the high-level goal of turning around the aircraft is achieved by the four subgoals of preparing for arrival, servicing the aircraft, maintaining the aircraft, and preparing for departure. The roles of *Airline Staff* and *Airport Staff* in this figure are in fact *aggregate roles*; that is, they are sets of roles, such as aircraft maintenance engineers, cleaners, and airline crew, which are described in lower-level role-goal models. The *Manager* role is responsible for overseeing the entire turnaround and re-allocating resources if there is a delay in turning around one aircraft.

4.2   Withholding Design Commitment

The requirements elicitation proceeded by our group being given an overview of the aircraft turnaround process, including the staff involved, and constructing a high-level goal and role model that represented our understanding of the system. These diagrams were improved and refined over a series of six round-table meetings with the stakeholders, in which the role and goal models were distributed to each stakeholder before a meeting, and were then used as shared artifacts to guide conversations. Over the course of these meetings, other models including the interaction models, environment models, and agent types were progressively introduced as we gained further understanding of the system.

Withholding design commitment was achieved by basing conversations between stakeholders on the role-goal models and using the role-goal models as a facilitator to open up the discussion. In this regard, the goal models took a similar role as the guiding rules described by Tjong et al. [24], whose aim is to detect uncertainties in order to trigger questions to be asked of the client.

The role and goal models were helpful in triggering communication about the specific challenges of the domain, and for identifying missing parts of the system. For example, one stakeholder commented from a single glance at the high-level goal model that air traffic controllers play a role in aircraft turnaround, and this induced discussion about how the system should handle new traffic entering the airport. In subsequent iterations, the air traffic controller role was deemed unnecessary for the system and was dropped, but changes related to this remained.

Our experience indicates that having models evolve over time lead to a clearer solution, as early concerns regarding concepts such as resources were delayed without jumping to a pre-conceived solutions. Later in the development process, successive versions of the models were used as a reminder to the design decisions that were made. This gave the research team something to fall back on when discussions started to get too complex for some stakeholders or drifting off from original high-level goals. The example of the air traffic controller role illustrates this, in which the models were updated to reflect this role, but even after its removal, parts of the model related to it remained. This is consistent with the findings described by MacLean and Bellotti [16].

Our industry partners are comfortable with the role and goal models, although this is perhaps to be expected as they are software engineers. However, Paay et al. [19] have used role and goal models as shared artifacts in the social-technical domain with non-technical stakeholders such as ethnographers to similar effect.

4.3   Including Agent Types as an SRS

We delay the system boundary definition and the SRS sign-off using the same technique: by leaving both until the high-level design.

The major divergence we take from the typical AOSE methodology is to include the agent types, including the activities they perform, as part of the SRS. As discussed in Section 2, methodologies typically use roles, goal, and interaction models as requirements, while agent types are part of the architectural design.

In this project, the SRS consisted of the role and goal models, the interaction models, the environment model, and the agent types. Combining the environment model and the agent types defines the functionality of the system, while the role and goal models help to motivate this functionality. For this particular simulation system, there was a one-to-one mapping between roles and agents.

Figure 2 shows part of the agent type specification for the *Engineer* agent, which is responsible for performing routine and non-routine maintenance on the aircraft. The agent type specification includes which activities the agent will undertake in order to fulfil its responsibilities.

Signing-off on the SRS. We believe that roles, goals, and interactions do not provide sufficient detail to define system behaviour. While role and goal models specify the goals that the system will achieve, and the roles (and their responsibilities) that will help to achieve them, they do not define functionality; that is, how the system will behave to achieve these goals. For example, the model in Figure 1 specifies the goals that need to be achieved to turnaround the aircraft. Role descriptors for the three roles in this figure outline the responsibilities to ensure the turnaround goals are achieved. However, this does not define which activities will be performed to achieve the goals. In some cases, one can extrapolate the activities from the responsibilities and goals, but this is not always the case.

Our approach of including the environment model and agent types, including activity descriptions and their effect on the environment, specifies the behaviour of the system. From Figure 2, one can see that activity descriptors are similar

Name:	Engineer	
Description:	Play the role of *Engineer* by performing routine and non-routine aircraft maintenance.	
Activities:		

Activity name: Routine maintenance	
Trigger:	Informed by ground staff of the aircraft ID of the aircraft that is ready for maintenance
Precondition:	Wheel chocks of the aircraft ID are in position
Tasks:	1. Perform the routine maintenance on the specified aircraft 2. Inform *Pilot* of the aircraft ID, and that routine maintenance is complete on the aircraft
Postcondition:	Aircraft with the specified ID is safe to fly

Activity name: Non-routine maintenance
. . .

Environment considerations:	1. Aircraft 2. Aircraft information 3. Flight schedule 4. Aircraft gate number 5. Staff schedule

Fig. 2. Agent type specification for the *Engineer* agent

to the functional requirements that one would find in a non-agent-based SRS, and it is at this point that the major stakeholders will be able to sign-off on the models.

Figure 3 presents a possible template for an agent-based SRS, based on Wiegers' SRS template [26]. Using a template leads to requirements being presented in a consistent manner across different projects, however, we acknowledge the need to be flexible with specifications depending on the system.

Our template differs from Wiegers' template mainly by emphasising the importance of motivations (using role and goal models) and the environment, which are central to the agent paradigm. Wiegers considers both the purpose of the system and the environment, but these are secondary in the SRS. In addition, the functional requirements section from Wiegers' template is replaced by agent types, which define the behaviour.

A sign off is an agreement that overall goals are important, and that the defined system will achieve these goals. In our project, all stakeholders came to a solution that all were satisfied with. We see this as a benefit in itself.

Furthermore, the stakeholders commented that the behaviour of the system was clearer when the agent types were included, even though the mapping from roles to agents was one-to-one. This is perhaps partly due to the similarity

Title information

Revision history

Table of contents

1 Introduction

1.1 Purpose
1.2 Intended audience
1.3 Project scope
1.4 Definitions, acronyms, and abbreviations
1.5 References

2 Product Description

2.1 High-level level motivation model
2.2 User classes
2.3 Product features
2.4 Design constraints
2.5 Assumptions

3 Goal models and motivational scenarios

3.1 Motivational scenarios
3.2 Goal models

4 Role and organisational models

4.1 Organisational model(s)
4.2 Role 1
4.3 Role 2
etc ...

5 Domain/Environment model

5.1 Physical environment
5.2 Virtual Environment
5.3 Environment perspective
5.4 Overall interaction

6 Agents types and interaction models

6.1 Interaction models
6.2 Agent type 1
6.3 Agent type 2
etc ...

7 Scenarios

7.1 Scenario 1
7.2 Scenario 2
etc ...

8 External interfaces

8.1 User interfaces
8.2 Hardware interfaces
8.3 Software interfaces

9 Endorsement

9.1 Sign-off

Fig. 3. A software requirements specification template using Sterling and Taveter's models [23]

between activities and functional requirements, but the stakeholders commented that this was due to the fact that they were able to make a clear judgement as to whether the behaviour fulfilled their expectations. In our view, this justifies the decision to include the agent types in the SRS.

Defining the System Boundary. Including agent types in an SRS has a second effect: it completely defines the system boundary. Role and goal models define the entire socio-technical system, with no commitment to which roles will be played by which agents. As Cheng and Atlee [5] discuss, integrated systems pose problems in defining the system boundary, which can be solved by assigning responsibilities to different parts of the system, including the software system being constructed, human operators/users, and external systems. Our notion of a system boundary is exactly this: by describing the responsibilities of roles in the entire system, we can define the system boundary by specifying which agents will fulfil which roles, whether these agents are software agents, humans, or external systems.

For example, consider the organisation model in Figure 4, which describes the relationships between the roles in the system. A possible mapping between roles and agents is one in which software agents play all of the relevant roles, making the system a complete simulator of the turnaround process. Alternatively, we can define another system boundary in which the *Manager* role is played by a human, and thus the dotted arrows in Figure 4 define the interactions between the user and the software. One can see that assigning one role to a human instead of an agent changes the system and its interface greatly. In the first instance, the system is a complete simulation of the aircraft turnaround process. In the second instance, the result is an interactive system in which managers are able to assess different resource allocation mechanisms.

In this project, the system boundary was left undefined for most of the requirements elicitation process. The stakeholders were comfortable with the lack of a system boundary, and this was not explicitly mentioned to them during the requirements elicitation. However, as software engineers themselves, they did not see any great benefit for this project, because they felt only one system boundary was sensible. However, they also did not find that it was detrimental to the project. We did not find that delaying the definition of the system boundary had any adverse effects on the progression of the system, although this was not a controlled experiment. In addition, we found that conversations about the system, including details about roles and goals, continued after the agent types had been assigned, due to the system functionality becoming clearer.

To our group, the benefits of not defining a system boundary are illustrated by the project. The system was intended to be a simulation of the air traffic turnaround domain, with all roles, including those in Figure 1, being played by software agents (the first boundary in the previous paragraph). One discussion that took place late in the requirements elicitation process indicated that there may have been scope for the system boundary to be changed to the second boundary, in which the *Manager* role is partly played by a human. Had the system boundary been defined at the start of the requirements elicitation, this discussion may not have taken place.

5   Related Work

Guizzardi and Pereni [12] have also recognised the importance of stakeholder involvement. Like us, they consider the goals of all stakeholders, and the interdependencies between these goals, as an initial step in understanding requirements. Yu [27–29] advocates the agent-oriented paradigm as a tool for helping to establish the *why* of a system, which helps stakeholders to understand the

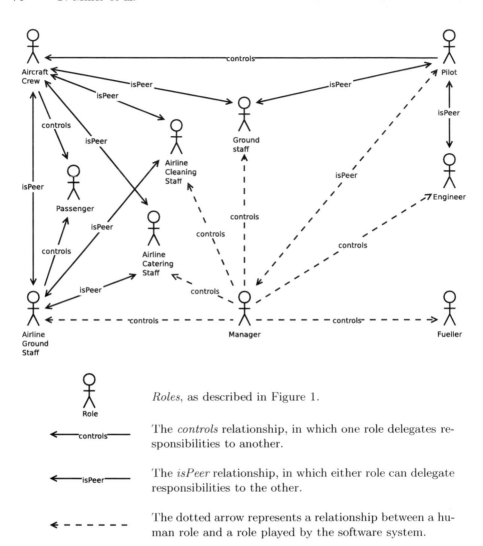

Fig. 4. The organisational model for the ATS system

problem at hand. Similar to us, Yu uses high-level motivation models, in this case, specified in i^*, to share understanding between stakeholders. The i^* models contain significantly more information than our motivation models, including concepts such as activities, resources, and dependencies between all of these. We explicitly aim to reduce the number of concepts and the amount of syntax to keep models simple. Yu offers no specific *techniques* for engaging stakeholders, as the focus of the work appears to be on the tools and notations for recording motivations.

We are not the first authors to identify that high-level conceptual models in agent methodologies are not sufficient to define behaviour. Ferber et al. [8] identify two approaches for specifying behaviour of a multi-agent system. The first approach resembles that of specifying individual requirements of a system, with the addition of nominating the agent that is undertaking each task, thus specifying an observer's view of system behaviour. The second approach involves assigning behaviour to *role instances*, and specifying behaviour from the viewpoint of the individual instance. Interactions between roles are specified as behaviour similar to protocol specifications. This approach is closer to our approach than the first approach, however, we feel that the intermediate representation between roles and agents is unnecessary.

The KAOS methodology [6] defines the behaviour of systems using *agent/action* definitions. These are similar to our agent types, in that they define the agent and the actions that the agent can perform. When applying the KAOS methodology to an example of a meeting schedule, van Lamsweerde et al. [25] comment that the last stages of the *goal elaboration* process, in which goals are refined an analysed, "were performed in parallel with the agent/action identification and goal operationalisation". This provides further evidence that committing to some agent or activity design is necessary to define behaviour.

The Prometheus methodology [20], like KAOS, does not consider roles as part of the elicitation, modelling, or specification process. Similar to us, they identify that functionality must be considered to define behaviour. A Prometheus specification contains the system goals, but with no indication of the roles that achieve them. *Functionalities*, which are natural language descriptions of behaviour, are used to define the system behaviour.

The agent paradigm has been applied in many industry systems. Munroe et al. [18] and Belecheanu et al. [1] describe several applications of agent technology in industry, and discuss key issues that agent proponents face to have their approaches accepted widely into industry.

Maiden et al. [17] is the most closely related work to ours of which the authors are aware. They use several different methodologies and notations, including the agent-oriented i^* methodology, to capture the requirements of an air-traffic control system. The purpose of uses different notations and methodologies is to capture the differing viewpoints of the stakeholders within the project. Maiden et al do not offer any particular methods for engaging stakeholders, however, using different approaches has a positive side effect of being able to cross-validate the different models against each other.

Iterative and incremental lifecycle models are used to achieve similar goals to our approach: shared understanding between stakeholders. Our project used an iterative elicitation process, in which the models were refined and more detail added in each iteration. The hierarchical structure of the motivation models are particularly well suited to such a process, as earlier iterations focus on the high-level goals, and the goal hierarchy is expanded in subsequent iterations. The use of aggregate roles, discussed in Section 4.1 has similar benefits, as role models are added and refined in later iterations.

This approach also fits within an iterative/incremental lifecycle model for the overall project. The hierarchical nature of the models would allow partial determination of the system behaviour, which could be designed, implemented, and tested, before continuing with modelling in the next iteration. Such a process would be likely to increase the shared understanding due to the concrete feedback of a system implementation, however, this would be complementary to our approach: within each iteration, our approach would be applied.

6   Conclusions and Related Work

AOSE models are useful as a shared artifact for communication between stakeholders and software engineers. We find that using the agent-oriented models of Sterling and Taveter [23] as part of requirements elicitation allows meaningful conversations between all stakeholders about abstract concepts, with goals as the catalyst. The role of the goal models is not simply to lead to the development of a system, but also as a way to think through problems and to reach agreements. By making these accessible to all stakeholders, and by keeping stakeholders involved in discussions as long as possible in the requirements elicitation process, we aim to increase the quality of requirements specifications.

In this paper, we proposed three changes to the typically AOSE requirements engineering process that we believe help to engage stakeholders: 1) withholding design commitment; 2) delaying the definition of the system boundary; and 3) delaying the sign-off of the SRS to be as late as possible without affecting system development.

Our experience with an industry partner suggests that not committing to a specific design solution early in the requirements elicitation gave the team an opportunity to further explore and understand the specific challenges related to the high-level goals of the socio-technical system.

We propose delaying the definition of the system boundary and the signing-off of the requirements by including the agent types as part of the SRS. As far as we know, we are the first authors to consider this, rather than including these as part of the architectural or detailed design. By defining which agents will play which roles, we define the behaviour of the system, and implicitly define the system boundary. The experience with our industry partner indicates that this decision is justified.

Our approach is particularly valuable in projects that contain a diverse group of stakeholders. The lightweight notation and the focus on input from all stakeholders encourages participation. In projects where stakeholder background is diverse, this participation is a necessity if all stakeholders are expected to understand parts of the varying domains that are relevant to the system. In projects where stakeholder background is uniform, the process and models can still be used to arrive at a shared understanding about the system, but the advantages are likely to be less when compared to projects with diverse stakeholders.

References

1. Belecheanu, R.A., Munroe, S., Luck, M., Payne, T., Miller, T., McBurney, P., Pěchouček, M.: Commercial applications of agents: Lessons, experiences and challenges. In: Proceedings of the Fifth International Joint Conference on Autonomous Agents and Multiagent Systems, pp. 1555–1561. ACM Press, New York (2006)
2. Berry, D., Kamsties, E., Krieger, M.: From contract drafting to software specification: Linguistic sources of ambiguity - a handbook version 1.0 (2000)
3. Bresciani, P., Perini, A., Giorgini, P., Giunchiglia, F., Mylopoulos, J.: Tropos: An Agent-Oriented Software Development Methodology. Autonomous Agents and Multi-Agent Systems 8(3), 203–236 (2004)
4. Button, G., Sharrock, W.: Occasioned practices in the work of software engineers. In: Jirotka, M., Goguen, J. (eds.) Requirements Engineering: Social and Technical Issues, pp. 217–240. Academic Press, London (1994)
5. Cheng, B., Atlee, J.M.: Research directions in requirements engineering. In: Briand, L., Wolf, A. (eds.) Proceedings of the International Conference on Software Engineering, pp. 285–303 (2007)
6. Dardenne, A., Lamsweerde, A., Fickas, S.: Goal-directed requirements acquisition. Science of Computer Programming 20(1-2), 3–50 (1993)
7. Easterbrook, S., Nuseibeh, B.: Using viewpoints for inconsistency management. Software Engineering Journal 11(1), 31–43 (1995)
8. Ferber, J., Gutknecht, O., Jonker, C.M., Müller, J.P., Treur, J.: Organization models and behavioural requirements specification for multi-agent systems. In: Demazeau, Y., Garijo, F. (eds.) Proceedings of the 10th European Workshop on Modelling Autonomous Agents in a Multi-Agent World, Multi-Agent System Organisations, pp. 1–19 (2001)
9. Garcia, A., Medinilla, N.: The ambiguity criterion in software design. In: International Workshop on Living with Uncertainties. ACM, New York (2007)
10. Gause, D.: User driven design – the luxury that has become a necessity, a workshop in full life-cycle requirements management. In: ICRE 2000, Tutorial T7 (2000)
11. Gause, D., Weinberg, G.: Exploring Requirements: Quality Before Design. Dorset House Publishing Co., Inc., New York (1989)
12. Guizzardi, R., Perini, A.: Analyzing requirements of knowledge management systems with the support of agent organizations. Journal of the Brazilian Computer Society (JBCS)-Special Issue on Agents Organizations 11(1), 51–62 (2005)
13. Juan, T., Pearce, A., Sterling, L.: ROADMAP: Extending the Gaia methodology for complex open systems. In: Proceedings of the First Int. Conf. on Autonomous Agents and Multi-Agent Systems, pp. 3–10. ACM Press, New York (2002)
14. Jureta, I., Faulkner, S.: Clarifying goal models. In: Grundy, J., Hartmann, S., Laender, A., Maciaszek, L., Roddick, J. (eds.) ER (Tutorials, Posters, Panels & Industrial Contributions). CRPIT, vol. 83, pp. 139–144 (2007)
15. Kamsties, E., Berry, D., Paech, B.: Detecting ambiguities in requirements documents using inspections. In: Proceedings of the First Workshop on Inspection in Software Engineering (WISE 2001), pp. 68–80 (2001)
16. MacLean, A., Bellotti, V., Young, R.M.: What rationale is there in design? In: Diaper, D., Gilmore, D.J., Cockton, G., Shackel, B. (eds.) Proceedings of the 3rd Int. Conf. on Human-Computer Interaction, pp. 207–212 (1990)
17. Maiden, N., Jones, S., Manning, S., Greenwood, J., Renou, L.: Model-driven requirements engineering: Synchronising models in an air traffic management case study. In: Persson, A., Stirna, J. (eds.) CAISE 2004. LNCS, vol. 3084, pp. 368–383. Springer, Heidelberg (2004)

18. Munroe, S., Miller, T., Belecheanu, R., Pěchouček, M., McBurney, P., Luck, M.: Crossing the agent technology chasm: Lessons, experiences and challenges in commercial applications of agents. Knowledge Engineering Review 21(4), 345–392 (2006)

19. Paay, J., Sterling, L., Vetere, F., Howard, S., Boettcher, A.: Engineering the social: The role of shared artifacts. International Journal of Human-Computer Studies 67(5), 437–454 (2009)

20. Padgham, L., Winikoff, M.: Developing Intelligent Agent Systems: A practical guide. John Wiley and Sons, Chichester (2004)

21. Pavón, J., Gómez-Sanz, J.: Agent oriented software engineering with INGENIAS. In: Mařík, V., Müller, J.P., Pěchouček, M. (eds.) CEEMAS 2003. LNCS (LNAI), vol. 2691, p. 394. Springer, Heidelberg (2003)

22. Randall, D., Hughes, J., Shapir, D.: Steps toward a partnership: ethnography and system design. In: Jirotka, M., Goguen, J. (eds.) Requirements Engineering: Social and Technical Issues, pp. 241–254. Academic Press, London (1994)

23. Sterling, L., Taveter, K.: The Art of Agent-Oriented Modelling. MIT Press, Cambridge (2009)

24. Tjong, S.F., Hartley, M., Berry, D.: Extended disambiguation rules for requirements specifications. In: Alves, C., Werneck, V., Marcio Cysneiros, L. (eds.) Proceedings of Workshop in Requirements Engineering, pp. 97–106 (2007)

25. Van Lamsweerde, A., Darimont, R., Massonet, P.: Goal-directed elaboration of requirements for a meeting scheduler: problems and lessons learnt. In: Proceedings of the Second IEEE International Symposium on Requirements Engineering, pp. 194–203. IEEE Computer Society, Los Alamitos (1995)

26. Wiegers, K.E.: Software requirements, 2nd edn. Microsoft Press, Redmond (2003)

27. Yu, E.: Modeling organizations for information systems requirements engineering. In: Proceedings First IEEE International Symposium on Requirements Engineering, pp. 34–41. IEEE, Los Alamitos (1993)

28. Yu, E.: Towards modelling and reasoning support for early-phase requirements engineering. In: Proceedings of the 3rd IEEE International Symposium on Requirements Engineering (RE 1997), p. 226. IEEE Computer Society, Los Alamitos (1997)

29. Yu, E.: Agent-oriented modelling: software versus the world. In: Wooldridge, M.J., Weiß, G., Ciancarini, P. (eds.) AOSE 2001. LNCS, vol. 2222, pp. 206–225. Springer, Heidelberg (2002)

30. Zambonelli, F., Jennings, N.R., Wooldridge, M.: Developing multiagent systems: The Gaia methodology. ACM Transactions on Software Engineering Methodology 12(3), 317–370 (2003)

Towards Requirement Analysis Pattern for Learning Agents

Shiva Vafadar and Ahmad Abdollahzadeh Barfourosh

Intelligent System Lab,
Computer Engineering and IT Faculty
Amirkabir University of Technology
vafadar@aut.ac.ir, ahmad@ce.aut.ac.ir
http://ceit.aut.ac.ir/ISLab

Abstract. Learning is a capability that can be incorporated into software agents to handle the complexity of dynamic and unexpected situations, exploiting available artificial intelligence (AI) techniques. Despite design techniques for learning agents have been discussed in agent oriented software engineering literature, how to identify and analyze the requirements for learning agents is still poorly addressed. In this paper, we introduce a pattern for requirement analysis of learning agents. This analysis pattern contains a group of related, generic meta-classes of learning and their relations in a domain neutral manner which can be described as elements of conceptual modeling of learning requirement of agents. The applicability of the pattern has been investigated through the development of a book trading case study.

Keywords: Agent Oriented Software Engineering (AOSE), Analysis Patterns, Requirements Analysis, Learning.

1 Introduction

Today software systems are used in more complex application domains which demand for software systems with autonomic properties [8]. This complexity often arises from open networked and heterogeneous environments with dynamic and unpredictable scenarios in which software is expected to operate. Enriching software systems with the capability of improving while operating can benefit from available artificial intelligence (AI), and agent oriented software engineering aims at providing methods to support developing systems with this property [22]. One of the capabilities which can help intelligent software agents to perform more appropriately in dynamic and volatile situations is learning. An agent being considered as intelligent is, among other things such as autonomy and socialability, usually expected to be able to learn [19]. We entitle this expected feature, learning requirement of the agent.

Every expected feature of the system to be built should pass through a complete development process from requirements to test activities. Machine learning techniques for agent based systems have been proposed [16],[17] and issues in

D. Weyns and M.-P. Gleizes (Eds.): AOSE 2010, LNCS 6788, pp. 79–90, 2011.

designing software agents with learning capabilities have been discussed [15], [9] but techniques for requirement analysis of an agent's learning is still poorly addressed. To overcome this shortage, we focus our research on requirement analysis as the starting point.

Requirements analysis addresses the identification and specification of the functional and non-functional (or quality) characteristics expected for the system to be developed, and analyze them in terms of ways to operationalize them. Therefore, requirements analysis activities encompass the problem domain as well as the solution domain, with the aim to provide effective information for the system design. More specifically, first activities of requirements analysis are focused on the problem domain analysis and the elicitation of expected features of the system-to-be, but late requirements analysis activities focus on a deeper understanding of these system features, thus providing information for architectural and design concerns in terms of available candidate. The latter tries to provide required information for moving smoothly from requirements to high level design of the system. Taking the perspective of a requirements engineer who may not be expert in AI techniques, we believe that providing methods for supporting analysis of learning as one of the expected capabilities for the agent would be beneficial.

Based on this view, in this paper we present a pattern based approach for analyzing agent's learning capability. A main novelty of this work is its focus on the late analysis phase of the development of learning agents in order to provide deeper understanding of this feature, which abstracts from the approach learning, is realized in design and implementation. More precisely, we use AI literature as resources from which to extract generic concepts and issues of learning and their relationships, we represent these concepts and their relationships by using domain modeling techniques (linguistic analysis technique [1]), and organize them in the form of analysis pattern. Analysis patterns are a group of related, meta-classes and their relations which present issues of conceptual modeling for analyzing requirements [5] [6] in a domain-neutral manner. Analysis patterns are particularly useful for conceptual modeling because they provide abstractions of situations that occur frequently, allowing developers to reuse chunks of prior knowledge in new situations.

In order to evaluate the pattern we use a case study (which is a book trading system) and apply the pattern on it. By comparing the results of applying the pattern on the case study with required information for design and implementation of learner agent during software development, we can assess the applicability of our pattern on developed application.

The remainder of this paper is organized as following. Section 2 introduces software analysis patterns and their role on software development. It also describes related works of this research. In Section 3, we present analysis pattern for learning agents and introduce its participants. Section 4, introduces book trading system which is used as our case study. This section also discusses preliminary results of applying the pattern on the case study. In sections 5 and 6, respectively, we discuss the results, explain our further works and conclude.

2   Background and Related Work

2.1   Software Analysis Patterns

A well-accepted approach for sharing software engineering experiences to the wider community of software developers is through the use of software patterns. However, software patterns have been introduced by design patterns but they have spread in other fields of software development such as requirements [21], analysis [5] [6] and architecture [4] as well.

An analysis pattern is a group of related, generic objects (meta-classes) and expected interactions defined in a domain-neutral manner [5] [6]. Analysis patterns resemble the notion of chunks of formalized knowledge that are at a higher level of abstraction than individual classes. Identification of analysis patterns involves the creation of domain-independent abstractions [4] because these abstractions represent frequently. These experiences are introduced to the software engineering community as strategies and patterns for analyzing software systems [5].

Various analysis patterns have been introduced in literature. In order to reuse these patterns for analyzing software systems, three generic reuse steps of retrieval, adaptation, and integration are suggested [14]. By following these steps, software analyst should identify potentially useful patterns in application domain by retrieving them among repository of patterns. Then s/he should adapt the pattern to the domain of interest by instantiating meta-classes. Integrating various patterns of the application domain is the final step which will lead to application conceptual model.

2.2   Related Work

It was obvious to generalize from object-oriented patterns to agent-oriented ones. A comprehensive view on agent-oriented patterns has been presented in [13]. According to this categorization, various patterns have been introduced for different phases of agent-oriented software development. Patterns at analysis phase usually deal with organizational and interactional properties of agent-based systems. Instances of these patterns are Structure-in-5, Pyramid [11], Mediator [18] and social patterns [7]. Our analysis pattern for learning agents can be classified in this category of patterns though it is not in organizational or interactional sub-category. As we concentrate on analyzing AI characteristics of an agent, we believe that this classification should be extended by adding a new sub-category which deals with intelligence properties of agents.

According to [13], patterns of internal architecture design are categorized to structural, interactional and strategic. Strategic patterns focus on design of specific notions of agency such as autonomy, reactivity and proactivity. Reactive agent, deliberative agent [10] and learning design pattern [15] [9] are examples of this category's patterns. However, these patterns deals with intelligence characteristics of agents but their focus is on design concerns such as designing several algorithms of machine learning for the agent. They present main software classes (and required attributes and methods) and their interaction to improve reuse and maintainability of the design [15]. Another method presented to improve the quality of design (with respect to transparency, reusability, code replication and etc.) considers learning as an aspect in agent architecture [9]. The difference between these researches and our work is the difference between design and analysis patterns. While design patterns represent a group of software objects, their attributes and methods to improve reusability and maintenance of software design, analysis patterns deal with types (not implementation classes) for generating conceptual model of application. Our focus is on analysis phase which tries to understand learning characteristic in application domain and provide required information for design phase. By using our analysis pattern, analyst produces a conceptual model which specifies learning in the problem domain. Designer uses this model for producing software class diagram by applying learning design patterns (to have a higher-quality design artifact) or by following conventional design methods.

Our work is also related to the other researches that focus on analyzing agents requirements associated with AI techniques such as reasoning [2] and autonomy [20]. Similarity between our works is trying to find software engineering approaches for analyzing AI requirements of agents. However, they present a semi-formal language for reasoning and autonomy of agents while we follow a pattern based approach for analyzing learning capability.

3   Analysis Pattern for Learning Agent

The analysis pattern for learning agents is a pattern that is used in late requirement analysis. It is supposed that during early requirements analysis, requirements engineer identifies that customer needs an intelligent agent that learns while acting. To have a deeper understanding of required learning capability, s/he should analyze it and generate a conceptual model of the learner agent. Software analyst can uses our pattern as a guideline to generate conceptual model of the learning agent of the application domain. The goal is moving smoothly from requirements to high level design.

To use this pattern, the first parts of the pattern description (context, problem and forces) are used to identify its applicability in the application domain. If there are agents in the system that are mapped with the context and forces of the pattern, the learning pattern is a good candidate to apply. After retrieving the pattern, it should be adapted in the application domain. For adaptation, conceptual classes of the pattern should be instantiated by recognizing related concepts in the application domain. In the following, we describe the pattern by using the template suggested in [12] for analysis patterns of agent based systems.

Name: Learning Pattern
Classification: Analysis
Problem: How should an agent be analyzed to specify its learning capability?

Context: An agent-based system which in a role needs to improve its performance while executing its tasks and getting experience. This role needs learning capability in order to carry out one or more tasks or achieving a goal.

Domain of Application: the pattern is general. It can be used in different application domains.

Forces:

- Performing the task(s) or achieving the goal(s) is not possible without learning or learning makes it possible in higher quality or less time.
- Agent's knowledge (which can be related to the process of doing the task or primitive knowledge or rules) is not complete and it can be improved by getting experience.
- The agent can perform some tasks in order to get some experience or there is adequate training data which help the agent to improve its behavior.
- The agent can receive feedback from the environment after doing the task.

Solution: To solve the mentioned problem, we suggest using the following model for analysis learning requirement. As figure 1 shows, there are 13 participants in the suggested model. In the following, we explain these meta-classes.

- **Agent:** Indicates the agent which its learning requirement is analyzed.
- **Goal:** Indicates the goal(s) that the agent is responsible for. Identifying the goal(s) of the agent is the first step of analyzing activity. Since agents are goal-oriented entities, the goals an agent tries to achieve plays vital role in agent analysis. Learning is a technique that can help the agent to achieve its goals. Therefore, the kind of the learning is expected from the agent is influenced by the goal(s) it is responsible for.
- **Task:** Specifies the tasks that the agent can perform. We can specify the tasks the agent can perform and then identify which of them needs improvement by incorporating learning. At the other hand, we may know that to

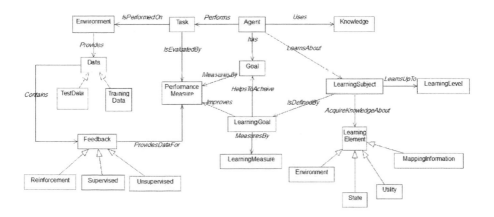

Fig. 1. Analysis Pattern for Learning Agents

achieve its goals or improve its behavior agent must have learning capability. Therefore, we should recognize that what kind of tasks the agent should be able to perform to learn (such as the tasks required for exploration and experience generation). Both approaches are necessary for determining the required tasks.

- **PerformanceMeasure:** embodies the criterion for success of an agent's behavior for achieving its goal. An agent has learning capability if its performance improves during performing the tasks. This improvement is measured by performance measure. Therefore, performance measure is a factor for evaluating learning capability of agent and it has an important role for defining learning goal.

- **LearningGoal:** Denotes improvement in agent's performance measure which is expected by incorporating learning. It also specifies in which duration this improvement is expected. It affects on learning elements of the agent because the amount of improvement defines which parts of the agent should improve their behavior to attain learning goal. It is affected by many meta-classes such as agent goal, its performance measure, input data and its quality, feedback is available for the agent, tasks the agent can perform, prior knowledge and its quality. For example if the input data is not adequate or its quality is low, requirements engineer may decide extend duration which agent can achieve its learning goal.

- **LearningSubject:** is the subject which agent learns about.

- **LearningElement:** Defines issues that agent should learn to achieve learning goal. On the other hand, it defines learning goal in more details with respect to the subjects agent can have learning on such as: *State* which is mapping from conditions on the current state to the actions, *Environment* which is relevant properties of the world from percept sequence, *Mapping-information* which is information about the way world evolves, results of possible actions the agent can take on the environment, *Utility* which is information indicating the desirability of the world state and action

- **Feedback:** Defines the type of the feedback is received by the agent which can be supervised, unsupervised or reinforcement. The feedback is one of the major issues that affect on selecting appropriate leaning algorithm during design. Therefore, during analysis we should specify what type of feedback is obtained for agent in application domain.

- **Knowledge:** Defines the agent's knowledge. It contains the knowledge the agent has prior to start his actions. This knowledge is defined according to the tasks the agent should perform, The knowledge that the agent expected to achieve during performing the tasks and the knowledge is required to achieve learning goal.

- **Environment:** Defines the environment the agent is acting on and all of its participants. Environment is an important factor in analyzing agent. How well an agent can behave depends on the nature of the environment. Therefore, the environment that the agent is situated in directly affects the appropriate design for the agent. In this model, environment meta-class models the external world from the agent's perspective. The properties of the environment from agent's point of view such as fully observable vs. partially observable, deterministic vs. stochastic, episodic vs. sequential, static vs. continuous, single agent vs. multi-agent should be defined during analysis. These characteristics also influence learning algorithms which are selected during design. On the other hand, environment is also an intermediate medium that provides all the data that the agent learns from. Identifying these properties, functions and constraints of the environment during analysis provides adequate information for understanding constraints on the learning.

- **Data:** Defines the raw data that is received from environment (and all its participants) and is used as learning input. Therefore, it has a vital role in learning process. Amount of data and its quality has an important role for deciding about learning algorithm and it is an important criterion which affects our expectation from learning. Information which is related to data helps requirements engineer to decide about trade offs between duration and quality of learning. Test Data and Training Data are different types of data that should be considered during analysis.
- **LearningMeasure:** Defines the measure for evaluating learning capability of the agent. It can be described by criterion such as preciseness and speed.
- **LearningLevel:** Describes level of the learning we expect from the agent which can have a wide range from remembering the information to knowledge based inductive learning.

Resulting Context:

- Using learning pattern for modeling learning capability of the agent considers concepts of the learning in the conceptual model of the learning agent. Therefore, it generates a more complete model of these agents
- Pattern focuses on learning concepts. Consequently, using this pattern for analyzing an agent does not produce a complete, comprehensive model for agents. Therefore, this pattern should be used after analyzing the role in order to add concepts which are related to the learning.
- Using learning analysis pattern generates a model with more conceptual classes. This may increase the complexity of the model because of increasing the number of meta-classes in the model.

Related Patterns: The output of the pattern is a conceptual model that is the input of the design activity. There are two patterns that are directly related to the design of learning agents. 1- The learning design pattern [15]: The intent of this pattern is to add machine learning algorithms to an object oriented design. It introduces knowledge representation, algorithm, performance evaluation and training example generator classes as the elements of machine learning to the design. 2- The learning aspect pattern[9] : This pattern presents an aspect-oriented solution to make agent components easier to maintain and reuse. This pattern contains a learning aspect which extends the agent classes to introduce the learning protocol. It also has two crosscutting interface which are InformatioGathering and LeanringKnowledge.

4   Case Study: Book Trading System

In order to investigate applicability of our pattern, we apply it on a case study. In this section, we define a Book Trading System (BTS) and present the results of applying the pattern on learner agent of the system. As this is the first iteration of our evaluation activity, we deliberately select a simple case study. Our system is an extension on Book Trading examples that comes with JADE 3.1. We modify the scenario as it includes some agents that sell books and other agents which buy them on behalf of their users. Buyer's goal is purchasing the cheapest book while seller's goal is to achieve the highest profit. In this case, we also consider learning as an expected capability for the seller agent. Seller should explore various prices for each book and try to find best price which increases its profit.

4.1   Developing the Case Study

First, we develop our case study using existing methods for developing agent based systems. The aim of this step is to generate artifacts of software development process that are related to the learning capability. Our focus is on analysis, therefore we use Tropos methodology [3] because of its emphasize on requirements analysis. We also implemented the system by using JADE framework. In this way, we modified and extended book trading example by adding required objects and methods. Figure 2 shows an instance of the analysis artifacts of the system. It is the goal model of the Book Trading System which illustrates stakeholders' goal analysis. As the figure shows, the seller uses the system to achieve the goal; finding eBuyers. The system helps seller to propose the books and find the best selling price for each book which has the positive contribution on his/her softgoal (increase the profit). The buyer uses the system in order to find eSellers and compare their prices which helps him/her to pay lowest price as his/her softgoal.

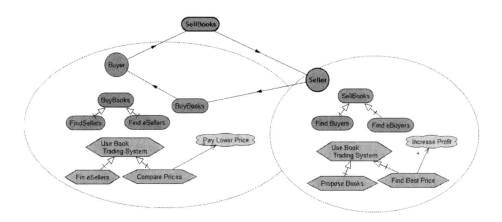

Fig. 2. Goal Diagram for BTS's Stakeholders

4.2   Applying Analysis Pattern on the Case Study

Using an analysis pattern for modeling a system contains three main steps; retrieval, adaptation, and integration. In our case study, in retrieval step, we choose learning pattern for seller agent because it is expected to be able to learn. For adaptation, we instantiate conceptual classes of the pattern by recognizing related concepts in the application domain. For example, in this case study Agent meta-class is instantiated to Seller because it is the learning agent of the system and LearningSubject is Book. Similarly, all related meta-classes are instantiated. Figure 3 shows seller agent conceptual model which is the result of applying the pattern.

To evaluate the applicability of our pattern, we investigate how it can be realized during design and implementation. To achieve this goal, we compared the artifacts of analysis, design and implementation in our case study. The conceptual model of the seller agent has been considered as the output of the analysis activity via using the analysis pattern. It was compared with implementation model which contains agents, classes, attributes and methods in the developed system in JADE. The results show that, Agent, Task, Environment, Input, PerformanceMeasure and Knowledge are the meta-classes of the model which there are design and implementation elements for them. These concepts have been highlighted as yellow meta-classes in figure 3. While Goal, Learning-Goal, LearningElement and LearningMeasure are meta-classes which are used for understanding the domain of the application and they are not instantiated as a design or implementation element. These classes are related to non-functional properties of learning and provide important information for designer that can help him/her for selecting appropriate algorithm for learner agent. They are also important for designing test cases of the agent and therefore can be useful for testers as other stakeholders of the analysis artifacts. These concepts have been shown as white meta-classes in figure 3.

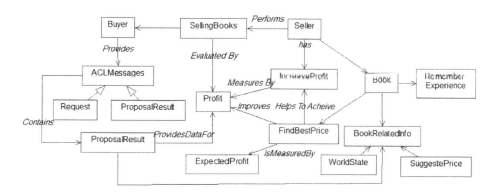

Fig. 3. Seller's Conceptual Model in Book Trading System

5   Discussion

This first experience on using our pattern for analyzing learning capability of agents shows that using it during analysis helps us to produce conceptual model of learner agent easier and specify domain information that is related to the learning capabilities of the agents. Some of the classes of derived conceptual model are converted to the software agents, classes, attributes or methods while the others are used to understand the application domain and provide required information for making decisions about suitable learning algorithms for the agent. By having this pattern, software analyst is provided by a guideline, which describes main issues of learning and their relations. Using this guideline helps analyst to easily recognize related issues of learning in the problem domain and document them. Following this approach can save time and effort for requirements analysis. This issue becomes more important when we take into account that software analyst may not be an expert in learning. Therefore, s/he may ignore some information that is important for learner agent designers. Using analysis pattern for learner agent helps requirement analyst to overcome this shortage and provide required information for designer.

Although our results provide some evidences about the applicability of our pattern in agent based systems, they also point out limitations in our research, which we consider as part of our future work agenda to improve the pattern. We discuss them briefly here below:

1. Using the same group of subjects for developing the case study and applying the pattern on it may affect the evolution results related to applicability of the pattern. To improve evaluation process and omit this side effect, developing the case study and applying the pattern on it should be performed by different subjects.
2. It is assumed that the pattern will be used by software analysts who may not have adequate knowledge about learning and other AI techniques. The evaluation of the pattern by the authors of this work (who are working on learning and are familiar with its concepts) may affect evaluation results. Involving software analysts who are dealing with conventional software systems should be considered in future work.
3. We evaluated our pattern according to its applicability on the case study. This confirms our pattern but it does not help us to discover pattern's weaknesses. We can extend our evaluation method and criteria by adding other factors such as coverage of the concepts. For example we may compare the results of applying the pattern on the case study with the results of using other techniques for domain modeling (e.g. use cases) and find out the weaknesses and shortages.
4. Our pattern is not limited or binded to any specific methodology. In this paper, we used Tropos as a sample methodology to develop our case study. We selected Tropos' requirements analysis methods and produced goal-oriented requirements models that include agents' goals and task that fit seamlessly to the corresponding pattern's elements. This suggests that our pattern may

be used as a supplementary document for analyzing learner agents modeled by any methodology. We also may consider extending Tropos (and other methodologies) to cover all the concepts of the pattern as further work.

5. Currently, our pattern is general. To have a more detailed pattern, we take into account decomposing the proposed pattern to some sub-patterns which makes it more comprehensive and complete. For example, we should extend environment meta-class and describe main important issues of environment that should be considered during analysis of learning.

6. We intentionally selected a simple case study for evaluating our pattern in the first iteration. More complex case studies in various domains in further iterations will help to evaluate the pattern when it tackles more complex learning problems.

6   Conclusion

In this paper, we introduced analysis pattern for learning capability of software agents that can be used by software requirements analysts. This pattern is defined in the terms of domain neutral meta-classes (and their relations) that can be identified as elements of conceptual modeling for analyzing and understanding the learning requirements of agents. According to this pattern, for analyzing the learning capability of an agent goals, tasks, learning goal, environment, data and feedback, knowledge, learning elements, learning measure and learning level should be considered. Conceptual models of learner agents in various domains can be constructed by applying the pattern on the application domain. In this way, these meta-models are instantiated and their instances in the domain are recognized. By using this pattern, the required information for understanding the learning requirement is provided during analysis phase. This will help the software analysts who are not expert in AI or learning to provide required information for designer to decide about learning algorithm and methods according to the application domain constraints. Preliminary evaluation of the pattern has been illustrated and we identified a set of suggestion for improving it.

Acknowledgments. The authors would like to thank Anna Perini for her time and comments on the earlier versions of this paper. This research is partially supported by ITRC.

References

1. Abbott, R.: Program Design by Informal English Descriptions. J. Communications of the ACM 26(11) (1983)
2. Bosse, T., Jonker, C.M., Treur, J.: Requirements Analysis of an Agent's Reasoning Capability. In: Akoka, J., Liddle, S.W., Song, I.-Y., Bertolotto, M., Comyn-Wattiau, I., van den Heuvel, W.-J., Kolp, M., Trujillo, J., Kop, C., Mayr, H.C. (eds.) ER Workshops 2005. LNCS, vol. 3770, pp. 48–63. Springer, Heidelberg (2005)
3. Bresciani, P., Giorgini, P., Giunchiglia, F., Mylopoulos, J., Perini, A.: Tropos: an agent-oriented software development methodology. J. Autonomous Agents and Multi-Agent Systems 8(3), 203–236 (2004)

4. Buschmann, F., Meunier, R., Rohnert, H., Sommerlad, P., Stal, M.: Pattern-Oriented System Architecture. A System of Patterns, vol. 1, pp. 325–343. Wiley, Chichester (1996)
5. Coad, P., North, D., Mayfield, M.: Object Models: Strategies, Patterns, and Applications. Prentice Hall, Upper Saddle River (1995)
6. Fowler, M.: Analysis Patterns: Reusable Object Models. Addison-Wesley, Reading (1997)
7. Fuentes, R., Gómez-Sanz, J.J., Pavón, J.: Requirements Elicitation for Agent-Based Applications. In: Müller, J.P., Zambonelli, F. (eds.) AOSE 2005. LNCS, vol. 3950, pp. 40–53. Springer, Heidelberg (2006)
8. Ganek, A.G., Corbi, T.A.: The dawning of the autonomic computing era. J. IBM Systems 42(1), 5–18 (2003)
9. Garcia, A.F., Kulesza, U., Sardinha, J.A.R.P., Milidi, R.L., Lucena, C.J.P.: The Learning Aspect Pattern. In: 11th Conference on Pattern Languages of Programs, PLoP 2004 (2004)
10. Kendall, E.A., Murali Krishna, P.V., Pathak, C.V., Suresh, C.V.: Patterns of intelligent and mobile agents. In: 2nd International Conference on Autonomous Agents, pp. 92–99 (1998)
11. Kolp, M., Giorgini, P., Mylopoulos, J.: Multi-Agent Architectures as Organizational Structures. Autonomous Agents and Multi-Agent Systems 13(1), 3–25 (2006)
12. Oluyomi, A., Karunasekera, S., Sterling, L.: Description templates for agent-oriented patterns. J. Systems and Software 81(1), 20–36 (2008)
13. Oluyomi, A., Karunasekera, S., Sterling, L.: A Comprehensive View of Agent Oriented Patterns. Autonoumous Agents and Multi Agent Systems 15, 337–377 (2007)
14. Purao, S., Storey, V.C., Han, T.: Improving Analysis Pattern Reuse in Conceptual Design: Augmenting Automated Processes with Supervised Learning. J. Information System Research 14(3), 269–290 (2003)
15. Sardinha, J.A.R.P., Garcia, A.F., Milidi, R.L., Lucena, C.J.P.: The Agent Learning Pattern. In: 4th Latin American Conference on Pattern Languages of Programming, SugarLoaf, PLoP 2004, Fortaleza, Brazil (2004)
16. Shoham, Y., Powers, R., Grenager, T.: Multi-agent reinforcement learning: a critical survey, Technical Report, Stanford University (2003)
17. van den Herik, H., Hennes, D., Kaisers, M., Tuyls, K., Verbeeck, K.: Multi-agent learning dynamics: A survey. In: Klusch, M., Hindriks, K.V., Papazoglou, M.P., Sterling, L. (eds.) CIA 2007. LNCS (LNAI), vol. 4676, pp. 36–56. Springer, Heidelberg (2007)
18. Weiss, M.: Patterns for motivating an agent-based approach, conceptual modelling for novel application domains (AOIS@ER). In: Jeusfeld, M.A., Pastor, Ó. (eds.) ER Workshops 2003. LNCS, vol. 2814, pp. 229–240. Springer, Heidelberg (2003)
19. Weiss, G.: Multiagent Systems: a Modern Approach to Distributed Artificial Intelligence. MIT Press, Cambridge (1996)
20. Weiss, G., Fischer, F., Nickles, M., Rovatsos, M.: Operational modelling of agent autonomy: theoretical aspects and a formal language. In: Müller, J.P., Zambonelli, F. (eds.) AOSE 2005. LNCS, vol. 3950, pp. 1–15. Springer, Heidelberg (2006)
21. Withall, S.: Introduction to Software Requirements Patterns, 1st edn. Microsoft Press, Redmond (2007)
22. Zambonelli, F., Omicini, A.: Challenges and Research Directions in Agent-Oriented Software Engineering. J. Autonomous Agents and Multi-Agent Systems 9(3), 253–283 (2004)

Test Coverage Criteria
for Agent Interaction Testing

Tim Miller[1], Lin Padgham[2], and John Thangarajah[2]

[1] Department of Computer Science and Software Engineering, University of
Melbourne, Australia
`tmiller@unimelb.edu.au`
[2] Department of Computer Science, RMIT University, Melbourne, Australia
{`lin.padgham,johnt`}`@rmit.edu.au`

Abstract. By the very definition of complex systems, complex behaviour
emerges from the interactions between the individual parts. This emergent behaviour may be difficult or impossible to predict by analysing the
parts. As a result, systematic and thorough testing of the interactions
of complex systems, including multi-agent systems, is an important part
of the verification and validation process. This paper defines two sets of
test coverage criteria for multi-agent interaction testing. The first uses
only the protocol specification, while the second considers also the plans
that generate and receive the messages in the protocol. We describe how
an existing debugging agent can be used as a test oracle for assessing
correctness of a test, and how the Petri Net representation of the debugging agent can be annotated to support test coverage measurements.
This work both specifies, and shows how to measure, the degree of thoroughness of a set of test cases. It also provides a basis for the future
specification of test case input, designed to provide good coverage.

1 Introduction

Like other types of complex systems, the overall behaviour of multi-agent systems
emerges from the interaction of their parts. Often, this emergent behaviour is difficult or even impossible to identify without running the system. This increased
complexity makes verification and validation of these systems a non-trivial task.
Furthermore, the fact that the behaviour cannot be accurately predicted implies
that manual test case generation is unlikely to test the more complex behaviour.
Automated test generation offers one solution to help with this problem.

Previous work on testing multi-agent systems [2,3,13,16,21,24] has contributed to testing frameworks and automated test case generation. However, none
have explicitly focused on testing interactions, the source of complexity in many
systems. In many multi-agent methodologies, such as Prometheus, Tropos and
OMaSE [4], interactions are captured via interaction protocols in design
diagrams.

Our focus in this paper is on using protocol specifications, as well as information about how the interacting agents use these specifications, to define and

D. Weyns and M.-P. Gleizes (Eds.): AOSE 2010, LNCS 6788, pp. 91–105, 2011.

measure systematic interaction testing. We also describe how correctness can be determined using the debugging agent of Poutakidis et al. [19]. Section 2 defines two sets of *test coverage criteria* for interaction testing, the first using only the protocol specification, and the second including information about the plans involved in receiving and sending messages for a particular protocol. Section 3 describes the use of Poutakidis et al.'s "debugging agent" as a test oracle for determining whether a set of interacting agents is correctly following a valid protocol. Modifications to this debugging agent are made to automatically measure how well a test set achieves the coverage criteria. We finish with a discussion of relationships to previous work and a comment on future work.

2   Test Coverage Criteria

To measure the quality of a set of test cases, a criterion is necessary. Standard control-flow and data-flow criteria [14] that are defined for imperative programming languages are based on program statements and predicates, so are not directly applicable to agent interaction. However, many of the underlying ideas are valid. In this section, we define two sets of criteria based on the control-flow of interactions. This control-flow is extracted from the design models. The first set is based on the ordering of messages, which we obtain from protocol specifications. We refer to these as *protocol-based* criteria. The second set also considers the plans that send and receive the messages in protocols. We refer to these as *plan-based* criteria. We describe and compare each of these.

These criteria are demonstrated on an example. Figure 1 shows an AUML2 interaction diagram [9] of the FIPA Query Protocol specification [7]. In this example, the initiator agent can query whether some information is true (*query-if*), or query information about an identified object (*query-ref*). The participant can refuse or agree to this query. If the participant agrees, then it will inform the initiator of the response, or report a failure.

2.1   Protocol-Based Coverage Criteria

Based on protocols specified in a standard protocol language such as AUML2 interaction diagrams, it is possible to construct a *protocol graph* that shows all possible orderings of messages[1]. Figure 2 shows the protocol graph corresponding to the FIPA Query Interaction Protocol [7].

The *conversation IDs* annotated to each message identify six conversations that have happened using this protocol, in which a conversation is a possible chaining of messages.

Criterion Definition. Our coverage criteria are based on graph traversal of the protocol graph. For protocol coverage, we define three criteria:

---

[1] Our coverage criteria are then based on these orderings. We are not concerned with the content of messages, nor the time at which they are sent, only the relative ordering.

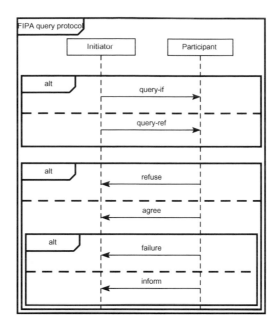

Fig. 1. An AUML2 interaction diagram of the FIPA Query Interaction Protocol

Message coverage. Every message in the protocol must be sent at least once.

Pairwise message coverage. For every message, start node, and end node in the protocol, all directly proceeding messages/nodes must be executed after the first message/node at least once; that is, we must test every case in which one message can be followed by another.

Message path coverage. Every possible interaction sequence permitted by the protocol must be executed at least once.

These three criteria correspond to node, arc, and path coverage of a graph. Figure 2 contains a minimal set of conversations that, if fully executed, achieve these criteria on the protocol graph.

Achieving path coverage is sometimes not possible as a protocol may be defined as an infinitely iterative or recursive structure, leading to an infinite number of paths. Workarounds include achieving only non-cyclical path coverage, or using heuristics such as the 0-1-*many* rule, which specifies that we test only three of these paths: paths containing 0 loops, 1 loop, and more than one loop.

Coverage Measures. Spillner [20] defines *coverage measures* for integration testing criteria. Coverage measures are defined as "*the ratio between the test cases [inputs] required for satisfying the criteria and those of these which have been executed*". These measures can be applied to test sets to determine how complete they are for a particular program.

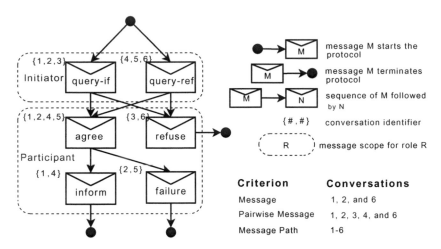

Fig. 2. A protocol graph for the FIPA Query interaction protocol specified, and the conversations required to achieve coverage criteria

The interaction coverage measures (IC) for our three protocol-based criteria are defined as follows:

$$IC_{protocol\_message} = \frac{\#\text{messages sent at least once}}{\#\text{totalmessages in protocol}}$$

$$IC_{pairwise\_message} = \frac{\#\text{arcs executed}}{\#\text{total arcs in protocol}}$$

$$IC_{message\_path} = \frac{\#\text{paths executed}}{\#\text{total message paths in protocol}}$$

As an example, in Figure 2 the set of conversations 1, 2, and 6 achieves 100% for protocol message coverage (6 messages that are all executed), 82% for pairwise message coverage (11 arcs, 9 arcs covered), and 50% for message path coverage (6 different paths, 3 paths covered).

Protocol-based coverage criteria are intuitively useful for interaction testing because they are strictly related to the interactions that can occur between the agents. However, purely message-based criteria do not consider the internal structure of the agents. For example, an agent may be able to send or receive the same message in many different plans. Consequently, we develop an additional set of coverage criteria that take into account the plans of the agents, and the relationship of messages to these plans.

2.2 Plan-Based Coverage Criteria

We extract from the design artifacts, the information to build a *plan graph* for each protocol, of the kind shown in Figure 3. This graph represents the relationship between plans and messages for a particular protocol.

Plan graphs are built by extracting as nodes, those plans that send or receive any message in the protocol, and the messages themselves. In addition to the obvious send/receive links between plans and messages, we add a link between any two plans in the graph, which are connected by a chain (or multiple chains)

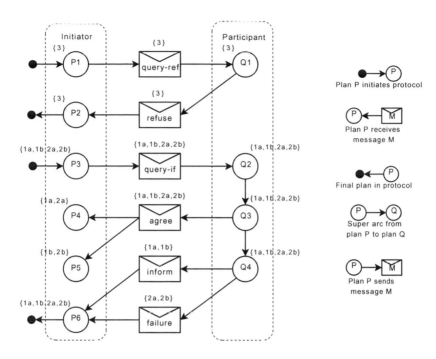

Fig. 3. A plan graph for the FIPA Query interaction protocol specified

of triggering links. We will call such links between plans *super-arcs* as they represent an entire plan structure. Figure 4 shows the internals of the super-arc between plan nodes $Q3$ and $Q4$ in Figure 3.

From Figure 3, one can see that the participant always agrees to a *query-if* request and always refuses a *query-ref*, so while the agents may follow the protocol, they do not use all parts of it. We also note that plans can send more than one message or receive more than one message, for example, plan $Q4$ sends both *inform* and *failure*.

Unlike other branches in the graph, the branch at $Q3$ is not a choice. Instead $Q3$ sends the message *agree*, and then triggers the plan $Q4$. For the purpose of test criteria, it is not necessary to model whether this is a choice or the ability to do more than one action because we need only measure whether the message was sent.

Criterion Definition. We define a set of coverage criteria using plan graphs, in a similar way to those we defined on the protocol graph. We note how these correspond to criteria in standard (non-agent-oriented) integration testing [20].

Message coverage. Every message in the plan graph is sent at least once. The analogous case in standard integration testing is ensuring that each method/function in the target component's interface is executed at least once.

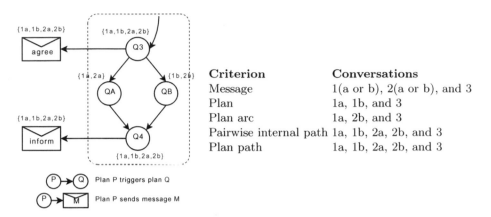

Criterion	Conversations
Message	1(a or b), 2(a or b), and 3
Plan	1a, 1b, and 3
Plan arc	1a, 2b, and 3
Pairwise internal path	1a, 1b, 2a, 2b, and 3
Plan path	1a, 1b, 2a, 2b, and 3

Fig. 4. Internal plan structure between plans $Q3$ and $Q4$ for the graph from Figure 3, and the conversations required to achieve coverage criteria for the entire protocol

Plan coverage. Every plan that sends or receives a message in the protocol is executed at least once. The analogous case in integration testing is ensuring that each method in the program that calls a method in the target component's interface is executed.

Plan arc coverage. Every occurrence of a message being sent by a plan and every occurrence of a plan being triggered (by a message, an event (a start node), or another plan) is executed at least once. This is different from plan coverage because a plan may be able to send more than one message (e.g. plan $Q4$ sending *inform* and *failure* in Figure 3). The analogous case in integration testing is ensuring that every call made to every method in the target component's interface is tested.

Pairwise internal path coverage. Every possible path, including paths in super arcs, between two pairwise messages, or between a first/last message in a protocol and its corresponding start/end node is executed at least once. This ensures that all paths that could be used to produce a particular message in the protocol, are tested. The analogous case in integration testing is ensuring that every path between two method calls from the target component's interface is executed. Note that pairwise messages cannot be determined from the plan graph, but must be determined from the protocol specification or protocol graph. For example, in Figure 3, one cannot determine that *agree* is sent directly before *inform*.

Plan path coverage. Every possible path through the structure induced by expanding super-arcs within the plan graph is executed at least once. The analogous case in integration testing is ensuring that every possible sequence of calls to every method in the target component's interface is tested. Even without the expansion of super-arcs this differs from message path coverage defined on the protocol graph, in that it addresses the case where the same message may be sent from, or received by, two different plans. (e.g. plan $P4$ and $P5$ receiving *agree* in Figure 3).

Again, some of the above criteria correspond to graph coverage criteria. Message and plan coverage combined correspond to node coverage. Plan arc coverage, and plan path coverage correspond to arc, and path coverage respectively. Pairwise internal path coverage corresponds to path coverage between plan nodes within a super arc, combined with arc coverage on the other arcs of the graph.

To illustrate, Figure 4 contains a minimal test sets that, when fully executed, achieve each criteria, using the plan graph from Figures 3 and 4.

Coverage Measures. We define coverage measures for these criteria in the same way as the protocol-based criteria: the ratio of executed nodes/arc/paths to the total number of nodes/arc/paths.

For example, in Figures 3 and 4, the set of conversations 1a, 2b, and 3 achieves 100% coverage for message coverage (6/6), plan coverage (10/10), and plan arc coverage (19/19), 85% for pairwise internal path coverage (11/13), and 55.5% for plan path coverage (5/7).

2.3 Comparison of Coverage Criteria

To compare these criteria, we are interested in any subsumption relationships between them. Test criterion A *subsumes* test criterion B if and only if any test set that achieves 100% coverage on criterion A also achieves 100% coverage on criterion B.

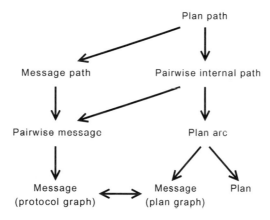

Fig. 5. The *subsumes* relation between the protocol-based and plan-based coverage

Figure 5 shows the subsumption relationship between our criteria. We know from graph theory that path coverage subsumes arc coverage, and arc coverage subsumes node coverage. This directly gives us the subsumption relation between the different protocol graph criteria (message path subsumes pairwise message, and pairwise message subsumes message).

In the plan graph, plan path subsumes plan arc, and plan arc subsumes message/plan coverage, directly from graph theory. Although neither message nor plan coverage are equivalent to node coverage, both are subsumed by it. Plan coverage does not subsume message coverage, because plans can send and receive multiple messages. For example, plan coverage of Figure 3 can be achieved by executing plans $Q4$ and $P6$ once each, which means either *inform* or *failure* will not be sent. There is also an additional coverage metric, pairwise internal path coverage, which sits between plan path coverage and plan arc coverage. The argument for this is straightforward: by definition it subsumes arc coverage, and if every path, including every path internal to a super arc, is executed, then every arc plus all super-arc paths must also be executed.

To compare the criteria for the two different types of graph, we make the assumption that all criteria are feasible. For example, in plan message coverage, we assume that the participating agents are programmed such that every message in a protocol is able to be sent by these agents. Otherwise, 100% coverage is not achievable. It is not uncommon for this assumption to be false, particularly when pre-existing protocols are used. For example, a developer using a third-party protocol may choose not to use some messages defined in a protocol.

If this assumption is relaxed, the result is simply that there is no subsumption relation between any of the criteria[2]. With this assumption of feasibility we can establish some relationships between the criteria based on the two different graphs. Firstly, we note that the two types of message coverage are equivalent. That is, they both require test cases that send every message in the protocol. The next relation is that pairwise internal path coverage subsumes pairwise message coverage. Pairwise internal path coverage is defined as executing all paths (including super arcs) between all pairwise messages, therefore, it trivially subsumes pairwise message coverage. Finally, we have that plan path coverage subsumes message path coverage. With our assumption of feasibility, this subsumption relation holds because if there is a path defined by the protocol, there must be a path in the plan graph that executes it. If all paths through the plan graph are executed, then this implies all paths in the protocol graph must also be executed.

We argue that the combination of message path coverage and pairwise internal path coverage is a minimum testing level to aim for in rigorous interaction testing. It tests the various plan combinations that may be used in moving from receipt of a message, to the production of the next message in the protocol, and also tests every possible conversation. Although there is some amount of exponential growth, this is likely to be substantially more limited than that required for testing all paths in the plan graph.

3   Measuring Correctness and Coverage Using a Debugging Agent

The model-based measure of correct behaviour of agent interaction is primarily whether the agents follow the specified interaction protocols. While the coverage

---

[2] This can be demonstrated by the examples in Figures 2 and 3: the agents are programmed such that the sequence $\langle query\text{-}ref \rightarrow agree \rangle$ is infeasible, therefore, pairwise message coverage is not achievable on the protocol graph, but pairwise internal path coverage is achievable on the plan graph.

measures we have defined can tell us how thoroughly a given set of test cases actually exercises the program under test, we require some way of knowing whether the agents interact as specified. To establish this we use the work of Poutakidis et al. [19] on debugging agent interactions. The monitor that is used in that work for detecting bugs, can equally well be used as a *test oracle*.

The IEEE Standard Glossary of Software Engineering Terminology [10] defines a test oracle as: *"any means of determining whether a system or component's behaviour is consistent with its specification."*

In Poutakidis et al.'s work, the agent platform is modified so that the debugging agent receives copies of all messages sent within the system. This debugging agent then raises an alert if a sent message does not follow one of the specified protocols, or if a protocol does not reach a specified end state. These are the two possible errors that can arise with respect to the agent interactions.

We use the infrastructure of Poutakidis et al. to collect information regarding our protocol graph interaction coverage criteria. This information can be collected by an independent observer. For the plan-graph coverage criteria, information must be known about the inner details of the participants. In current work, we are adapting Zhang et al.'s automated unit test framework [24] to measure plan-graph coverage criteria.

3.1   Petri-Net Representation for Protocols

Poutakidis et al. systematically translate AUML protocol specifications into Petri Nets, and executing these as agents interact, are able to ascertain whether the interaction is following a specified protocol.

A Petri Net is a bipartite graph containing two types of nodes: *places* and *transitions*. Places are represented with circles, and transitions are represented with rectangles (see Figure 6). Arcs connect transitions to places. The execution semantics of Petri Nets specifies that *tokens* can be located at places. A transition can be *fired* if all incoming places contain a token and the outgoing place is empty; when the transition fires, a token is placed at all outgoing places.

Poutakidis et al. define Petri Nets with two kinds of places: state places and message places. State places represent the state prior to a given message being received, or end states. When a Petri Net instance is initialised by the debugger, it has a token placed on its relevant message and state places. At each cycle all Petri Net instances are fired to completion, and then retained until the next cycle, when a token is added to the message place in the relevant Petri Nets. Poutakidis et al. define mappings from protocols to Petri Nets to model the possible protocol executions.

Figure 6(a) shows the Petri Net for the FIPA query protocol. When a *query-if* message arrives, this is identified as a start message for this protocol, and a new Petri Net instance is created. A token is placed in the *query-if* message place, and the corresponding state place. The Petri Net is then executed allowing the transition to fire producing a token on the outgoing state-place, P, as in Figure 6(b). The Petri Net is now in a state where, when a token is placed on either the *agree* or *refuse* message place, it can fire the relevant transition, producing a token in either R or T.

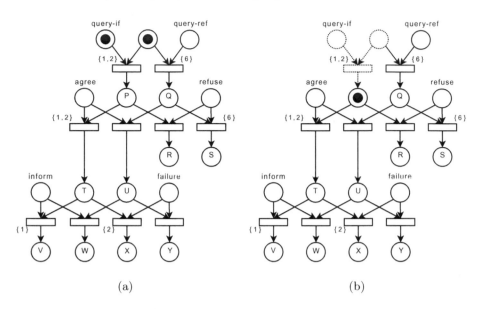

Fig. 6. An example of a Petri Net transformation

The debugging agent contains a copy of every protocol (and its corresponding Petri Net) used in the system. Each conversation held between a set of agents must contain a *conversation ID* to allow placement of a message into the correct Petri Net instance as there may be concurrent conversations. This requirement is supported by the FIPA standard for agent communication [6].

Each time the debugging agent receives a copy of a message, it first confirms whether the conversation ID corresponds to a current conversation. If not, it creates a Petri Net for *all* protocols that contain the received message as their initial message, initialises these appropriately, (as in Figure 6(a)). This is necessary because it has no way of knowing which protocol the sending agent is using if more than one protocol has that message as the initial message. The agent maintains a set of Petri Net instances for each conversation, until it becomes clear by a process of elimination, which protocol is being used.

If the message corresponds to an existing conversation, the debugging agent places the message in the appropriate message-place of all the Petri Nets in the set for the conversation. Those that do not have an appropriate place, or where the message place does not enable a transition, are removed from the set, because it is evident the conversation is not following this protocol. If the set becomes empty, then this indicates a fault: the agents are not following any known protocol. For example, if the Petri Net is in the state shown in Figure 6(b), and the debugging agent received the message *agree*, then this transition could fire. Alternatively, if the message was *refuse*, the transition could not fire because there would be no token at Q. This indicates a fault.

The process continues until the conversation is deemed to have terminated. If there are tokens remaining in any non-terminal places, this indicates a fault, because the conversation did not follow the protocol to completion.

3.2 Measuring Coverage Using Petri Nets

We adapt Poutakidis et al.'s debugging agent to measure the coverage corresponding to the protocol-based criteria defined in Section 2. First, we modify the oracle such that, when a transition is fired, the transition is annotated with the conversation ID, such as in Figure 6(a).This records all of the conversations that take place using a particular protocol. In this example, conversations 1, 2, and 6 from Figure 2 have been executed, and the appropriate transitions have been annotated.

To measure message coverage, we analyse each message place in the Petri Net and determine if at least one of its outgoing transitions has been fired (is annotated). If so, the message has been sent. We can then use the coverage measure definition from Section 2.1 to measure coverage.

To measure pairwise message coverage, we analyse each place in the Petri Net that represents an intermediate state; that is, all non-message-places between two transitions. If the incoming transition and at least one outgoing transition share at least one conversation ID, then this pair was executed. For example, the place P contains one incoming transition and two outgoing transitions. The incoming arc and the left outgoing transition both contain the conversation IDs 1 and 2, so this pair was executed in sequence. To show this is valid, we note that the unfolding rules specified by Poutakidis et al. [19] result in a graph such that any two places are linked by at most one path. As a result, each intermediate place in a Petri Net must have at least one input and one output transition, and all pairwise messages in a protocol are connected by exactly one such message place in the Petri Net representation. If the incoming and outgoing message place share a conversation ID, then the pair of messages must have been executed.

Finally, to measure message path coverage, we take each terminal place, and determine if the incoming transition to that place was fired; that is, contains at least one conversation ID. To demonstrate validity of this, we again note that Poutakidis et al.'s unfolding rules result in a graph such that any two places are linked by at most one path. Therefore, the final transition is unique to a path, so if this transition has been fired, the entire path must have been executed.

3.3 Measuring Coverage for Concurrent Conversations

To monitor multiple conversations over a single protocol, Poutakidis et al. create multiple instances of the same Petri Net. Using a single instance is not suitable because, upon testing to see if a message is valid, the Petri Net may be in a configuration such that the message is valid for another conversation, but not the current one. Creating multiple instances of a Petri Net is suitable for monitoring interactions, however, to measure coverage, the coverage information is spread over multiple Petri Nets for a single protocol.

One solution is to collate all information from all Petri Nets after a test suite has been executed. However, this is somewhat inefficient and cumbersome.

A more elegant solution is to adapt Poutakidis et al.'s solution to use *coloured Petri Nets* [11]. Coloured Petri Nets extend Petri Nets by (among other things) allowing tokens to carry a *value*. A transition can be fired only if all incoming places contain a token with the same shared value.

To handle concurrent conversations, each protocol corresponds to a single Petri Net in the test oracle. Rather than creating multiple copies for multiple conversations, tokens are given values corresponding to the conversation ID. Using this, the test oracle receives a message containing a conversation ID, and can determine at which place the correct token resides. From here, it can determine whether the message is valid.

Taking this approach, tokens remain at the terminal places after conversations have terminated. Therefore, measuring path coverage is as simple as counting the number of terminal places that contain at least one token, and dividing this by the total number of terminal places.

4   Related Work

Test coverage criteria are typically used on the code level, with criteria specifying that a set of test cases must achieve complete coverage of program statements or of all branches in a program [15], or of all methods/functions that call another module in a program [20]. Such criteria are applicable to testing multi-agent systems, however, they do not test interactions specifically, which is the aim of the work in this paper.

Model-based coverage criteria also exist [23]. These typically require the coverage of transitions in a semi-formal finite-state automata model, or of propositions or functions in a formal state machine model. Modelling the interactions within a system and using these model-based criteria would be sufficient to test agent interactions, however, we aim to leverage off the existing models in the system. AUML interaction diagrams are one of the most common forms of interaction models.

There has been recent work on automating test case generation in multi-agent systems, such as the Unit test framework of Zhang et al. [24] already mentioned in this work, and the eCAT system associated with Tropos [16,17,18]. eCAT is a testing tool that automates test case generation and execution. There are 4 test generation techniques employed in eCAT: *goal-oriented*, which is manual test generation using goal diagrams; *ontology-based*, where test cases are derived automatically from the specification of the agent interaction ontology; *random*, where values for test cases are randomly generated; and *evolutionary mutation*, where genetic algorithms generate test cases measured by the quality goals of the system. Our approach to testing correctness, and measuring thoroughness could complement any of these test case generation techniques.

Low et al. [13] consider test coverage criteria for BDI agents. They derive two types of control-flow graphs: one with nodes representing plans and arcs representing messages or other events that trigger plans; and one with nodes representing statements within plans and arcs representing control-flow between statements (a standard control-flow graph). Several coverage criteria are defined, based on node, arc, and path coverage, as well as some based on the success or failure of executing statements and plans. However, Low et al.'s work builds graphs over the entire program, and thus does not facilitate the modular and focused testing based on specific interaction protocols.

Low et al.'s coverage criteria relate to ours. Their plan graph is similar to our plan graph, except that they consider plans that are not related to interaction. As a result, their coverage criteria subsume ours; for example, their plan path coverage subsumes our plan path coverage. However, their criteria do not consider pairwise messages, as they do not focus on interaction protocols. Low et al. do not define specific coverage measures or how to calculate them, nor do they discuss test oracles.

We are not the first authors to consider the use of Petri Nets for testing. We discuss some of the most closely-related work.

Kissoum and Sahnoun [12] use Petri-Nets for testing agent interactions specified in AUML. Similar to our oracle approach, an AUML interaction diagram is converted into a Petri Net, although the method of conversion is different. All paths in the Petri Net are extracted and used as test cases. Kissoum and Sahnoun do not discuss how the sequences are used to determine the necessary input or how they can be used as an oracle. Instead, they provide a high-level overview of the framework.

Braberman et al. [1] propose test coverage criteria for real-time systems. In their method, real-time system behaviour, including timing constraints, are specified using a formal notation known as SA/SD-RT [8]. This is translated in a high-level Petri Net, which is simulated to obtain a *timed reachabililily tree*. From this, simulation can be used to generate abstract test cases. Braberman et al. leave the method for generating the final tests case and the oracle problem as future work.

Tjell [22] discuss the use of Petri Nets for monitoring the test outputs of a small car radio program. The system behaviour is modelled using Petri Nets, and all traces of the model are calculated. Traces of the program are collected during its execution, and the traces are checked to ensure that they are in the traces of the model. Expanding all traces of the model can result in a prohibitively large set, which is why our oracle reacts passively to the system behaviour by executing the Petri Nets on the fly

Desel et al. [5] present a technique for generating simulation traces for checking properties of a Petri Net. As a side effect of this technique, they propose that this can be used to generate test data for a program that implements the Petri Net. In their technique, the system behaviour is modelled as a Petri Net, with places representing propositions about the system, and transitions represent actions. A *cause-effect net* is extracted from the graph, which is a binary relation between all actions that cause the system to change state, and is represented using a restricted form of Petri Net. From this, test cases are generated by simulating the cause-effect net to determine the inputs (causes) and outputs (effects).

5 Discussion and Conclusion

Due to the complex emergent behaviour that results from agents interacting with each other, testing these interactions is an important part of the verification and validation process. The fact that emergent behaviour in complex systems is often difficult or impossible to identify without running these systems implies that using human test engineers to generate test cases manually is not sufficient, and automated test case generation techniques are required.

Whether test cases are generated automatically or manually, it is important to have a measure of the quality of the set of test cases. This paper has provided criteria by which to measure this, showing the subsumption relationships between these criteria, and discussing which we would practically aim for. We suggest that testing all paths through the protocol, combined with all plan paths between two messages achieves a high level of coverage, and is likely to be more feasible than plan path coverage, which subsumes both of these criteria. This paper has also shown how to collect these measurements as part of the testing process. We consider that these coverage definitions provide a sound basis for guiding test case generation where test cases are designed to give good coverage.

The work in this paper is one step towards a larger goal: model-based automated testing for multi-agent systems. Future work will define methods for automatically deriving test cases from design artifacts. With respect to interaction testing, we will attempt to automatically generate complete test suites that achieve message path coverage combined with pairwise internal path coverage, using design documents as the models.

References

1. Braberman, V., Felder, M., Marre, M.: Testing timing behavior of real-time software. In: International Software Quality Week (1997)
2. Caire, G., Cossentino, M., Negri, A., Poggi, A., Turci, P.: Multi-Agent Systems Implementation and Testing. In: The Fourth International Symposium: From Agent Theory to Agent Implementation, April 14-16 (2004)
3. Coelho, R., Kulesza, U., von Staa, A., Lucena, C.: Unit testing in multi-agent systems using mock agents and aspects. In: Proc. of the 2006 Intl. Workshop on Software Engineering for Large-Scale Multi-Agent Systems, pp. 83–90 (2006)
4. DeLoach, S., Padgham, L., Perini, A., Susi, A., Thangarajah, J.: Using three AOSE toolkits to develop a sample design. International Journal of Agent-Oriented Software Engineering 3(4), 416–476 (2009)
5. Desel, J., Oberweis, A., Zimmer, T., Zimmermann, G.: Validation of information system models: Petri Nets and test case generation. In: IEEE International Conference on Systems, Man, and Cybernetics, vol. 4, pp. 3401–3406. IEEE, Los Alamitos (2002)
6. FIPA. FIPA ACL message structure specification. Standard SC00061G, Foundation for Intelligent Physical Agents (December 2002)
7. FIPA. FIPA query interaction protocol specification. Standard SC00027H, Foundation for Intelligent Physical Agents (December 2003)
8. Hatley, D.J., Pirbhai, I.A.: Strategies for real-time system specification. Dorset House, New York (1988)

9. Huget, M., Odell, J.: Representing agent interaction protocols with Agent UML. In: Odell, J.J., Giorgini, P., Müller, J.P. (eds.) AOSE 2004. LNCS, vol. 3382, pp. 16–30. Springer, Heidelberg (2005)

10. IEEE. IEEE standard glossary of software engineering terminology. Technical Report 610.12-1990, Institute of Electrical and Electronic Engineers (1990)

11. Jensen, K.: Coloured Petri Nets. Springer, Heidelberg (1997)

12. Kissoum, Y., Sahnoun, Z.: A recursive colored Petri Nets semantics for AUML as base of test case generation. In: IEEE/ACS International Conference on Computer Systems and Applications, pp. 785–792. IEEE, Los Alamitos (2008)

13. Low, C., Chen, T.Y., Ronnquist, R.: Automated test case generation for BDI agents. Autonomous Agents and Multi-Agent Systems 2(4), 311–332 (1999)

14. Myers, G.J.: The Art of Software Testing. Wiley, New York (1979)

15. Myers, G.J., Sandler, C., Badgett, T., Thomas, T.M.: The Art of Software Testing, 2nd edn. Wiley, Chichester (2004)

16. Nguyen, C., Perini, A., Tonella, P.: Automated continuous testing of multi-agent systems. In: Fifth European Workshop on Multi-Agent Systems, Hammamet, Tunisia (December 2007)

17. Nguyen, C., Perini, A., Tonella, P.: eCAT: a tool for automating test case generation and execution in testing multi-agent systems (demo paper). In: Proceedings of AAMAS 2008, Estoril, Portugal, pp. 1669–1670 (2008)

18. Nguyen, C., Perini, A., Tonella, P.: Ontology-based test generation for multi-agent systems. In: Proceedings of AAMAS 2008, pp. 1315–1320 (2008)

19. Poutakidis, D., Padgham, L., Winikoff, M.: Debugging multi-agent systems using design artifacts: The case of interaction protocols. In: Alonso, E., Kudenko, D., Kazakov, D. (eds.) AAMAS 2000 and AAMAS 2002. LNCS (LNAI), vol. 2636, pp. 960–967. Springer, Heidelberg (2003)

20. Spillner, A.: Test criteria and coverage measures for software integration testing. Software Quality Journal 4(4), 275–286 (1995)

21. Tiryaki, A., Öztuna, S., Dikenelli, O., Cenk Erdur, R.: SUNIT: A unit testing framework for test driven development of multi-agent systems. In: Padgham, L., Zambonelli, F. (eds.) AOSE VII / AOSE 2006. LNCS, vol. 4405, pp. 156–173. Springer, Heidelberg (2007)

22. Tjell, S.: Model-based testing of a reactive system with coloured Petri Nets. Proceedings of INFORMATIK 94, 274–281 (2006)

23. Utting, M., Legeard, B.: Practical Model-Based Testing: A Tools Approach. Morgan-Kaufmann, San Francisco (2007)

24. Zhang, Z., Thangarajah, J., Padgham, L.: Automated unit testing for agent systems. In: 2nd International Working Conference on Evaluation of Novel Approaches to Software Engineering, Spain, pp. 10–18 (July 2007)

Using ASEME Methodology
for Model-Driven Agent Systems Development

Nikolaos Spanoudakis[1] and Pavlos Moraitis[2]

[1] Technical University of Crete, Dept. of Sciences,
University Campus, 73100 Chania, Greece
nikos@science.tuc.gr
[2] Laboratory of Informatics Paris Descartes (LIPADE), Paris Descartes University,
45 rue des Saints-Pères, 75270 Paris Cedex 06, France
pavlos@mi.parisdescartes.fr

Abstract. This paper shows how an AOSE methodology, the Agent Systems Engineering Methodology (ASEME), uses state of the art technologies from the Model-Driven Engineering (MDE) domain. We present the Agent Modeling Language (AMOLA) metamodels and the model transformation tools that we developed and discuss our choices. Moreover, the way that non-functional requirements are used throughout the software development lifecycle is discussed and presented with two real-world case studies. Finally, we compare ASEME with a set of existing AOSE methodologies.

1   Introduction

During the last years, there has been a growth of interest in the potential of agent technology in the context of software engineering. A new trend in the Agent Oriented Software Engineering (AOSE) field is that of converging towards the Model-Driven Engineering (MDE) paradigm. Thus, a lot of well known AOSE methodologies propose methods and tools for automating models transformations, such as Tropos [23] and INGENIAS [7], but this is done only for some of the software development phases.

This paper aims to show for the first time how the principles of MDE can be used throughout all the software development phases and how the AOSE community can use three different types of transformations in order to produce new models based on previous models. This approach has been used by the Agent Systems Engineering Methodology (ASEME)[1] [26], [28] and shows how an agent-based system can be incrementally modeled by gradually adding more information at each development phase using the appropriate type of model.

ASEME offers some unique characteristics regarding the used MDE approach. It covers all the classic software development phases (from requirements to implementation) and the transition of one phase to another is done through

---

[1] From the ASEME web site the interested reader can download the tools and metamodels used in this paper, URL: http://www.amcl.tuc.gr/aseme

D. Weyns and M.-P. Gleizes (Eds.): AOSE 2010, LNCS 6788, pp. 106–127, 2011.

model transformations. It employs three transformation types, i.e. model to model (M2M), text to model (T2M) and model to text (M2T). Thus, the analysts/engineers and developers just enrich the models of each phase with information, gradually leading to implementation. Moreover, the design phase model of ASEME is a statechart [10], a modeling paradigm well known to engineers, which can be implemented using a variety of programming languages or an agent-oriented platform.

Another important aspect of ASEME is the support of documentation of non-functional requirements even from the requirements analysis phase. These are propagated in the analysis phase where they are used for taking managerial decisions and selecting the technologies that will be used for design and development.

This paper presents the ASEME process showing the models transformations between the different development phases. The models that are used by ASEME are defined by the Agent Modeling Language (AMOLA, a first version is presented in [28]). Moreover, it emphasizes on the handling of non-functional requirements by ASEME. The next paragraph provides a background on metamodeling and models transformation followed by the definition of the AMOLA metamodels in section two. The ASEME MDE process is presented in section three discussing the used transformation tools. Section four presents how ASEME tackles the issue of non-functional requirements. In section five we evaluate ASEME using empirical results through the development of two real world systems. Related work is discussed in section six and the paper is concluded in section seven.

1.1   Metamodeling and Models Transformation

Model Driven Engineering (MDE) relies heavily on model transformation [25]. Model transformation is the process of transforming a model to another model. The requirements for achieving the transformation are the existence of metamodels of the models in question and a transformation language in which to write the rules for transforming the elements of one metamodel to those of another metamodel. The MDE approach has been argued to contribute to non-functional requirements capture, such as portability, interoperability and reusability [15].

In the software engineering domain a *model* is an abstraction of a software system (or part of it) and a *metamodel* is another abstraction, defining the properties of the model itself. However, even a metamodel is itself a model. In the context of model engineering there is yet another level of abstraction, the *metametamodel*, which is defined as a model that conforms to itself [13].

There are four types of model transformation techniques [16]:

- **Model to Model (M2M)** transformation. This kind of transformation is used for transforming a type of graphical model to another type of graphical model. A M2M transformation is based on the source and target metamodels and defines the transformations of elements of the source model to elements of the target model.

- **Text to Model (T2M)**transformation. This kind of transformation is used
  for transforming a textual representation to a graphical model. The textual
  representation must adhere to a language syntax definition usually using
  BNF. The graphical model must have a metamodel. Then, a transformation
  of the text to a graphical model can be defined.
- **Model to Text (M2T)** transformations. Such transformations are used
  for transforming a visual representation to code (code is text). Again, the
  syntax of the target language must be defined along with the metamodel of
  the graphical model.
- **Text to Text (T2T)** transformations. Such transformations are used for
  transforming a textual representation to another textual representation. This
  is usually the case when a program written for a specific programming language is transformed to a program in another programming language (e.g.
  a compiler).

In the heart of the model transformation procedure is the Eclipse Modeling Framework (EMF, [3]). Ecore is EMF's model of a model (metamodel). It
functions as a metametamodel and it is used for constructing metamodels. It
defines that a model is composed of instances of the *EClass* type, which can
have attributes (instances of the *EAttribute* type) or reference other EClass instances (through the *EReference* type). Finally, EAttributes can be of various
EDataType instances (such are integers, strings, real numbers, etc). EMF allows
to extend existing models via inheritance, using the *ESuperType* relationship for
extending an existing EClass.

A similar technology, the Meta-Object Facility (MOF), is an OMG standard
[19] for representing metamodels and manipulating them. MOF is older than
EMF and it influenced its design. However, the EMF meta-model is simpler
than the MOF meta-model in terms of its concepts, properties and containment
structure, thus, the mapping of EMF's concepts into MOF's concepts is relatively
straightforward and is mostly 1-to-1 translations [8]. EMF is also used today by
a large open source community becoming a de facto standard in MDE.

2   The AMOLA Metamodels

In this section we present the metamodels used in the ASEME MDE process.
Using these metamodels we can derive graphical tools for defining the models
and tools for automating the models tranformations.

2.1   The System Actor Goal Model (SAG)

The SAG model is a subset of the Actor model of the Tropos ecore model [31].
Tropos is, on one hand, one of the very few AOSE methodologies that deal with
requirements analysis, and, on the other hand it borrows successful practices
from the general software engineering discipline. This is why we have been inspired by Tropos. The reason for not using the Tropos diagrams as they are is

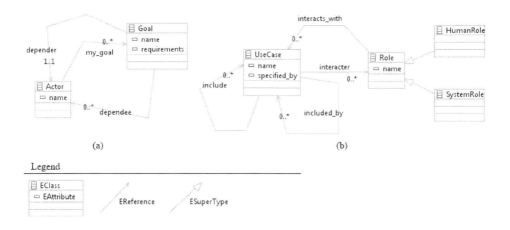

Fig. 1. The AMOLA SAG (a) and SUC (b) metamodels

that they provide more concepts than the ones used by AMOLA as they are also used for system analysis. However, as we will show later, AMOLA defines more well-suited diagrams for system analysis.

Thus, the AMOLA System Actors Goals diagram is the one that appears in Figure 1(a) employing the *Actor* and *Goal* concepts. The actor references his goals using the *EReference my_goal*, while the *Goal* references a unique *depender* and zero or more *dependees*. The reader should notice the choice to add the *requirements EAttribute* of *Goal*. Through this attribute, each goal is related to functional and non-functional requirements, which are documented in plain text form.

2.2   The System Use Cases Model (SUC)

In the analysis phase, the analyst needs to start capturing the functionality behind the system under development. In order to do that he needs to start thinking not in terms of goal but in terms of what will the system need to do and who are the involved actors in each activity. The use case diagram helps to visualize the system including its interaction with external entities, be they humans or other systems. It is well-known by software engineers as it is part of the Unified Modeling Language (UML).

In AMOLA no new elements are needed other than those proposed by UML, however, the semantics change. Firstly, the actor "enters" the system and assumes a role. *Agents* are modeled as roles, either within the system box (for the agents that are to be developed) or outside the system box (for existing agents in the environment). Human actors are represented as roles outside the system box (like in traditional UML use case diagrams). This approach aims to show the concept that we are modeling artificial agents interacting with other artificial agents or human agents. Secondly, the different use cases must be directly related to at least one artificial agent role.

The SUC metamodel containing the concepts used by AMOLA is presented in Figure 1(b). The concept *UseCase* has been defined that can include and be included by other *UseCase* concepts. It interacts with one or more roles, which can be Human roles (HumanRole) or Agent roles (SystemRole).

2.3   The System Roles Model (SRM)

An important concept in AOSE is the role. An agent is assumed to undertake one or many roles in his lifetime. The role is associated with activities and this is one of the main differences with traditional software engineering, the fact that the activity is no longer associated with the system, but, rather, with the role. Moreover, after defining the capabilities of the agents and decomposing them to simple activities in the SUC model we need to define the dynamic composition of these activities by each role so that he achieves his goals. Thus, we defined the SRM model based on the Gaia Role model [34]. Gaia defines the liveness formula operators that allow the composition of formulas depicting the role's dynamic behavior. However, we needed to change the role model of Gaia in order to accommodate the integration in an agent's role the incorporation of complex agent interaction protocols (within which an agent can assume more than one roles even at the same time), a weakness of the Gaia methodology. The AMOLA SRM metamodel is presented in Figure 2(a). The SRM metamodel defines the concept *Role* that references the concepts:

- *Activity*, that refers to a simple activity with two attributes, name (its name) and functionality (the description of what this activity does)
- *Capability* that refers to groups of activities (to which it refers) achieving a high level goal, and,
- *Protocol*. The protocol attributes *name* and *participant* refer to the relevant items in the Agent Interactions Protocol (AIP) model. This model is not detailed here-in. It is used for identifying the roles that participate in a protocol, their activities within the protocol and the rules for engaging (for more details consult [29]).

The *Role* concept also has the *name* and *liveness* attributes (the first is the role name and the second its liveness formula). The reader should note the *functionality* attribute of the *Activity* concept which is used to associate the activity to a generic functionality. For example, the "get weather information" activity can be related to the "web service invocation" functionality (see [27], [28]).

2.4   The Intra-Agent Control Model (IAC)

In order to represent system designs, AMOLA is based on statecharts, a well-known and general language and does not make any assumptions on the ontology, communication model, reasoning processes or the mental attitudes (e.g. belief-desire-intentions) of the agents, giving this freedom to the designer. Other methodologies impose (like Prometheus or INGENIAS [11]), or strongly imply

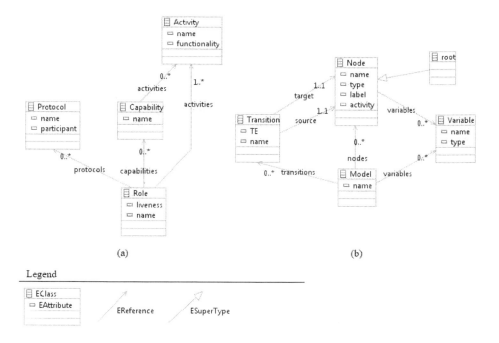

Fig. 2. The AMOLA SRM (a) and IAC (b) metamodels

(like Tropos [11]) the agent mental models. Of course, there are some developers who want to have all these things ready for them, but there are others who want to use different agent paradigms according to their expertise. For example, one can use AMOLA for defining Belief-Desire-Intentions based agents, while another for defining procedural agents [26].

The inspiration for defining the IAC metamodel mainly came from the UML statechart definition. Aiming to define the statechart using the AMOLA definition of statechart [30], the IAC metamodel differs significantly from the UML statechart. However, a UML statechart can be transformed to an IAC statechart, although some elements would be difficult to define (UML does not cater for transition expressions and association of variables to nodes and uses statecharts to define a single object's behaviour). Thus, the IAC metamodel, which is presented in Figure 2(b), defines a *Model* concept that has *nodes, transitions* and *variables* EReferences. Note that it also has a *name* EAttribute. The latter is used to define the namespace of the IAC model. The namespace should follow the Java or C# package namespace format. The nodes contain the following attributes:

- *name*. The name of the node,
- *type*. The type of the node, corresponding to the type of state in a statechart, typically one of AND, OR, BASIC, START, END (see [10]),
- *label*. The node's label, and
- *activity*. The activity related to the node.

Nodes also refer to *variables*. The *Variable* EClass has the attributes *name* and *type* (e.g. the variable with *name* "count" has *type* "integer"). The next concept defined in this metamodel is that of *Transition*, which has four attributes:

- *name*, usually in the form <source node label> TO <target node label>
- *TE, the transition expression*. This expression contains the conditions and events that make the transition possible. Through the transition expressions (TEs) the modeler defines the control information in the IAC. TEs can use concepts from an ontology as variables. Moreover, the receipt or transmission of an inter-agent message can be used (in the case of agent interaction protocols). For the formal definition of the TE and some examples see [26] or [29].
- *source*, the source node, and,
- *target*, the target node.

3   The ASEME Model-Driven Process and Tools

ASEME is described in detail in [26]. It is a complete process incorporating all the traditional software engineering methodology phases, however, using the SPEM 2.0 process metamodel [21] it can be modified to provide an agile process. Figure 3, a screenshot from the EPF[2] modelling tool, shows on the left side the ASEME method library and its various properties. From top to bottom the most important are the:

- *Work Product Kinds*, we have defined two product kinds, models (graphical models, e.g. SAG, SUC, etc) and text (textual representation, e.g. a computer program).
- *Role sets*, where the different human actors implicated in the software development process are identified.
- *Tools*, the various tools used in the process, in this case the transformation tools.
- *Processes*, can be *delivery processes*, which provide the project manager with an initial project template, showing the project milestones with the work products to be delivered and needed resources, or *capability patterns* that allow project managers to use one or more method libraries to compose their project-specific process.

In Figure 3, the reader can see two defined capability patterns, the first named ASEME and containing the six software development phases, and a more compact one, the ASEME MDE process where the model-driven development process for a single agent system is depicted. This process shows the nine tasks needed for developing an agent-based system:

1. *Edit SAG model*. The business consultant of the software development firm identifies the actors involved in the system to be along with their goals.

---

[2] The Eclipse Process Framework (EPF) aims at producing a customizable software process engineering framework. URL: http://www.eclipse.org/epf/

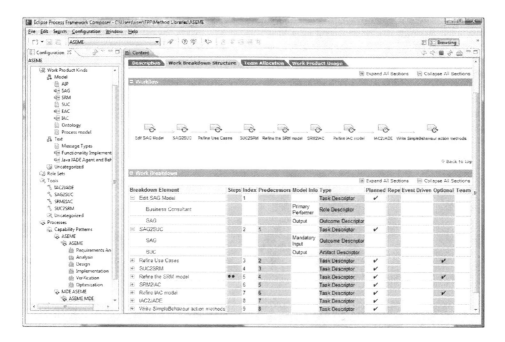

Fig. 3. The ASEME MDE Process

2. *SAG2SUC.* An automated task, as the reader can see in the figure this task has only a mandatory input model (SAG) and an output model (SUC). It creates an initial SUC model based on the previously created SAG model.
3. *Refine Use Cases.* The analyst works on the SUC model and refines the general use cases using the include relationship. He/she also identifies which actors will be implemented defining them as human or artificial agent actors. The overall system design is enriched by identifying the tasks that have to be carried out by the actors.
4. *SUC2SRM.* An automated task, it has only a mandatory input model (SUC) and an output model (SRM). It creates an initial SRM model based on the previously created SUC model.
5. *Refine the SRM model.* The analyst works on the SRM model by defining the liveness formulas that will describe the dynamic compilation of the previously identified tasks.
6. *SRM2IAC.* An automated task, it has only a mandatory input model (SRM) and an output model (IAC). It creates multiple initial IAC models based on the previously created SRM model, one for each role.
7. *Refine the IAC model.* The designer works on each IAC model by defining the conditions and/or events that will enable the transitions from one task to the other.

8. *IAC2JADE*. An automated task, it has only a mandatory input model (IAC) and an output model (Java JADE[3] Agent and Behaviours code). It creates a JADE Agent class and multiple JADE Behaviour classes for each IAC model.

9. *Write SimpleBehaviour action methods*. The programmer writes code only for the JADE *SimpleBehaviour* class descendants'*action* methods.

The following paragraphs discuss the employed transformations automation tools that are used in the presented ASEME MDE process.

3.1   The ASEME M2M Transformation Tools (SAG2SUC and SUC2SRM)

The Atlas Transformation Language (ATL) [14] was used for model to model (M2M) transformations. Another alternative to ATL would be the Query-View Transformation (QVT) language [20], however, ATL was better documented on the internet with a user guide and examples, while the only resource located for QVT was a presentation. Therefore, and as the requirements of both languages (ATL and QVT) are the same the decision was to choose the better documented one. Such transformations are the SAG2SUC and SUC2SRM.

The ATL rules for the SAG2SUC transformation are presented in Figure 4. At the top of the right window, the IN and OUT metamodels are defined followed by rules that have an input model concept instance and one or more output concept model instances. The first rule (*Goal2UseCase*) takes as input a SAG Goal concept and creates a SUC UseCase concept copying its properties. The ATL is declarative and has catered for the cases that a concept references another. The *depender* and *dependee* references of a SAG Goal are both transformed to *participator* references of the SUC UseCase. The ATL engine searches the rules to find one that transforms the types of the EReference (i.e. the SAG Actor concepts to a SUC Role). It finds the second rule (*Actor2Role*) and fires it, thus creating the EReference type objects and completing the first rule firing. At the left hand side of Figure 4 the reader can see the files relevant to this transformation: a) the *SAG.ecore* and *SUC.ecore* metamodel files, b) the *SAG2SUC.atl* rules file, c) the *SAGModel.xmi* file containing the SAG model in XML format and d) the *SUCModelInitial.xmi* file containing the automatically derived initial SUC model.

3.2   The ASEME T2M Transformation Tool (SRM2IAC)

The trick in text to model transformations is to define the meta-model of the text to be transformed. This can be done in the form of an EBNF syntax (for languages with a grammar) or through string manipulation. Efftinge and Völter [6] presented the xtext framework in the context of the Eclipse Modeling Project

---

[3] The Java Agent Development Environment (JADE) is an open source framework that adheres to the FIPA standards, URL: http://jade.tilab.com

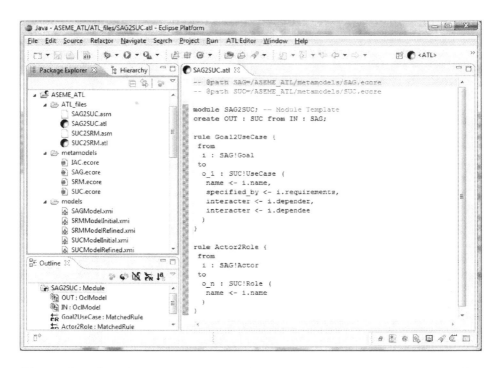

Fig. 4. The eclipse ATL project for the SAG2SUC and the SUC2SRM M2M transformations

(EMP[4]). According to their work, an xText grammar is a collection of rules. Each rule is described using sequences of tokens. Tokens either reference another rule or one of the built-in tokens (e.g. STRING, ID, LINE, INT). A rule results in a meta type, the tokens used in the rule are mapped to properties of that type. xText is used to automatically derive the meta model from the grammar. Then a textual representation of a model following this grammar can be parsed and the meta-model is automatically generated.

Rose et al. [24] described an implementation of the Human-Usable Textual Notation (HUTN) specification of OMG [18] using Epsilon, which is a suite of tools for MDE. OMG created HUTN aiming to offer three main benefits to MDE: a) a generic specification that can provide a concrete HUTN language for any model, b) the HUTN languages to be fully automated both for production and parsing, and, c) the HUTN languages to conform to human-usability criteria. The HUTN implementation automates the transformation process by eliminating the need for a grammar specification by auto defining it accepting as input the relevant EMF meta-model. This is the main reason for choosing HUTN for ASEME.

---

[4] The Eclipse Modeling Project provides a unified set of modeling frameworks, tooling, and standards implementations, URL: http://www.eclipse.org/modeling/

A T2M transformation is used for transforming a liveness formula to a state-chart (IAC model). We first use an iterative algorithm (see [30]) that creates the HUTN model, which is then automatically transformed to an IAC model. The usage of the HUTN technology also helped a lot in debugging the algorithm as the output was in human-readable format.

3.3   The ASEME M2T Transformation Tool (IAC2JADE)

The last transformation type used in the ASEME process is M2T. The platform independent IAC model must be transformed to a platform dependent one and to executable code.

We used the Xpand language offered by the Eclipse. Another commonly used M2T transformation language (in EMP) is the Java Emitter Templates (JET). JET uses JSP-like templates, thus it is easy to learn for developers familiar with this technology.

The advantages of Xpand are the fact that it is source model independent, which means that any of the EMP parsers can be used for common software models such as MOF or EMF. Its vocabulary is limited allowing for a quick learning curve while the integration with Xtend allows for handling complex requirements. Then, EMP allows for defining workflows that allow the modeler to parse the model multiple times, possibly with different goals.

In ASEME, the developer uses the IAC2JADE tool that automatically generates the message receiving and sending behaviours and the composite behaviours that coordinate the execution of simple behaviours. Thus, the user just needs to program the action methods of simple behaviours.

4   Non-functional Requirements in ASEME

Throughout this section, and aiming to present the way that ASEME handles non-functional requirements, some parts of the requirements and system analysis of two real-world agent-based systems are presented.

4.1   A Real World Case Study: The ASK-IT Project

In this first case study, the requirements were to develop a system that allows a user to access a variety of location-based services supported by a brokering system. The system should learn the habits of the user and support him while on the move. It should connect to an OSGi[5] service for getting the user's coordinates using a GPS device. It should also handle dangerous situations for the user by reading a heart rate sensor (again an OSGi service) and call for help. A non-functional requirement for the system is to execute on any mobile device with

---

[5] The OSGi (Open Services Gateway initiative) Alliance is a worldwide consortium of technology innovators that advances a proven and mature process to assure interoperability of applications and services based on its component integration platform, URL: http://www.osgi.org

the OSGi service architecture. The broker has access to a variety of existing web services but should also provide added value services. For more details about the real-world system, which will be referred to as ASK-IT for the remainder of this document, the reader can refer to [17].

A subset of the SAG model capturing the ASK-IT system requirements is presented in Figure 5. This model was created after identifying the stakeholders relevant to this project [26]. Such were the:

- *User*: The user is a mobility impaired person that wants to get infomobility services tailored to his needs (e.g. find the nearest toilet that is accessible according to his type of impairment). This user is assumed to wander in the environment having access to the internet and wherever possible access to local area networks using technologies like Wi-Fi. He also has constant access to devices and services that are on his person and move around with him. Such can be a GPS device. He also needs assistance in handling dangerous situations (e.g. if he has a heart attack).
- *Broker*: This is the ASK-IT B2C (Business to Consumer) Operator. He is interested in aggregating services offered by diverse service providers either globally or locally. Whenever a user makes a request he matches the request to his repository of available services and selects the most relevant one to request on behalf of the user.
- *Added Value Service Providers*: These service providers can provide a simple service or they can introduce new added value services through the aggregation of one or more simple services accessed through the broker. A simple service provider offers map information for a specific city. An added value service provider offers map information for any city including the capability to add points of interest offered by many independent providers.

The stakeholders are modeled as actors. A stakeholder, who is assisted by a software, introduces a new actor, usually named as *personal assistant*. Thus,

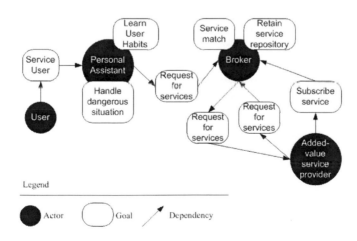

Fig. 5. The SAG model for the ASK-IT project

in Figure 5, the above three stakeholders are represented by four actors, the user, his personal assistant, the broker and the added value service provider. The user needs to get location based services and for that he is dependent to his personal assistant. The latter has three individual goals, to adequately service his user, to learn his/her habits and to autonomously handle a dangerous situation. The personal assistant depends on the broker (BR) for getting services. The broker represents a network operator or portal stakeholder who acts as a service aggregator and offers the services to its users. Its goals include the maintenance of a service repository, finding the best service for a user and accessing several web services offered by third parties. Moreover, he depends for getting added-value services to the "Added-value service provider" (AVSP), who provides specialized services for users with special needs or capabilities. For example, an organization of mobility impaired persons maintains a repository of accessible streets and buildings and can provide trip planning services to such persons. For offering their service they depend on the broker themselves in order to get maps or public transport routing options.

The *requirements per goal* (RPG) is a simple model aiming to associate SAG goals to requirements presented in plain text mode. For adding the goal requirements the engineer should add the answers to the following questions:

- Why does the actor have this goal and why does he depend to another for it (this is the most important question and its answer is usually the goal's name)
- What is the outcome of achieving the goal (identify related resources)
- How is he expected to achieve this goal (identify the task to be performed for reaching this goal)
- When is this goal valid (identify timing requirements)

The *requirements per goal* are documented in the *requirements* EAttribute of the *Goal* concept of the SRM model, see Figure 2(a). A non-functional requirement for the personal assistant's service user goal is to be executed on a mobile device. Another is that it should reply to a user request within 10 seconds (see Table 1).

The SUC model presented in Figure 6 is part of the use cases for ASK-IT. Actually, it is a part focusing in the personal assistant (PA) role. The reader should notice at this point that the general use cases correspond to the goals of

Table 1. A portion of the Requirements Per Goal (RPG) model for the Personal Assistant Actor in ASK-IT project

Personal Assistant goals	
Service User	Delivery of the service within 10 seconds
	The service is offered from a mobile device with the OSGi service architecture
	The user can request a mapping or a routing service

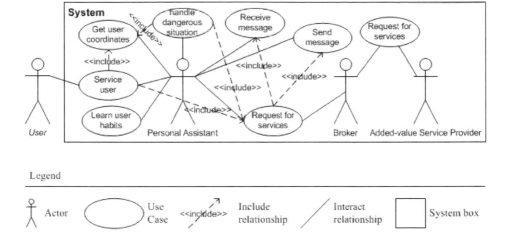

Fig. 6. A portion of the SUC model of the ASK-IT project

the requirements analysis phase. It is also important to note that at this phase the task of the system modeler is not to identify goals and dependencies between actors, like in the SAG, but to analyze the behavior of the system in order to achieve specific tasks. However, at the highest level of abstraction these tasks correspond to the system goals. The difference is that the know-how related to this phase is not that of the business modeler or the business consultant, it is that of the systems engineer or analyst.

A portion of the SRM for the personal assistant (PA) is presented in Figure 7. In his liveness model, the root formula states that he executes forever the "service user" capability in parallel with the "handle dangerous situation" capability. Each of these capabilities is detailed in the following two formulas whose left hand side terms are named after them. Other capabilities are further detailed in following formulas.

Role: Personal Assistant (PA)
Protocols: request for services; service requester (SR)
Liveness:
personal assistant = (service user)$^\omega$ || (handle dangerous situation)$^\omega$
service user = get user order. get user coordinates. get user preferences. request for services
    SR. present information to the user. learn user habits.
handle dangerous situation = invoke heart rate service. determine user condition. [get user
    coordinates. request for services SR]
request for services SR = search broker. [*send request message. receive response message*]
learn user habits = learn user preference. update user preferences.

Fig. 7. A portion of the SRM model of the Personal Assistant role of the ASK-IT project

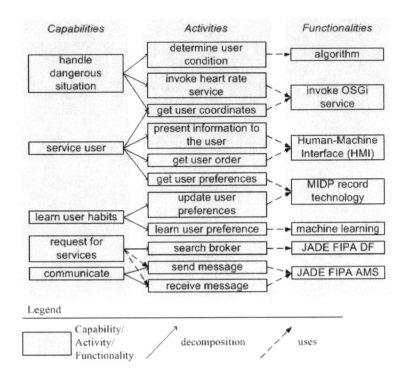

Fig. 8. Functionality Table for the personal assistant role of the ASK-IT project

The Functionality Table (FT) is where the analyst associates each activity participating in the liveness formulas of the SRM to the technology or tool (functionality) that it will use (see an example of FT in Figure 8 for the capabilities of the PA). The *communicate* capability includes the "send message" and "receive message" activities and is shared by all agents as proposed by FIPA[6]. This is the point where the analyst proposes the use of a platform for instantiation, e.g., in our example, JADE. This strategic choice also defines the programming language that will be used, in this case Java.

Returning to the ASK-IT example, the non-functional requirement for the PA to execute on any mobile device running OSGi services reveals that such a device must at least support the Java Mobile Information Device Profile (MIDP), which offers a specific record for storing data. Therefore, the activities that want to store or read data from a file must use the MIDP record technology.

The functionality table is defined in the SRM model adding a "functionality" property to each activity. However, a decision maker would prefer to see this information in a tabular format (like in Figure 8) in order to gain a quick understanding about the technologies involved in developing each agent.

---

[6] The Foundation for Intelligent Physical Agents (FIPA) is an IEEE Computer Society standards organization that promotes agent-based technology and the interoperability of its standards with other technologies, URL: http://www.fipa.org

4.2   A Real World Case Study: The Market-Miner Project

In the Market-Miner project [27], we developed an autonomous product pricing agent situated in a firm monitoring for changes of the prices of competitors along with changes in firm policies and deciding on the prices of the products on the self.

During the analysis phase we identified the actors and the use cases related to our agent system. We documented these findings using the ASEME System Use Cases (SUC) model (see Figure 9). For our system, the system actor is the Market-miner Product Pricing Agent (or MIPA), while the external actors that participate in the system's environment are the user, external systems of competitors, weather report systems (as the weather forecast influences product demand, like in the case of umbrellas) and municipality systems (as local events like concerts, sports, etc, also influence consumer demand).

Having defined the involved actors we started identifying general use cases (like *interact with user*) and then we elaborated them in more specific ones (like *present information to the user* and *update firm policy*) using the ≪ include ≫ relation. After refining the use cases, the SUC model was transformed to the System Roles Model (SRM), see Figure 10(a).

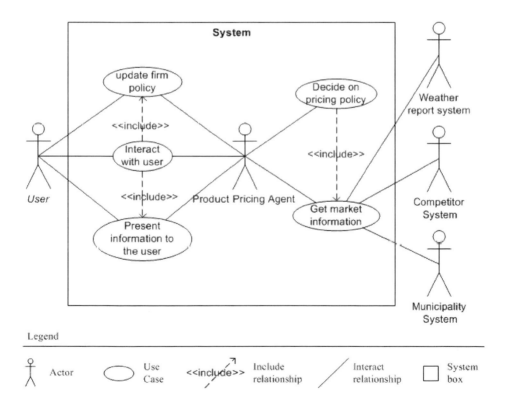

Fig. 9. An extract from the MIPA System SUC Model

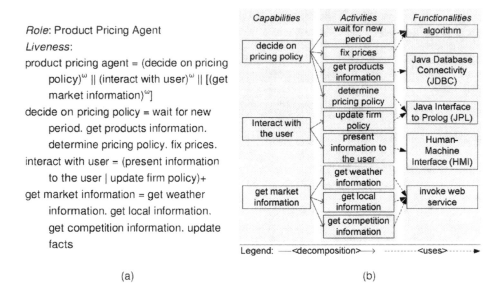

Role: Product Pricing Agent

Liveness:

product pricing agent = (decide on pricing
    policy)$^\omega$ || (interact with user)$^\omega$ || [(get
    market information)$^\omega$]

decide on pricing policy = wait for new
    period. get products information.
    determine pricing policy. fix prices.

interact with user = (present information
    to the user | update firm policy)+

get market information = get weather
    information. get local information.
    get competition information. update
    facts

(a)

(b)

Fig. 10. MIPA Role Model (a) and the Functionality Table (b)

The next step was to associate each activity to a functionality, i.e. the technology that would be used for its implementation. In Figure 10(b) the reader can observe the capabilities, the activities that they decompose to and the functionality associated with each activity. The choice of these technologies is greatly influenced by non-functional requirements. For example the system will need to connect on diverse firm databases. Thus, the JDBC[7] technology was selected, as it is database provider independent. Moreover, the different information channels that are currently used depend on the same functionality, i.e. a web service invocation. Thus, in the future, new information channels such as a financial channel where from to get relevant news, such as a financial crisis, can be integrated in the system using the same functionality. In this way, this model allows for the easy extensibility of the system (another usually desired non-functional requirement).

5   ASEME Evaluation

For evaluating our work we used two case studies on the development of two real-world systems. The first, a module of the ASK-IT project [17], included programming for semantic service matching and interfaces to other modules that were based on OSGi, a service oriented architecture. The ontology was developed using

---

[7] The Java Database Connectivity (JDBC) is a standard for database-independent connectivity between the Java programming language and a wide range of databases providing a call-level API for SQL-based database access, URL: http://java.sun.com/javase/technologies/database/

the Protégé[8] ontology editor and its beangenerator add-on, which generates java files representing an ontology that can be used with the JADE environment. The second is the Market-Miner project [27], where we used Prolog for implementing the decision making capability of the agent. Again, we used the Protégé editor for creating the ontology.

These projects used different implementation platforms, the first the JADE platform, while the second a Java CASE (Computer-Aided Software Engineering) tool, IBM Rational Rhapsody (URL: *http://www.ibm.com*). For the latter it was needed to transform the SRM model to an IAC model manually (as Rhapsody does not offer an import tool for statechart models) using the process defined in [30].

Table 2 shows a quick comparison of ASEME with existing AOSE methodologies. It has been inspired by a similar table in [32] from which we use some criteria (rows). The first row shows the levels of abstraction supported by the methodologies. Only ASEME maintains three levels of abstraction throughout the software development phases. Some do not support abstraction at all, while others do a phase-based abstraction (e.g. define agent interactions and roles in the analysis phase and focus in the specific agent development in the design phase). The next row shows the MDE support for the different software development phases. ASEME supports all the phases, many methodologies support some phases and INGENIAS allows the modeler to define his own transformations. The third row shows if a methodology covers all the software development phases, i.e. requirements analysis, system analysis, design, implementation, verification and optimization. The forth row shows what kind of agents each methodology supports and the fifth row indicates which methodologies define an intra-agent control model that allows an agent to coordinate his capabilities, thus supporting a modular development approach. The sixth row shows that ASEME is the only methodology to use a uniform representation of inter-agent protocols and the intra-agent control allowing for an easy integration of protocols in an agent specification. In Table 2 "n/a" means not applicable.

The last two rows are related to the non-functional requirements capture capability of the methodologies. Only three of the reviewed methodologies address this issue as the seventh row suggests. In Tropos, NFRs are either operationalized (also in MaSE) or are transformed to operational rules in the Late Requirement Analysis phase. Finally, only in ASEME they are used for selecting implementation technologies and tools in the analysis phase while in Tropos they are used for offering alternatives of implementations (also in the form of redundant sub-systems).

6   Related Work

A number of works in AOSE have introduced concepts and ideas from the model-driven engineering domain. Most of them just introduce an MDE technique for

---

[8] Protégé is a free, open source ontology editor and knowledge-base framework, URL: `http://protege.stanford.edu`

Table 2. ASEME compared with existing AOSE methodologies

Methodology	ASEME	Gaia	Tropos	INGENIAS	PASSI	Prometheus	MaSE
Abstraction	all phases	n/a	phase-based	n/a	phase-based	phase-based	n/a
MDE phases	all	n/a	some	defined by the modeler	some	n/a	some
Phases coverage	all	some	all	some	some	some	some
Agent nature	hetero-geneous	hetero-geneous	BDI-like agents	agents with goals and states	hetero-geneous	BDI-like agents	not specified
Intra-agent control (IAC)	yes	no	no	no	no	no	yes
Uniform representation of IAC and inter-agent protocols	yes	no	no	no	no	no	no
Non-functional requirements capture phase	yes	no	yes	no	no	no	yes
Associate non-functional requirements to system analysis choices	Yes	no	yes	no	no	no	no

transforming one of their models to another in one phase, e.g. from a Tropos plan decomposition diagram to a UML activity diagram in [23] and from a BDI (Belief-Desire-Intention) representation in XML format to JACK platform code in [12]. Almost all AOSE methodologies define a single, usually huge metamodel covering all the requirements, analysis and design phases [1].

Other works aim to create a single meta-model that can be used by different AOSE methodologies in a specific phase, like in [9], where the authors defined a meta-model (PIM4Agents) that can be used to model MAS in the PIM level of MDA, and in [1], where the authors try to envisage a unifying MAS meta-model. Finally, a more recent work [7] presents an algorithm to generate model transformations by-example that allows the engineer to define himself the transformations that he wants to apply to models complying with the INGENIAS metamodel.

ASEME furthers the state of the art by being the first AOSE methodology to propose a model-driven approach covering all the development phases. Thus, the developer only at the requirements analysis phase starts a model from scratch (SAG). All the other models are launched through a transformation that initializes them. Then, the developer adds the new information related to the specific model.

Regarding the use of non-functional requirements (NFRs), Tropos [2] provides a means for documenting them in the requirements analysis phase as soft goals. Then, Tropos uses them in two ways. The first is to evaluate identified tasks as helping or restricting the soft-goals. The second is to identify tasks that pursue the soft-goals (in which case soft goals become functional requirements).

Another approach is that proposed by Danny Weyns [33]. In his work, the author addresses the issue of NFRs by selecting appropriate architectures that each addresses a family of NFRs. For example, he proposes that selecting an agent-based approach to software development contributes to the NFRs openness, adaptability and scalability. Moreover, additional NFRs are modeled in quality attribute scenarios. These consist of three parts, a) *stimulus*: an event occuring in the system, b) *environment*: the environment conditions at the time of the stimulus occurence, and, c) *response*: the activity to be executed when the stimulus arrives.

In ASEME the way to cater for NFRs has been influenced by the work of Pérez et al. [22], who believe that non-functional requirements need a way to influence the way to implement a system or task, and this is what ASEME uniquely achieves compared to the other AOSE methodologies. In ASEME we do not define specific situations as NFRs, we allow quality requirements to be inserted in each goal requirements in the SAG model. Thus, they influence all analysis phase decisions including the technology selection for achieving the goal. Moreover, ASEME could allow for the catering of quality attribute scenarios if they are defined as agent interaction protocols (which define preconditions and results along with the different interested actors activities).

7 Conclusion

In the previous sections, we presented the formal definition of the AMOLA metamodels, which have been inspired by previous works but are original in the way that they uniquely extend those works and insert new semantics, thus assisting the ASEME process. We also presented the models transformations that occur in the different phases of ASEME.

The platform independent model of ASEME, i.e. the IAC, is a statechart which can be transformed to a platform specific model in C++ or Java (using commercial CASE tools) or in the JADE agent platform. This is another originality of ASEME, it is the first AOSE methodology to provide a PIM model that is compatible with existing software tools (i.e. the statechart) giving multiple platform choices to the developers.

The models used are common in the software engineering community, which means that any engineer can quickly adapt to the ASEME process. Model transformations are automated throughout the software development process.

Moreover, ASEME documents quality or non functional requirements at the requirements analysis phase and allows these to influence the architectural decisions of the analyst(s) when selecting technologies (e.g. reasoning, communication, etc) for realising system tasks. The possiblity of the ASEME IAC model to be transformed to a process model allows for simulating the analysis model even before design and validate the system functional and several non-functional requirements including scalability and robustness.

ASEME has been successfully used for the development of two real world systems ([17], [27]) and is currently used for development of a robotic system [4]. Moreover, we are working on automating the transformation of the IAC model to a process model as there are a number of existing tools in the market that perform system simulation, verification and optimization on such models. In [5] we proposed transformation templates for doing this transformation manually and performed simulations that showed that the ASK-IT system could deliver the service to the end user in 10 seconds (thus achieving a non-functional requirement, see Table 1).

Acknowledgements. We thank the reviewers of the AOSE workshop for their valuable, constructive comments. We also thank the European Union and the Ambient Assisted Living (AAL) Joint Programme (HERA Project, AAL-45061) for partially funding and for supporting this work.

References

1. Bernon, C., Cossentino, M., Pavón, J.: Agent-oriented software engineering. Knowledge Eng. Review 20(2), 99–116 (2005)
2. Bresciani, P., Perini, A., Giorgini, P., Giunchiglia, F., Mylopoulos, J.: Tropos: An agent-oriented software development methodology. Autonomous Agents and Multi-Agent Systems 8, 203–236 (2004)
3. Budinsky, F., Brodsky, S.A., Merks, E.: Eclipse Modeling Framework. Pearson Education, London (2003)
4. Chatzilaris, E., Kyranou, I., Orfanoudakis, E., Paraschos, A., Vazaios, E., Spanoudakis, N., Vlassis, N., Lagoudakis, M.G.: Kouretes 2010 spl team description paper. In: RoboCup 2010 Team Description Papers, Singapore (2010)
5. Delias, P., Spanoudakis, N.: Simulating multi-agent system designs using business process modeling. In: Proceedings of the 8th European Workshop on Multi-Agent Systems (EUMAS 2010), Paris, France, December 16-17 (2010)
6. Efftinge, S., Völter, M.: oaw xtext: A framework for textual dsls. In: Eclipse Summit 2006 Workshop: Eclipse Modeling Symposium (2006), http://www.eclipsecon.org/summiteurope2006/
7. García-Magariño, I., Rougemaille, S., Fuentes-Fernández, R., Migeon, F., Gleizes, M.P., Gómez-Sanz, J.J.: A tool for generating model transformations by-example in multi-agent systems. In: Demazeau, Y., Pavón, J., Corchado, J.M., Bajo, J. (eds.) 7th International Conference on Practical Applications of Agents and Multi-Agent Systems (PAAMS 2009), Salamanca, Spain, March 25-27. Advances in Soft Computing, vol. 55, pp. 70–79. Springer, Heidelberg (2009)
8. Gerber, A., Raymond, K.: Mof to emf: there and back again. In: Burke, M.G. (ed.) Proceedings of the 2003 OOPSLA Workshop on Eclipse Technology eXchange, Anaheim, CA, USA, pp. 60–64. ACM, New York (2003)
9. Hahn, C., Madrigal-Mora, C., Fischer, K.: A platform-independent metamodel for multiagent systems. Autonomous Agents and Multi-Agent Systems 18(2), 239–266 (2009)
10. Harel, D., Kugler, H.: The rhapsody semantics of statecharts (or, on the executable core of the uml) - preliminary version. In: Ehrig, H., Damm, W., Desel, J., Große-Rhode, M., Reif, W., Schnieder, E., Westkämper, E. (eds.) INT 2004. LNCS, vol. 3147, pp. 325–354. Springer, Heidelberg (2004)
11. Henderson-Sellers, B., Giorgini, P.: Agent-oriented methodologies. Idea Group Pub., USA (2005)
12. Jayatilleke, G.B., Padgham, L., Winikoff, M.: A model driven component-based development framework for agents. Comput. Syst. Sci. Eng. 20(4) (2005)
13. Jouault, F., Bézivin, J.: Km3: A dsl for metamodel specification. In: Gorrieri, R., Wehrheim, H. (eds.) FMOODS 2006. LNCS, vol. 4037, pp. 171–185. Springer, Heidelberg (2006)

14. Jouault, F., Kurtev, I.: Transforming models with atl. In: Bruel, J.-M. (ed.) MoDELS 2005. LNCS, vol. 3844, pp. 128–138. Springer, Heidelberg (2006)
15. Kleppe, A.G., Warmer, J., Bast, W.: MDA Explained: The Model Driven Architecture: Practice and Promise. Addison-Wesley Longman Publishing Co., Inc., Boston (2003)
16. Langlois, B., elena Jitia, C., Jouenne, E.: Dsl classification. In: 7th OOPSLA Workshop on Domain-Specific Modeling (2007)
17. Moraitis, P., Spanoudakis, N.I.: Argumentation-based agent interaction in an ambient-intelligence context. IEEE Intelligent Systems 22(6), 84–93 (2007)
18. OMG: Human-Usable Textual Notation V1.0 (2004)
19. OMG: Meta Object Facility (MOF) Core Specification Version 2.0 (2006), http://www.omg.org/cgi-bin/doc?formal/2006-01-01
20. OMG: Meta Object Facility (MOF) 2.0 Query/View/Transformation Specification Version 1.0 (2008), http://www.omg.org/spec/QVT/1.0/PDF/
21. OMG: Software and Systems Process Engineering Meta-Model Specification, version 2.0 (2008)
22. Pérez, F.J., Laguna, M.A., González-Carvajal, Y.C., González-Baixauli, B.: Requirements variability support through mda^{tm} and graph transformation. Electr. Notes Theor. Comput. Sci. 152, 161–173 (2006)
23. Perini, A., Susi, A.: Automating model transformations in agent-oriented modelling. In: Müller, J.P., Zambonelli, F. (eds.) AOSE 2005. LNCS, vol. 3950, pp. 167–178. Springer, Heidelberg (2006)
24. Rose, L.M., Paige, R.F., Kolovos, D.S., Polack, F.: Constructing models with the human-usable textual notation. In: Busch, C., Ober, I., Bruel, J.-M., Uhl, A., Völter, M. (eds.) MODELS 2008. LNCS, vol. 5301, pp. 249–263. Springer, Heidelberg (2008)
25. Sendall, S., Kozaczynski, W.: Model transformation: The heart and soul of model-driven software development. IEEE Software 20(5), 42–45 (2003)
26. Spanoudakis, N.: The Agent Systems Engineering Methodology (ASEME). Ph.D. thesis, Paris Descartes University (2009)
27. Spanoudakis, N., Moraitis, P.: Engineering an agent-based system for product pricing automation. Engineering Intelligent Systems for Electrical Engineering and Communications 17(2-3), 139–151 (2009)
28. Spanoudakis, N.I., Moraitis, P.: The agent modeling language (amola). In: Dochev, D., Pistore, M., Traverso, P. (eds.) AIMSA 2008. LNCS (LNAI), vol. 5253, pp. 32–44. Springer, Heidelberg (2008)
29. Spanoudakis, N.I., Moraitis, P.: An agent modeling language implementing protocols through capabilities. In: Proceedings of the 2008 IEEE/WIC/ACM International Conference on Intelligent Agent Technology (IAT 2008), Sydney, NSW, Australia, December 9-12, pp. 578–582. IEEE, Los Alamitos (2008)
30. Spanoudakis, N.I., Moraitis, P.: Gaia agents implementation through models transformation. In: Yang, J.-J., Yokoo, M., Ito, T., Jin, Z., Scerri, P. (eds.) PRIMA 2009. LNCS, vol. 5925, pp. 127–142. Springer, Heidelberg (2009)
31. Susi, A., Perini, A., Mylopoulos, J., Giorgini, P.: The tropos metamodel and its use. Informatica (Slovenia) 29(4), 401–408 (2005)
32. Tran, Q., Low, G.: Comparison of ten agent-oriented methodologies. In: Agent-oriented methodologies [11]
33. Weyns, D.: Architecture-Based Design of Multi-Agent Systems, 1st edn. Springer Publishing Company, Heidelberg (2010) (incorporated)
34. Zambonelli, F., Jennings, N.R., Wooldridge, M.: Developing multiagent systems: The gaia methodology. ACM Trans. Softw. Eng. Methodol. 12(3), 317–370 (2003)

Towards the Automatic Derivation of Malaca Agents Using MDE*

Inmaculada Ayala, Mercedes Amor, and Lidia Fuentes

E.T.S.I. Informatica, Universidad de Malaga
{ayala,pinilla,lff}@lcc.uma.es
http://caosd.lcc.uma.es

Abstract. The automatic transformation of software agent designs into implementations for different agent platforms is currently a key issue in the MAS development process. Recently several approaches have been proposed using model driven development concepts to specify generic agent metamodels and/or define a set of transformation rules from the design phase for different agent implementation platforms. However, all these approaches propose different sets of transformation rules for each target agent platform, thereby making the integration of new agent platforms more difficult. In this paper we propose transforming PIM4Agents, a generic agent metamodel used at the design phase, into Malaca, an agent specific platform-neutral metamodel for agents. With only one set of transformations it is possible to specify platform-neutral agents and to generate a partial implementation in Malaca, which can be executed on top of different FIPA compliant platforms.

Keywords: Agent Oriented Software Engineering, Model driven engineering, Malaca, PIM4Agents, Code generation.

1 Introduction

In order to make agent-based computing a widely accepted paradigm for the emerging application areas, advanced development processes of software engineering should be adopted. This process must be supported by agent development tools that alleviate the complexity of programming with agent platforms by providing facilities to express domain concepts at a higher level of abstraction.

Model-Driven Engineering (MDE) [1] is an approach for Software Development that promotes the use of models and metamodels to formally represent domain concepts. One important contribution of MDE is that a software system is obtained through the transformation of different metamodels defined at different abstraction layers. These transformations, defined by means of a model transformation language, allow deriving a PSM (Platform-Specific Metamodel) from a PIM (Platform-Independent Metamodel). The application of MDE ideas can bring important benefits to the development of Multi-Agent Systems (MAS)

---

* This work has been supported by the Spanish Ministry Project RAP TIN2008-01942 and the regional project FamWare P09-TIC-5231.

D. Weyns and M.-P. Gleizes (Eds.): AOSE 2010, LNCS 6788, pp. 128–147, 2011.

as shown in [10,21,8,20]. With MDE it is possible to specify a MAS in a platform-independent model, focusing on the domain model, and later transform it automatically to different design or implementation models, bridging the traditional gap between design and implementation.

One recent and notable effort in this direction is [2]. This work proposes a PIM for MAS (PIM4Agents) and a set of vertical transformations from this metamodel to different agent platform models, concretely JADE [3] and JACK [4]. However, this work has some drawbacks that we will address in this paper. Although PIM4Agents can be used in theory to derive PSMs for any agent platform, in practice the DSL4MAS Development Environment (DDE) tool [5] provided by the authors only supports the transformation to JADE and JACK. This means that other platforms which have emerged recently such as Andromeda [6], or different versions of JADE (e.g. LEAP, Android) are not currently covered by this proposal. But, what is the cost of including a new agent plaform in this proposal? It requires the definition of a new set of transformation rules, from PIM4Agents into the metamodel of the new agent plaform, and from the new agent platform metamodel into code. This is a very complex task, sometimes impossible to perform properly in this and in other approaches [25] due to: (i) the metamodel of the target agent platform must be available, which is not always the case; (ii) sometimes the target metamodel is not specified completely, and some mappings to the target metamodel are made in an ad-hoc manner; (iii) this task also requires some expertise in a transformation language; and (iv) also the transformations from the target platform metamodel to code have to be implemented, requiring in depth knowledge of the target agent implementation framework.

In order to bridge the gap from design to implementation, we previously defined a set of transformations from different agent methodologies to Malaca, an agent model able to be executed in different agent plaforms [7]. Although Malaca can be used as an agent model at the detailed design phase, its model is also a PSM. Nevertheless, we had a similar problem to [2], since we had to define different transformation rules to go from different design models (e.g. Tropos) to Malaca. As a solution in [8] we proposed defining a generic agent metamodel modelling the most common elements covered by the existing agent-methodologies. In this direction, and instead of defining a new MAS metamodel, we studied the feasibility of using one of the approaches proposed recently [2,0]. Finally we decided to use PIM4Agents since this metamodel meets the following requirements: (i) it is possible to represent concepts from different agent types (e.g. BDI, reactive agents), (ii) it is easy to specify MAS for different domains; (ii) the DDE tool helps to specify different views of MAS.

Therefore, as a solution for the automatic derivation of MAS to different agent platforms, in this paper we propose transforming specifications from PIM4Agents to Malaca. With Malaca the automatic derivation of MAS is greatly simplified, since Malaca is platform neutral, so no transformation from Malaca to different agent platforms is required. This is possible since Malaca separates the distribution of messages through different transport services in a distribution aspect (implemented as a plug-in), following the aspect-oriented principles (AOSD[1]). With this approach we obtain the benefits of using a generic platform independent metamodel to specify the design of a MAS at a high level of abstraction, and by executing the set of transformation rules presented in this paper, it is possible to automatically generate a partial implementation of the agents conforming to the Malaca metamodel. These agents could be executed in several agent platforms simply by selecting the appropriate distribution aspect (e.g. JADE). So, the incorporation of new agent platforms to this proposal has a lower cost since instead of requiring the specification of metamodels and coding a new set of transformations rules, only the implementation of a new distribution aspect is needed.

The structure of this paper is as follows. Section 2 provides a brief overview of MDE, and it introduces PIM4Agents and Malaca metamodels. Section 3 describes our main contribution, by showing the transformation rules implemented in ATL to transform agents from the PIM4Agents metamodel to Malaca and we illustrate how to use them with an example. Section 4 outlines some of the problems and limitations of our approach. Finally, Section 5 provides related work and Section 6 draws some conclusions.

2   Background

In this section we introduce the concept of MDE and the two agents' metamodels used in our approach, the PIM4Agents and Malaca metamodels (MalacaMM).

2.1   Model Driven Engineering

Model-Driven Engineering (MDE) [10,1] is an approach for Software Development where models are no longer simple mediums for describing software systems or facilitating inter-team communication. Models are now first class citizens of the software development process, and even the code is managed as a model. Using MDE, a software system is obtained through the definition of different models at different abstraction layers.

The best known MDE initiative is the OMG initiative Model-Driven Architecture (MDA) [1]. MDA is an approach to MDE based on the use of models, specified as conforming to the OMG standards. A model is often presented as a combination of drawings and text (the text may be in a modelling language or in natural language). Regarding a set of models, MDA sets down how those models are prepared, and the relationships between them. In MDA, a platform is a set of subsystems and technologies that provides a set of functionality through interfaces and specified usage patterns, which any application supported by that platform can use without concern for the details of how the functionality provided by the platform is implemented. MDA distinguishes between platform-independent models (PIM) and platform-specific models (PSM). Models of a

---

[1] Aspect-Oriented Software Development, `http://aosd.net/`

certain abstraction layer are derived from models of the upper abstraction layer, by means of model transformations. A model transformation specifies how an output model is constructed based on the elements of an input model. Model transformations expressed in a well-defined model transformation language [11] can be compiled and executed, automating the process of constructing a target model given a source model. Thus, using model transformations a detailed design model can be automatically constructed from an architectural design model, for instance. A model transformation encapsulates, somehow, the knowledge of how elements of a modelling approach are transformed into elements of another modelling approach.

An MDE approach usually combines the following [12]:

- *Domain Specific Modelling Languages* (DSMLs) which are used to formalize the system in a particular domain (e.g. avionics mission computing, online financial services, etc.). DSMLs are described using metamodels, which define the relationships between concepts in a domain. Developers use DSMLs to build applications using elements of the type system captured by metamodels and express design intent declaratively rather than imperatively.
- *Transformation engines and generators* that analyse certain aspects of models and then synthesizes various types of artifacts, such as source code, simulation inputs, XML deployment descriptions, or alternative model representations. The ability to synthesize artifacts from models helps ensure the consistency between application implementations and analysis information associated with functional and QoS requirements captured by models.

One of the most popular transformation engines is ATL (ATLAS Transformation Language) [13]. This is a hybrid model transformation language that allows both declarative and imperative constructs to be used in transformation definitions. In the field of Model-Driven Engineering (MDE), ATL provides ways to produce a set of target models from a set of source models using different kinds of rules differing in the way they are triggered (standard rules, lazy rules and unique lazy rules). Developed on top of the Eclipse platform, the ATL Integrated Environment (IDE) [14] provides a number of standard development tools (syntax highlighting, debugger, etc.) that aim to ease development of ATL transformations, including also a library of ATL transformations.

2.2   PIM4Agents

Domain Specific Modelling Language for MultiAgent System (DSML4MAS) [2] is an approach that tries to fill the gap between agent methodologies and agent-based development tools by using MDE principles. This approach provides PIM4Agents, which is a PIM for MAS, and a tool (DDE) [5] that provides a graphical modeling framework to design MAS. The PIM4Agents metamodel tries to include concepts that are present in most agent architectures and it is an approach for agent modeling standardization. It has several views that are focus on a specific aspect of multiagent systems:

- Multiagent view includes main building block of a MAS (agents, interactions, ...)
- Agent view describes the agent by means of its capabilities and roles.
- Behavioural view describes how plans are composed by complex control structures and simple atomic tasks.
- Organization view defines how agents cooperate within the MAS. This view has a sub-view named Collaboration view.
- Role view covers agent roles.
- Interaction view describes the agent interaction using protocols.
- Environment view contains the set of resources that an agent or organization can use, create or share

Moreover, with the DDE Tool, it is possible to edit a different diagram for each view. Since we are interested in deriving agent designs we will focus on the Agent and the Interaction views.

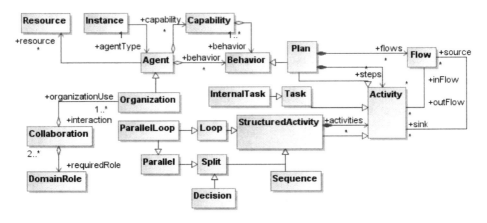

Fig. 1. PIM4Agengs metamodel reflecting the agent view in UML

Figure 1 shows the metamodel of the agent view. In PIM4Agents, an agent is an autonomous entity capable of acting in the environment and can access a set of resources (information, knowledge or ontologies). PIM4Agents agents can also perform some domain roles derived from their *Collaboration* with other agents and they can be members of an *Organization*. *Collaboration* and *Organization* are two related concepts, the former defines the social structure of *Agent* elements whilst the latter defines which agents can take part in it. On the one hand, *Collaboration* can bind *DomainRoles* to *Protocol Actor*. On the other hand, an *Organization* is a special kind of *Collaboration* that also has the same characteristics of an Agent (it can perform *DomainRole* and has *Capability*). Agents can also perform a set of *Behaviors*, which can be separated into a set of internal processes represented by *Plan* elements. A *Plan* is composed by a set of *Flow* and *Activity*. The concepts *StructuredActivity* and *Task* are specializations of an *Activity*. The *StructuredActivity* focuses on complex control structures like

Sequence, Loop, Split, etc., and *Task* focuses on atomic activities like sending or receiving a message. Also the *InternalTask* element is used to define agent internal code.

In the interaction view metamodel (figure 2) the main component is the *Protocol*, which refers to a set of *Actor* elements that interacts with it and to a set of *MessageFlows* that specifies how the exchange of messages is performed. On the one hand, an *Actor* has a set of *activeStates*, which corresponds to *MessageFlow*. The *Actor* can again refer to a set of *Actors* as sub-actors, meaning that the set of agents performing the super-actor is split into the sub-actors. In general, the sub-actors are determined at design time, but filled with the particular instances that perform this kind of Role at run-time (an example of *Actor* and *Subactor* is depicted in figure 8). On the other hand, a *MessageScope* defines the *Messages* and the order in which these arrive. In particular, this means that Messages are connected via a None, Parallel, Loop, Sequence, XOR, and OR operator. Furthermore, the MessageFlow refers to a TimeOut that specifies the latest point in time a Message should be sent. Beside the Messages that can be sent, the MessageFlow may also refer to Protocols that are initiated at some specific point in time in the parent Protocol in order to execute nested Protocols.

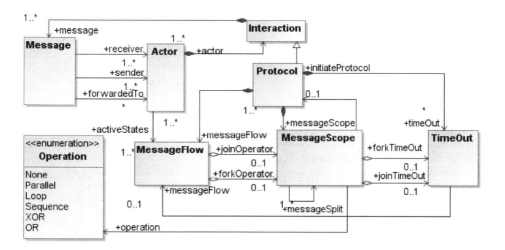

Fig. 2. Partial PIM4Agents metamodel reflecting the interaction view in UML

2.3 Malaca

Most existing agent architectures focus on the type of agent (BDI, reactive, ...), but do not provide direct support for handling and reusing properties and functionality separately. This approach results in agent design and implementations being quite complex, brittle and difficult to understand, maintain, and reuse in practice. The main feature of the internal architecture of a Malaca [7] agent is that it represents separately application-specific functions from extra-functional agent properties. This separation improves the internal modularization of the agent architecture, which is based on the composition of components and aspects, and contributes to enhance the adaptation, reuse and maintenance of the software agent. The Malaca agent model is used from the detailed design phase right through to implementation. At the detailed design stage two XML-based domain-specific languages (MaDL and ProtDL) are used to design the internal architecture of each agent of the system and its interaction [7].

MaDL metamodel which is partially given in figure 3, presents the concepts and constructs available in MaDL to describe an agent architecture. The *Agent-Description* provides a description of the agent architecture by means of the agent functionality (the actions that an agent is able to perform described by means of components) and the agent interaction (how the agent communicates with other agents). The agent functionality is provided by reusable software components, which offer the set of core services implementing the application-dependent functionality. The agent interaction is supported by *Representation*, *Distribution* and *Coordination* aspects. One extra benefit of Malaca is that it is possible to add new aspects extending the *Aspect* element of the Malaca metamodel. The *AspectWeaving* element describes the aspect composition with base components, using aspect composition rules (*AspectCompositionRule* element is composed of a ordered list of *ApplyAspect* elements).

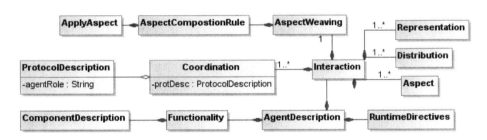

Fig. 3. Partial view of the MaDL metamodel in UML

The way the agent interacts is described at the architectural level by a set of aspects. Each aspect covers a different property of agent communication. Based on the FIPA [15] communication model, three issues are considered essential for an effective communication: the use of an interaction protocol, a common language representation format for the ACL and a MTS (Message Transport Service) to distribute messages. In Malaca, each one is supplied by different aspects (coordination, representation and distribution) decoupling these interaction issues. Specifically, the distribution aspect copes with the use of MTS, facilitating the use of different agent platforms just by plugging in the agent architecture the aspect implementing a specific platform. Any interaction protocol supported by the agent is controlled by a coordination aspect (class *Coordination*). This aspect uses a description of the interaction protocol in ProtDL to coordinate message interchange with the agent internal behaviour. The description of this aspect also indicates the role played by the agent.

The UML class diagram in figure 4 depicts the metamodel of a protocol description in ProtDL (ProtDLMM), which includes a description of the ACL messages interchanged during the interaction and a description of the internal behavior of each participant role (*RoleDescription* element). A finite state machine (FSM) is used to represent each participant role. Each FSM is represented by a set of state transition rules enclosed by the *FiniteStateMachine* class and each rule is defined in a *StateTransitionRule* class. The transition from a state to another carries out the execution of the agent functionality (defined in the *StateTransitionRule* by the attribute *executeTransition*). The *TransitionDescription* class encloses the description of the set of agent actions that are invoked during protocol execution using a Process model (figure 4). A *TransitionDescription* carries out the description a *ProcessComponent*, which can be either a single (or atomic) action, or a composite process composed of a set of processes related by a typical control construct.

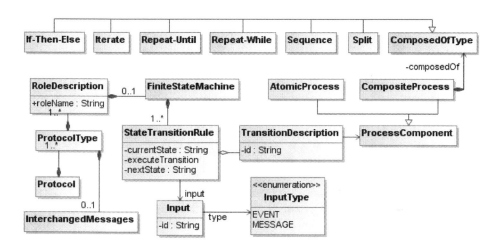

Fig. 4. Partial view of ProtDL metamodel in UML

3   From PIM4Agents to Malaca

MDE ideas and techniques enhance AOSE enabling reuse at the domain level. The DSML4MAS approach applies MDE and using PIM4Agents as a PIM provides a set of mapping functions to transform PIM4Agents model to JACK and JADE (see figure 5). However, one of the problems in this approach is found when trying to implement the MAS for an agent platform different from these. This decision requires expert knowledge to derive the appropriate mappings to the new agent platform. To solve this problem, we propose a mapping from PIM4Agents to Malaca, an agent architecture that can be executed on top of any agent platform using the appropriate plug-in. An overview of our approach can be seen in figure 5 (right side).

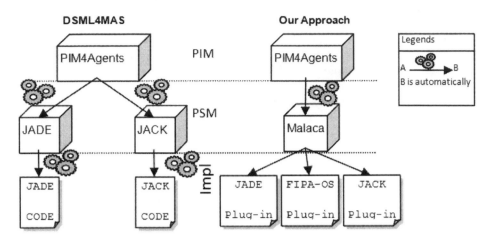

Fig. 5. The overall picture: From PIM4Agents metamodel to Jade and Jack (left side) and from PIM4Agents metamodel to Malaca metamodel (right side)

With this approach we obtain the benefits of using a general platform independent metamodel to specify the design of a MAS, and transform it (using the set of transformation rules presented in this paper) automatically into a set of Malaca agents in accordance with Malaca. The benefit of using Malaca as PSM is twofold: The incorporation of new agent platforms (i.e. PSMs) to this proposal has a lower cost since instead of requiring the specification of PSM metamodels and coding a new set of transformations rules, only the implementation of a new plug-in is needed; and the implementation of a MAS for different agent platforms does not require transforming and implementing it for each platform, instead, it just involves selecting and using the appropriate agent platform plug-in for each Malaca agent. This plug-in receives the incoming messages and delivers outgoing messages to an agent platform, hiding platform specific dependencies. The development of this plug-in consists of implementing a high-level interface *MTSAdapter* to send and receive messages.

3.1   Transformation Rules

Malaca defines a metamodel in two parts: the specification of the agent architecture (figure 3); and the specification of interaction protocols (figure 4), in MaDL and ProtDL languages respectively. The following sections summarize main mappings between PIM4Agents concepts and MaDL and ProtDL concepts. This section introduces this transformation process, which requires several ATL mapping rules.

The mapping rules included do not constitute an exhaustive list. We have only included those that help to comprehend the most relevant model mappings required for the use case scenario. Each mapping rule consists of (i) a head that defines which concepts from the source metamodel are mapped to which concepts of the target metamodel and (ii) a body that defines how attribute information of the target metamodel is derived. Some mapping rules are applied automatically (simple ATL rules), while the application of other rules depends on the previous application of other mapping rules or must be invoked by other rules (ATL lazy rules).

Rules for MaDL

MaDL Rule 1.

> Head: *PIM4Agents!Agent → MaDL!AgentDescription*
> Body: Each *Agent* from PIM4Agents is mapped to an *AgentDescription* in MaDL with the same associated interactions. By default, *Representation* is mapped to ACL and *Distribution* is mapped to JADE.

This rule maps an *PIM4Agents!Agent* to an *AgentDescription* in MaDL. *Distribution* and *Coordination* are mapped by default to JADE and ACL respectively, but *Coordination* is mapped using *PIM4Agents!Protocol* associated to the *Agent* and *AspectWeaving* is mapped using MaDL Rule 5 (MR5). To derive *Functionality* element the MR3 is used.

MaDL Rule 2.

> Head: *PIM4Agents!AgentInstance → MaDL!AgentDescription*
> Body: Each *AgentInstance* from PIM4Agents is mapped to an *AgentDescription* in MaDL with the same associated interactions and the same identifier at runtime. By default, *Representation* is mapped to ACL and *Distribution* is mapped to JADE.

This rule is very similar to MR1 and it is only applied for the deployment diagram specified with the DDE Tool. With this diagram, transformation rules can derive agents' names and how many agents are used at runtime. An *AgentDescription* element is derived for each *AgentInstance* present in the deployment diagram, with the same identifier.

MaDL Rule 3.

> Head: *PIM4Agents!DomainRole → MaDL!Coordination*
> Body: Each *DomainRole* that is associated to a *Protocol* is mapped to *Coordination* element in MaDL.

If a *DomainRole* is associated to a *Protocol* in PIM4Agents (means of a *Collaboration* element), then a *Coordination* element in MaDL is derived.

MaDL Rule 4.

> Head: *PIM4Agents!InternalTask → MaDL!ComponentDescription*
> Body: Each *InternalTask* from PIM4Agents is mapped to an *ComponentDescription* in MaDL.

This rule maps a *PIM4Agents!InternalTask* to a *ComponentDescription* in MaDL which is a set of identifiers that makes possible to identify the component at the deployment phase in order to assign it a concrete implementation.

MaDL Rule 5.

  Head: *PIM4Agents!Agent → MaDL!AspectCompositionRule*
  Body: For each *Agent* in PIM4Agent an *AspectCompositionRule* is
  derived for *RECVMSG InterceptionPoint*.

This rule derives a *AspectCompositionRule* element for the *RECVMSG Interception Point*. By default, the aspects applied when a message is received are *Representation* and *Coordination* for each *PIM4Agents!Protocol* associated to the *Agent* entity. Likewise, similar rules are defined for the *SENDMSG InterceptionPoint*.

MaDL Rule 6.

  Head: *PIM4Agents!DomainRole → MaDL!ApplyAspect*
  Body: For each *DomainRole* in PIM4Agent an *ApplyAspect* is derived for *RECVMSG InterceptionPoint*.

To specify the applied aspects in the *AspectCompositionRule* MR6-like rules are defined. This rule is for *Coordination* aspect but there are other rules for *Representation* and *Distribution*.

Rules for ProtDL

ProtDL Rule 1.

  Head: *PIM4Agents!Protocol → ProtDL!Protocol*
  Body: Each *Protocol* from PIM4Agents is mapped to a *Protocol* in
  Malaca.

This rule maps a *PIM4Agents!Protocol* to a *Protocol* in Malaca with the same ID, interchanged messages and actors.

ProtDL Rule 2.

  Head: *PIM4Agents!Actor → ProtDL!RoleDescription*
  Body: Each *Actor* is mapped to a *RoleDescription* associated to a
  specific *Protocol*.

Each *Actor* in the *PIM4Agents!Protocol* is mapped to a *RoleDescription* in *ProtDL!Protocol*. The *RoleDescription* has the same *ID* as the *Actor*. The *Actor activeStates* (figure 2) are mapped to the states of the *RoleDescription*'s *FiniteStateMachine*.

ProtDL Rule 3.

  Head: *PIM4Agents!MessageFlow, PIM4Agents!MessageFlow →
  ProtDL!StateTransitionRule*
  Body: From two *MessageFlow* this rule creates a StateTransition-
  Rule that begins in the first MessageFlow and ends in the second
  one.

This rule is linked to PR2 and it is used to derive the *StateTransitionRule* of a *FiniteStateMachine*. The occurrence of two consecutive *MessageFlows* (for a given *Protocol* and *Actor*) is mapped to a *StateTransitionRule*. The first *MessageFlow* is mapped to the current state while the second one is mapped to the next state.

ProtDL Rule 4.

    Head: *PIM4Agents!MessageFlow, PIM4Agents!MessageFlow* →
    ProtDL!TransitionDescription
    Body: From two *MessageFlow* this rule creates a *TransitionDescription* that begins in the first *MessageFlow* and ends in the second one.

This rule is linked to PR2 and it is very similar to PR3. The occurrence of two consecutive *MessageFlows* is mapped to a *TransitionDescription* which describes a message sending.

ProtDL Rule 5.

    Head: *PIM4Agents!Plan,String* → *ProtDL!RoleDescription*
    Body: Creates a *RoleDescription* from a *Plan* and a *String* that is the name for the *Role*.

This lazy rule maps a *Plan* (associated to a given *Actor* or *Agent* denoted by the *String* that is passed as an argument) to *RoleDescription*, identified with the same *String*. During its application, PR5 needs a special function (helper) to ignore *ReceiveMessage Activity* (Malaca does not consider it as a *Process* but as a *MESSAGE InputType* for a *StateTranstionRule*). Then the PR9 is applied.

ProtDL Rule 6.

    Head: *PIM4Agents!Activity, PIM4Agents!Activity* →
    ProtDL!StateTransitionRule
    Body: From two *Activity* this rule creates a *StateTransitionRule* that begins in the first *Activity* and ends in the second one.

This rule is very similar to PR4 but it considers *Activities* instead of *MessageFlows* to generate *StateTransitionRule*(s) of the *FiniteStateMachine*.

ProtDL Rule 7.

    Head: *PIM4Agents!Activity, PIM4Agents!Activity* →
    ProtDL!TransitionDescription
    Body: From two *Activity* this rule creates a *TransitionDescription* that begins in the first *Activity* and ends in the second one.

This rule maps an *Activity* (or a *StructuredActivity*) to a *TransitionDescription*. The description of the *TransitionDescription* is derived from the application of the following rules.

ProtDL Rule 8.

    Head: *PIM4Agents!InternalTask* → *ProtDL!ProcessComponent*
    Body: Each *InternalTask* is mapped to a *ProccesComponent* that have an *AtomicProcess* whose type is *DoActionType*.

The rule maps a PIM4Agents *InternalTask* of to a ProtDL *DoActionType* atomic process.

ProtDL Rule 9.

> Head: *PIM4Agents!Split* → *ProtDL!ProcessComponent*
> Body: Each *Split* is mapped to a *ProccesComponent* that have a
> *CompositeProcess* whose type is *SplitType*.

Each PIM4Agents *StructuredActivity* is mapped to a ProtDL *CompositeProcess*.
As an example, this rule maps *Split* to a *ProccesComponent* with a *Composite-
Process* that is a *Split*. PR8 is used to map the *BasicTasks* of the *StructuredAc-
tivity*.

ProtDL Rule 10.

> Head: *PIM4Agents!Protocol, PIM4Agents!Organization* →
> *ProtDL!Protocol*
> Body: Each *Protocol* which is from an *Organization* is mapped to a
> *Protocol*.

This rule maps each PIM4Agents *Protocol* within an *Organization* to a ProtDL
Protocol. The application of this rule generates a *Protocol* which includes a
RoleDescription which corresponds to a set of actions describing the behaviour
of the agent during the interaction. If there is no PIM4Agents *Plan* associated
to the protocol, then just the message interchanged is described (PR3).

3.2   Use Case Scenario

To illustrate the MDE process, the Conference Management System (CMS) case
study will be used. Conference program committee (PC) sends a call for papers,
when this is received by the authors they decide wether to submit a paper or
not. If an author submits his paper for the conference, PC assigns a submission
number to it and informs the author of this. This case study was used and
evaluated in our previous paper [16] and it was also used in the PIM4Agents
work [2]. The design of the CMS system has been derived from the DDE tool
using a tutorial [17]. The full example consists of 7 diagrams but for simplicity we
will only consider the diagrams shown in figures from 6 to 9, which corresponds
to a multiagent system, a collaboration, a protocol and a plan.

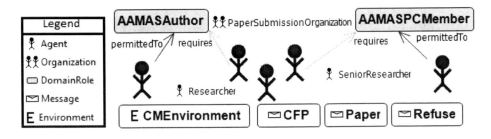

Fig. 6. PIM4Agents Multi-Agent system diagram in the DDE Tool

Figure 6 shows the MAS diagram of the CMS system in the DDE Tool. The representation of the agents, organizations and roles is straightforward in the PIM4Agents model. In order that agents are able to interact, they must be members of an *Organization*. Agents involved in paper submission process (*Researcher* and *SeniorResearcher*) are members of the*PaperSubmissionOrganization*. This *Organization* has two roles; to model authors and program committee members.

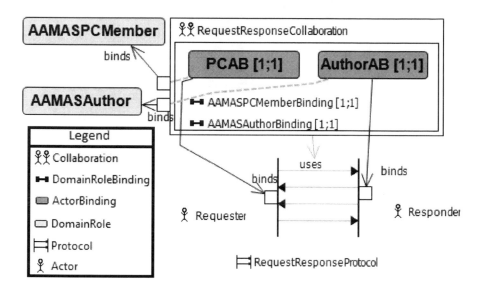

Fig. 7. PIM4Agents collaboration diagram in the DDE Tool

Figure 7 shows the collaboration diagram of the MAS in DDE Tool. This diagram links an *Organization DomainRole* (*ResponderRole* and *RequesterRole*) to *Protocol Actor* elements (*Responder* and *Requester*) by means of *ActorBinding* elements (*ResponderAB* and *RequesterAB*).

Figure 8 shows the protocol diagram of the *PaperSubmission* protocol, which covers the interaction between the *Requester* and *Responder* actors in the submission phase. *Requester* sends a *Request* that can be answered by *Responder* with a *Propose* or a *Refuse* message.

Figure 9 depicts the plan HandleCFP, which is executed by the *Responder* when it receives a *Request*, and it decides whether to submit a paper or to send a refuse message and relax. At run-time, the *Requester* is performed by *Researcher*, while the *SeniorResearcher* act as *Responder*.

Figure 10 presents a partial result of the application of rules MR1, MR3,MR4, MR5 and MR6 to the *Researcher* agent, because a deployment diagram is not made, MR2 is not applied. MR1 take the information from MAS diagram (figure 6) and generates the basic structure of the *Researcher AgentDescription*. This rule calls to lazy rule MR5 to get *AspectCompositionRule* for *RECVMSG InterceptionPoint* and this last rule calls to MR6-like rules to derive *ApplyAspect* elements. After the application of the MR1, MR3 and MR4 are applied: MR3

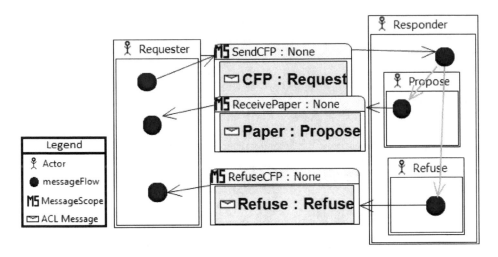

Fig. 8. PIM4Agents protocol diagram of the paper submission protocol in the DDE Tool

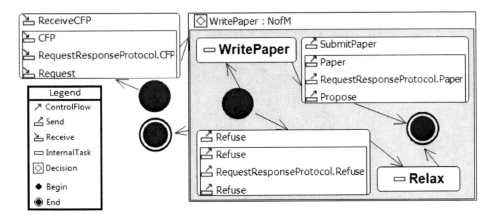

Fig. 9. PIM4Agents plan diagram for the HandleCFP plan in the DDE Tool

takes *AAMASAuthor DomainRole* from MAS diagram and it generates a *Coordination* element from *PaperSubmission Protocol* (*Protocol* and *DomainRole* are linked means of related organization diagram); MR4 is applied to *HandleCFP* (figure 9) *InternalTask* elements to get *ComponentDescription* elements.

Figure 11 presents a partial result of the application of rules PR10, PR5, PR6 and PR7 (in this order) to the *Responder* actor in the *PaperSubmission* protocol. After the application of the rule PR10 to the protocol diagram of figure 8 and the collaboration diagram in figure 7, the rule PR5 is applied to the *HandleCFP* plan (figure 9) and generates a ProtDL *RoleDescription* for the role *Responder*. Rules PR6 and PR7 are also applied to the *HandleCFP* plan to derive the states and *StateTransitionRules* of the *FiniteStateMachine* of the *Responder*.

- ⬦ Agent Description Type
  - ⬦ Functionality Type
    - ⬦ <componentDescription> Component Description Type WritePaperOntology
    - ⬦ <componentDescription> Component Description Type RelaxOntology
  - ⬦ Interaction Type
    - ⬦ Aspect Description malaca.model_impl.Distribution
    - ⬦ Coordination Type RequestResponse
    - ⬦ Aspect Description malaca.model.CoordinationAspect
    - ⬦ Aspect Weaving Type
      - ⬦ <aspectCompositionRule> Aspect Composition Rule Type SEND_MSG
        - ⬦ Apply Aspect Type
        - ⬦ Apply Aspect Type
      - ⬦ <aspectCompositionRule> Aspect Composition Rule Type RECV_MSG
        - ⬦ Apply Aspect Type
        - ⬦ Apply Aspect Type

Fig. 10. Partial MaDL *AgentDescription* of the *Researcher* agent in XMI format from EMF editor

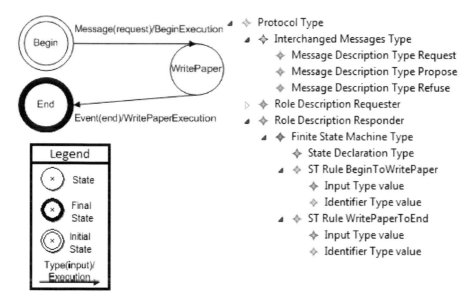

Fig. 11. Partial ProtDL *RoleDescription* of the *Responder* role in *PaperSubmission* protocol in XMI format (right side) from EMF and equivalent state transition diagram (left side)

4   Discussion

This section shows some comparative results between the code generated with the DDE tool and the configuration files generated by our approach, for the CMS case study. Although we have defined a systematic mapping from PIM4Agents to Malaca, it is not possible to generate a complete ProtDL and MaDL specifications since: (i) DDE neither supports the specification of important message details (at least a rough description), nor significant protocol design features; and (ii) PIM4Agents metamodel does not support the event-driven composition mechanism, which Malaca uses to model agent reactions to external events. In addition, some concepts related to the MAS social organization cannot be mapped to Malaca (such as the *Organization* concept), because Malaca is focused on the specification and configuration of the agents internal architecture. We are studying the possibility of extending the Malaca metamodel with social organization concepts, in order to express and validate that a set of agents belongs to the same organization. For example, in PIM4Agents organization concepts define which agents can collaborate, what protocols they can use and it defines resources and capabilities for each member. This is very useful to define large MAS because agents belonging to the same organization usually share large amount of resources and have common capabilities. On the other hand, the FAML metamodel[18] has other interesting concepts, for example rules for agents membership of an organization (policy) or system goals, these are useful for modeling the collaboration for BDI (Belief-Desire-Intention) agents, that have more complex social interactions.

Hence, some abstractions of PIM4Agents could not be mapped in Malaca; and some concepts present in Malaca could not be generated from the PIM4Agents metamodel. Then, the generated MaDL and ProtDL descriptions have to be completed by the developer (using the Malaca editor [7]) before executing the agents.This also happens in the implementations generated by the DDE tool (applying transformations to JADE and JACK as target implementation agent platforms). For the case study, which comprises the design of one protocol and two plans, the DDE tool generates 80 Java classes (for the JADE implementation). The generated classes provide the agent structure and interaction, and the developer has to add the application specific functionality. Comparing both approaches, we consider that completing the Java classes generated with the DDE tool is more error prone than using the Malaca Agent Development (MAD) tool to complete the configuration of the Malaca agents. Whereas in the DDE approach the developer has to deal with 80 classes, in the Malaca approach they only has to complete a single configuration file with the MaDL/ProtDL specification, with the aid of the MAD tool.

However, the code generated with DDE is not optimized. For example, in JADE several template classes encapsulating FIPA protocols are provided, but the DDE generator does not consider these templates in the code generation. Malaca offers similar template files for FIPA protocols, and the configuration files generated are optimized using these templates. As a result, it is possible to reuse protocol specifications in several case studies, avoiding the generation of code for the same protocol once again. It is also possible to reuse some protocol information, such as the ontology used, or the message content, for similar case studies, but in DDE this is not possible. Hence, completing protocol implementation classes, scattered across several classes, requires greater effort in the DDE approach.

5   Related Work

The code generation is not a new issue and it has been approached by agent methodologies, using MDE or not, to bridge the gap between design and implementation. One of the first AOSE approaches that includes code generation was MaSE [19] that supports a complete tool-aided life cycle process from early requirements to code generation. Moreover, in some of them, such as Tropos [20] and INGENIAS [21], the life-cycle is an MDE process, but this is done only for some of the software development phases. Otherwise, ASEME [22] uses the principles of MDE throughout all the software development phases (from requirements to implementation). MDE is also looked at in [6], which applies MDE for mobile agents. It takes Agent-π, a metamodel for mobile devices, as PIM and provides transformations to two mobile-specific PSMs, Andromeda and JADE-Leap. Although the intention of these approaches was to cover the implementation phase, they have the same disadvantages as those mentioned for the PIM4Agents approach: (i) a different transformation is needed for every PSM; and (ii) the implementation of agents in JADE and other OO agent architectures is difficult to maintain and reuse. The problem is that normally the agent internal architecture consists of a collection of highly-coupled objects, making it difficult to extend. Since different agent concerns such as the agent domain-specific functionality are not very well modularized, every time the agent needs to be upgraded, the developer must inspect the implementation code, then change and re-compile it. An additional disadvantage of these approaches is that they use their own agent metamodel (and not a generic one) in the design phase.

In addition to this, there are agent methodologies that use metamodels to bring support to their processes but not for code generation. Aalaadin [23] specifies one of the first developed metamodels for MAS and it is focused on social aspects. Another methodology that focus on social aspects and defines a metamodel is Gaia [24], which also defines a specific mapping to JADE as PSM [25], but it is not an automatic process. ADELFE [26] and PASSI [27] are other methodologies that have metamodels.

Metamodels are also used to achieve a standard representation for MAS. The first attempt in this trend was the Unified MAS Metamodel proposal [28], which merged the metamodels of ADELFE, Gaia and PASSI. Recently, using the same method, FAML [18] metamodel was developed. Another approach is the Generic Metamodel, which proposes a basic metamodel that allows the generation of systems in different agent platforms.

6   Conclusion

This paper presents an MDE approach to developing MAS using the PIM4Agents metamodel as PIM and Malaca as PSM, focusing on the external and internal coordination of agents. Following an MDE approach we have defined mapping rules to generate a set of MaDL/ProtDL files. From these, implementation details are added and can be used to deploy and execute Malaca agents.

Our main contribution is the usage of platform neutral agent metamodels in MDE process. In other approaches to extend a proposal, i.e. to add a new target platform to the process, the following has to be done: (i) developing two new sets of model transformations (M2M and M2T) and (ii) finding or developing a new metamodel for the target platform, according to the case. In contrast, using platform neutral agent metamodels as Malaca, we only have to develop an appropriate distribution aspect to add a new target platform to the proposal. Moreover, if we compare our process with the PIM4Agent process, we conclude that in our approach the generated implementation is more optimized and easier to modify and extend. In addition, with MAD Tool it is possible to reuse protocols specifications and other information, but this cannot be done with DDE Tool.

PIM4Agents seems a very attractive and powerful metamodel. However, our approach also has many unresolved issues, since some PIM4Agents concepts cannot be mapped to Malaca, and vice versa. Therefore it is not possible to represent some PIM4Agent concepts, such as organizations, which are lost in the generation process. Likewise, some Malaca concepts, such as event driven processes, cannot been properly represented using the PIM4Agents design model. In order to deal with these limitations, we are working on both sides extending PIM4Agents and Malaca metamodels. Moreover, we are currently integrating the mapping rules presented in this paper in MAD tool to enhance the automated development.

References

1. Kleppe, A., Warmer, J., Bast, W.: MDA Explained: The Model Driven Architecture-Practice and Promise. Addison-Wesley Professional, Reading (2003)
2. Hahn, C., Madrigal-Mora, C., Fischer, K.: A platform-independent metamodel for multiagent systems. Auton. Agent Multi-Agent Syst. 18, 239–266 (2009)
3. Bellifemine, F., Rimassa, G., Poggi, A.: JADE - A FIPA-compliant Agent Framework. In: Proc. of PAAM 1999 (1999)
4. Busetta, P., et al.: JACK Intelligent Agents - Components for IntelligentAgents in Java. Tech. Rep. Agent Oriented Software (1998)
5. Warwas, S., Hahn, C.: The DSML4MAS Development Environment. In: Proc. AAMAS 2009, pp. 1379–1380 (2009)
6. Agüero, J., Rebollo, M., Carrascosa, C., Julin, V.: Agent Design Using Model Driven Development. In: PAAMS 2009. AISC, vol. 55, pp. 60–69 (2009)
7. Amor, M., Fuentes, L.: Malaca: A component and aspect-oriented agent architecture. Information and Software Technology 51, 1052–1065 (2009)
8. Amor, M., Fuentes, L., Vallecillo, A.: Bridging the gap Between Agent-Oriented Design and Implementation Using MDA. In: Odell, J.J., Giorgini, P., Müller, J.P. (eds.) AOSE 2004. LNCS, vol. 3382, pp. 93–108. Springer, Heidelberg (2005)
9. Beydoun, G., et al.: Synthesis of a generic mas metamodel. In: Garcia, A., Choren, R., Lucena, C., Giorgini, P., Holvoet, T., Romanovsky, A. (eds.) SELMAS 2005. LNCS, vol. 3914, pp. 1–5. Springer, Heidelberg (2006)
10. Zambonelli, F., Omicini, A.: Challenges and Research Directions in Agent-Oriented Software Engineering. Auton. Agent Multi-Agent Syst. 9, 253–283 (2004)

11. Czarnecki, K., Helsen, S.: Feature-based Survey of Model Transformation Approaches. IBM Systems Journal 45(3), 621–646 (2006)
12. Schmidt, D.C.: Guest Editor's Introduction: Model-Driven Engineering. Computer 39(2), 25 (2006), http://dx.doi.org/10.1109/MC.2006.58
13. Jouault, F., Kurtev, I.: Transforming models with ATL. In: Bruel, J.-M. (ed.) MoDELS 2005. LNCS, vol. 3844, pp. 128–138. Springer, Heidelberg (2006)
14. ATL, http://www.eclipse.org/m2m/atl/
15. FIPA, http://www.fipa.org/
16. Amor, M., Fuentes, L., Valenzuela, J.: Separating learning as an aspect in Malaca agents. In: Nguyen, N.T., Jo, G.-S., Howlett, R.J., Jain, L.C. (eds.) KES-AMSTA 2008. LNCS (LNAI), vol. 4953, pp. 505–515. Springer, Heidelberg (2008)
17. DDE tool, http://sourceforge.net/apps/trac/dsml4mas/wiki
18. Beydoun, G., et al.: FAML: A Generic Metamodel for MAS Development. IEEE Transactions on Software Engineering 99, 841–863 (2009)
19. DeLoach, S.A., Wood, M.: Developing Multiagent Systems with agentTool. In: Castelfranchi, C., Lespérance, Y. (eds.) ATAL 2000. LNCS (LNAI), vol. 1986, p. 46. Springer, Heidelberg (2001)
20. Susi, A., Perini, A., Mylopoulos, J.: The Tropos Metamodel and its Use. Informatica 29, 401–408 (2005)
21. Pavón, J., Gómez-Sanz, J., Fuentes, R.: Model driven development of multi-agent systems. In: Rensink, A., Warmer, J. (eds.) ECMDA-FA 2006. LNCS, vol. 4066, pp. 284–298. Springer, Heidelberg (2006)
22. Spanoudakis, N., Moraitis, P.: Using ASEME Methodology for Model-driven Agent Systems Development. In: Weyns, D., Gleifes, M.-P. (eds.) AOSE 2010. LNCS, vol. 6788, pp. 106–127. Springer, Heidelberg (2011)
23. Ferber, J., Gutknecht, O.: A meta-model for the analysis and design of organizations in multiagent systems. In: Proceedings of the Third International Conference on Multi–Agent Systems (ICMAS 1998), pp. 128–135 (1998)
24. Zambonelli, F., Jennings, N., Wooldridge, M.: Developing multiagent systems: The Gaia methodology. ACM Transactions on Software Engineering and Methodology 12(3), 417–470 (1998)
25. Moraitis, P., Spanoudakis, N.I.: The Gaia2Jade process for multi-agent systems development. Applied Artificial Intelligence 20(2-4), 251–273 (2006)
26. Picard, G., Gleizes, M.P.: The ADELFE methodology. In: Methodologies and Software Engineering for Agent Systems, The Agent–Oriented Software Engineering Handbook. Kluwer Academic Publishers, Dordrecht (2004)
27. Cossentino, M.: From requirements to code with the PASSI methodology. In: Henderson-Sellers, B., Giorgini, P. (eds.) Agent–Oriented Methodologies Idea Group Inc., Hershey (2005)
28. Bernon, C., Cossentino, M., Gleizes, M.-P., Turci, P., Zambonelli, F.: A study of some multi–agent meta–models. In: Odell, J.J., Giorgini, P., Müller, J.P. (eds.) AOSE 2004. LNCS, vol. 3382, pp. 62–77. Springer, Heidelberg (2005)

$\mathcal{F}_{or}\mathcal{MAAD}$: Towards a Model Driven Approach for Agent Based Application Design

Zeineb Graja, Amira Regayeg, and Ahmed Hadj Kacem

ReDCAD Laboratory
Faculty of Economics and Management
University of Sfax, Tunisia
zeineb.graja@acm.org,
{amira.regayeg,ahmed.hadjkacem}@fsegs.rnu.tn

Abstract. Current trends in multi-agent systems development show a move towards adopting the Model Driven Architecture (MDA) approach to improve the development process and the quality of the agent-based software. Our work has two main contributions. First, it presents a reformulation of the $\mathcal{F}_{or}\mathcal{MAAD}$ methodology in terms of the MDA paradigm by using the AML language. Second, it proposes a translation of each model to a formal language, $\mathcal{T}_{emporal}\mathcal{Z}$ that integrates linear temporal logic to the $\mathcal{Z}$ notation, in order to guarantee a formal verification of the models. Furthermore, we make extensions to the $StarUML$ tool to support the proposed models and use the transition rules. Our work is illustrated by developing an agent-based solution for the air traffic control problem.

Keywords: MDA, AML language, formal methods, refinement, verification.

1 Introduction

Current trends in Multi-Agent Systems (MAS) development show a move towards adopting the MDA approach to improve the development process and the quality of the agent-based software ([4], [5], [6], [7]). The basic motivation of MDA is that it allows improvement of an application development process. In fact, MDA suggests to use model transformation techniques to generate automatically PSM (Platform Specific Model) from PIM (Platform Independent Model). But most of the MDA methodologies are based on semi-formal notations and, hence, they don't enable formal reasoning about developed specifications. On the other hand, formal methods have gained a large acceptance in the MAS development thanks to their great power to express rigorously the concepts related to agents and multi-agent systems ([1], [2], [12]). The main advantage of formal methods is that they offer the possibility of carrying out reasoning for verification and validation purposes.

The aim of our work is the integration of formal techniques and MDA principals in one methodology for the development of MAS in order to take advantage of both of them. Thus, we propose a reformulation of $\mathcal{F}_{or}\mathcal{MAAD}$ methodology, based on a formal framework and dedicated for the design of multi-agent systems

D. Weyns and M.-P. Gleizes (Eds.): AOSE 2010, LNCS 6788, pp. 148–164, 2011.

application. The goal is to enrich $\mathcal{F}_{or}\mathcal{MAAD}$ with a *foreground design* based on a semi-formal language and allowing the use of the MDA transformation techniques to automatically generate an executable code. For this purpose, we have adopt the Agent Modeling Language (AML) ([8], [9]) as the formalism for the models representing steps of the $\mathcal{F}_{or}\mathcal{MAAD}$ methodology.

In order to guarantee a formal verification of the design models, we propose to translate the AML models of the *foreground design* to a *background design* which uses a formal language $\mathcal{T}_{emporal}\mathcal{Z}$ [10] that integrates linear temporal logic into the Z notation. The *background design*, enables us to use formal verification tools supporting raw Z notation, such as $Z/EVES$ [11], for verification purposes. Such tools allow us to perform syntax, type and domain checking of our specification and to reason about correctness by proving several properties. This *background design* is described in [12] and [13] allowing a formal verified specification of an agent based application.

This paper is structured as follows. Section 2 is dedicated to the description of related work. Section 3 presents a fragment of the AML meta-model. Section 4 describes the models proposed to cover the different phases of the $\mathcal{F}_{or}\mathcal{MAAD}$ approach. The translation rules are presented in section 5. Tools developed to support the use of the *foreground design* are described in section 6. Section 7 concludes the paper and outlines perspectives to our work.

2 Related Work

Related work describe two aspects for the development of Multi-Agent Systems (MAS). The first one is related to the application of the Model Driven Architecture (MDA) approach in some MAS design methodologies. The second one is about use of formal frameworks in MAS design.

2.1 MAS Design and MDA

In [7], the *ADELFE* methodology is extended by adding a model driven implementation phase using model transformation, domain specific modeling language (which are $AMAS - ML$ used at design time and μADL allowing the description of the agent micro-architecture) and code generation. This phase is composed of several transformation steps. The first one allows the micro-architecture extraction in a μADL model from the $AMAS - ML$ model. The second step consists in generating code skeletons for micro-components that will be filled up by the java developer by adding the necessary micro-components services. The last transformation permits the behavioral code skeleton generation from the behavioral rules expressed in the design phase with $AMAS - ML$.

The *Tropos* methodology is also based on the use of MDA principals throughout its process. In [6], transformations of plan decomposition into a *UML* activity diagram are defined according to the *Tropos* modeling language meta-model and the *UML* meta-model. *Tropos* allows code generation for the *JADE* platform using transformation techniques compliant with MDA's Query/View/Transformations requirements.

INGENIAS [4] is both a methodology and a set of tools for the development of MAS. Based on the results coming from *MESSAGE*, *INGENIAS* provides more complete and consistent meta-models and allows automatic code generation for different implementation languages and agent platforms.

These works show that the *MDA* approach contributes greatly to facilitate the MAS development and specially the code generation. But most of the methodologies using the MDA approach are based on semi-formal notations and, hence, they don't enable formal reasoning about developed specifications. At another hand, formal techniques contribute greatly to verification of MAS design. In the next subsection, we overview some formal frameworks for MAS development.

2.2 MAS Design and Formal Techniques

A very eminent work in the formalization of agent and multi-agent systems is that of Luck and d'Invero [1]. They provide formal definitions of a four-tiered hierarchy of entities which compose an agent-based system. They mainly consider static properties of agents and entirely ignore behavioral properties. These latter are dealt with in *DESIRE* using temporal logic. *DESIRE* [3] is a specification and design framework which supports agents based on recursive composition of interconnected tasks. The interaction and coordination among agents is specified as an interchange of information and control dependencies.

The $\mathcal{F}_{or}\mathcal{MAAD}$ methodology ([12], [13], [14]) is based on two principals. The first one indicates the use of a formal specification language covering individual (static and behavioral) aspects of agents (e.g., knowledge, goal and role) as well as collective aspects of a multi-agent application (e.g. collective behaviors and organization structure). This language integrates linear temporal logic into the Z notation and is called $\mathcal{T}_{emporal}\mathcal{Z}$. The second principal emphasis a formal methodology based on stepwise refinements to generate, step by step, individual agent behaviors starting from an abstract specification of a common goal. $\mathcal{F}_{or}\mathcal{MAAD}$ proposes also guidelines that help the designer to define a cooperation strategy for achieving the given common goal, to set an appropriate organization structure, then to identify the needed communication actions and finally to derive the intended agent behaviors. In order to guarantee the correctness of the designed specification, $\mathcal{F}_{or}\mathcal{MAAD}$ proposes, for each refinement step, an appropriate proof obligation ensuring that the refined specification preserves the properties of the application to develop.

Recently, a work on context driven dynamic agent organization is advanced in [2]. In this work, a formal specification in Z is given for an organization model for context driven dynamic agent organizations called *MACODO*. This specification consists of two main parts. The first part models state in a *MACODO* system by various sets and schemas. The second part models the behavior of a *MACODO* system by means of functions and operation schemas.

Whereas most of the cited works focus on a special aspect of MAS (*MACODO* on organizations, *DESIRE* on behavioral properties, Luck and d'Invero on static properties), the $\mathcal{F}_{or}\mathcal{MAAD}$ methodology consider both static and behavioral aspects as well as individual and organizational ones. But this methodology suffers from the lack of an implementation phase for code generation. The idea is to couple $\mathcal{F}_{or}\mathcal{MAAD}$ with the *MDA* approach.

Based on the $\mathcal{F}_{or}\mathcal{MAAD}$ methodology, our work aims to take advantage of the formal aspects (coming from $\mathcal{F}_{or}\mathcal{MAAD}$) and the *MDA* aspect for the development of MAS by combining them together.Thus, we propose a methodology with two levels. The first one is called *foreground design* and is dedicated for designers familiar with semi-formal languages. It allows MAS design through models expressed with the Agent Modeling Language (AML) based on the AML meta-model described in the next section. The second level is called *background design* and is intended for formal verification purposes. The term *background design* come from the fact that this level will be hidden to the designer and will run in background. We define also transformation rules to allow passage between these two levels. The *background design* being described in a previous work ([12]), this paper focuses on describing the *foreground design* and bridges between them.

3   AML Meta-model

The Agent Modeling Language (AML) ([8], [9]) is a semi-formal visual modeling language for specifying, modeling and documenting systems that incorporate features drawn from multi-agent systems theory. It is specified as an extension to UML 2.0 in accordance with major OMG modeling frameworks (MDA, MOF, UML, and OCL). The current version of AML offers support for the abstraction of architectural and behavioral concepts associated with multi-agent systems, i.e. ontologies, MAS entities, social aspects, behavior abstraction and decomposition, communicative interactions, services, observations and effecting interactions, mental aspects used for modeling mental attitudes of entities, MAS deployment and agent mobility [8].

The AML meta-model is structured as packages according to the various aspects of MAS abstractions: mental package, architecture package, behaviors package, etc. In the reminder of this section, we will present, as an example, a fragment of the architecture package and the mental one.

The architecture package defines the meta-classes used to model architectural aspects of MAS, such as entities (agents, environment, resources), social aspect, ontologies, etc. Fig. 1 is a fragment of the AML meta-model extracted from the architecture package. The meta-class *EntityType* is an abstract specialized Type. It is a superclass to all AML modeling elements which represent types of entities of a multi-agent system. The meta-class *AgentType* is a specialized *AutonomousEntityType* modeling a type of agents which means entities capable of autonomous behavior and have a mental state. *EnvironmentType* meta-class is a specialized *AutonomousEntityType* used to model types of environments, i.e. logical or physical surroundings of entities which provide conditions under which the entities exist and function. The meta-class *OrganizationUnitType* is a specialized *EnvironmentType* used to model types of organization units, i.e. types of social environments or their parts. An organization unit can contain coherent autonomous entity playing roles, having sets of goals and interaction with each other.

The mental package defines the meta-classes used to model mental aspects of MAS, i.e. mental attitudes of autonomous entities, which represent their believes and goals. It defines also meta-classes which can be used to model problem decomposition and complex problems, in particular representing intentionality in use case models and goal-based requirements modeling. Fig. 2 is a fragment of the mental package. We can distinguish two types of goals with the *AML* meta-model; when the goal holder can decide if his goal is achieved successfully, it's a *Decidable Goal*, otherwise it's an *Undecidable Goal*. A *Contribution* is a mental relationship that can model goal's decomposition.

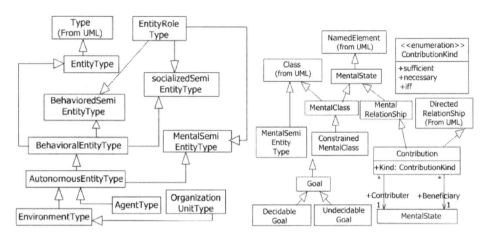

Fig. 1. An excerpt of the architecture package [8]

Fig. 2. An excerpt of the mental package [8]

4 $\mathcal{F}_{or}\mathcal{MAAD}$: Towards a Model Oriented Approach for MAS Design

The $\mathcal{F}_{or}\mathcal{MAAD}$ approach is based on two main phases. The first one is a specification phase in which the user requirements are described. The second one is a design phase in which a detailed specification is derived based on a succession of refinements of collective (inter-agents) and individual (intra-agent) behaviors. In this section, we will review the $\mathcal{F}_{or}\mathcal{MAAD}$ steps and associate to them the corresponding models.

4.1   Specification Phase

In this phase, we specify the requirements which correspond, for a society of agents, to a common objective that must be achieved by these agents and the environment in which the agents evolve. This phase is captured by the requirement specification model in which, each entity is modeled by a class, a society of agent is modeled by an organization unit type, the environment is modeled by an environment unit type and an objective is modeled by a decidable goal. The common objective of an agent organization is expressed through a constraint associated to this organization. Here we deal only with functional requirements. Dealing with quality requirements such as robustness, availability or performance is not yet supported by our methodology.

As an example, the requirement specification diagram in the air traffic control application is illustrated by the Fig. 3. The class *System* models the agents's environment which is composed of an organization of planes (called *Planes*). This organization contains at least two planes and must achieve the goal *SolveConflict*. The note attached to the class *Planes* is a constraint that corresponds to the objective of the organization *Planes* which consists in solving each potential conflict situation between two planes.

4.2   Design Phase

The $\mathcal{F}_{or}\mathcal{MAAD}$ design process follows seven refinement steps. The first step defines a cooperation strategy for achieving the common objective. It consists in decomposing the common objective into a set of sub-goals, called local goals. The definition of an organization structure is performed into two steps. First, we identify the roles by grouping local goals; then, we relate them with suitable relationships. Simultaneously, we assign roles to agents. The relationships between roles are translated at the agent level into organization links. Based on these links, we identify the needed collective behavior. Finally, we have to define an appropriate individual behavior for each agent. These steps will be given in details in the following sections.

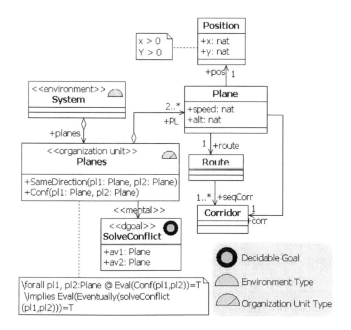

Fig. 3. A requirement specification model example

Cooperation Strategy Definition. This step consists in a decomposition of the common objective into local goals. In the *foreground design*, the cooperation strategy is defined onto two levels: the first one allows the description of the objective types and the decomposition relations between them using a class diagram; the second allows the instantiation of the objective classes using an object diagram. In the context of the air traffic application, the Fig. 4 shows that the objective *solveConflict* is decomposed into two goals; *detectConflict* which corresponds to the detection of a conflict between two planes and *resConflict* which corresponds to the detected conflict resolution. This decomposition is modeled by a contribution relationship from the AML language.

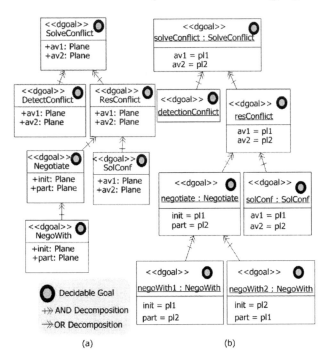

(a)   (b)

Fig. 4. A cooperation strategy definition model example: class level (a) and instance level (b)

Organization Structure Definition. The organization structure is depicted by the organization structure definition model composed of three diagrams: the role identification diagram, the organization structure diagram and the precedence order graph.

– Role identification diagram: this diagram describes the main roles needed to achieve the local goals. It is derived automatically from the cooperation strategy definition model by grouping local goals, instantiated from the same class, together. For example, the *negoWith1* and *negoWith2* goals (Fig. 4) are instances from the same goal class *NegoWith*. Thus, they are grouped to form the role *Negotiator* (Fig. 5).

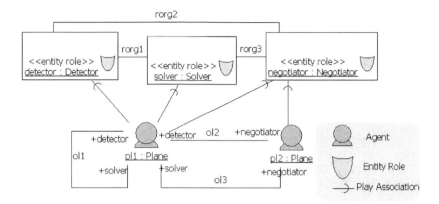

Fig. 5. An organization structure diagram example

- Organization structure diagram: this diagram is created by instantiating the roles identified in the previous diagram and creating the organization relations between them. In practice, we will identify common attribute values of the local goals of different roles. A common attribute between two roles indicates an organizational relation between them. As an example, the *solConf* local goal and the *negoWith1* local goal have two common attribute values *pl*1 and *pl*2. Thus, an organization relationship between the *solver* role and the *negotiator* role will be created (Fig. 5). Given the set of roles and the set of relations between them, we will identify necessary agents and assign the retained roles to them. Given the set of agents and their corresponding roles, we can generate automatically the organization links between agents. In fact, each organizational relation between two roles leads to an organizational link between the agents having these roles. Fig. 5 shows an example of a complete organization structure diagram. It depicts three roles: *detector*, *negotiator* and *solver* with respective types *Detector*, *Negotiator* and *Solver*, two agents: *pl*1 and *pl*2, three organizational relations: *rorg*1, *rorg*2 and *rorg*3 and three organizational links: *ol*1, *ol*2 and *ol*3.
- Precedence order graph: this activity diagram models the precedence order between local goals and serves to facilitate the identification of the necessary agents.

4.3   Collective Behavior Definition

The collective behavior of the agents is defined according to their organizational links. In fact, an organizational link established between two agents leads to a sequence diagram describing the messages exchanged between them. In the air traffic control application, the collective behavior definition model (Fig. 6) describes the negotiation protocol between two planes. The two notes attached to the lifelines in Fig. 6 are temporal constraints written in Latex format.

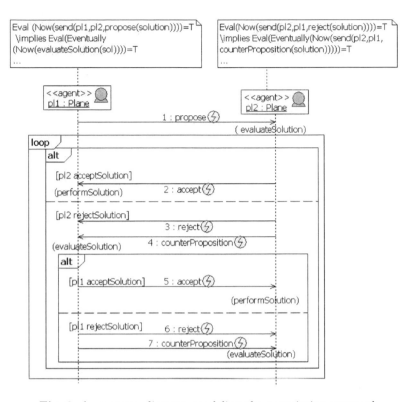

Fig. 6. A sequence diagram modeling the negotiation protocol

As an example, the constraint attached to the *Pl*1 lifeline states that when the plane *Pl*1 sends a solution proposition to the plane *Pl*2, *Pl*2 will eventually evaluate the proposed solution.

4.4 Individual Behavior Definition

The individual behavior definition model describes, with an activity diagram, the behavior of each type of agent. The agent actions and the sent messages are described with more details by a class diagram. Fig. 7 details some agent actions as behavior fragments. The agent type *Plane* has three behavior fragments which are *Perform*, *Perceive* and *Evaluate*. The behavior fragment *Perform*, as an example, contains one action which is *performSolution*.

5   Translation to $\mathcal{T}_{emporal}\mathcal{Z}$

In order to verify some properties in our models, we propose to use formal verification techniques. The formal verification is applied after each step of the design methodology and is composed of two parts. The first part allows one to translate automatically the models to the $\mathcal{T}_{emporal}\mathcal{Z}$ formal language. The

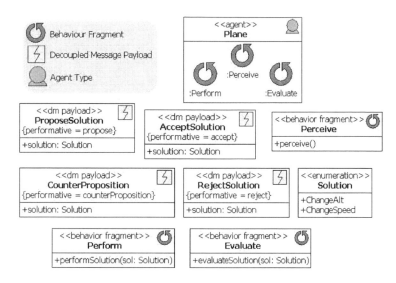

Fig. 7. An individual behavior definition model example

second one consists in verifying some theorems. The $\mathcal{T}_{emporal}\mathcal{Z}$ formal language was presented in [10] and is the result of the integration of the temporal operators into Z schemas. Thanks to this integration, we can express both structural as well as behavioral aspect of a MAS.

5.1 Translation of the Requirement Specification Model

This translation is done by mapping each class C into a Z schema called C whose declarative part contains the attributes of the class C and the predicative part contains the constraints related to that class.

In the case of the air traffic control, the *Position* class will lead to the *Position* schema, the *Plane* class will lead to the *Plane* schema describing a plane and the *Planes* class will lead to the *Planes* schema representing an organization of planes.

Position
$x : \mathbb{N}$
$y : \mathbb{N}$
$x > 0$
$y > 0$

Plane
speed : $\mathbb{N}$
alt : $\mathbb{N}$
route : *Route*
pos : *Position*
corr : *Corridor*

Planes
$PL : \mathbb{F}$ *Plane*

5.2 Translation of the Cooperation Strategy Definition Model

As depicted in Fig. 8, the translation of the cooperation strategy definition model to $\mathcal{T}_{emporal}\mathcal{Z}$ completes the specification of type *Formula* [12] with the atomic formulas (local goals) and leads to the *Implementation0* schema.

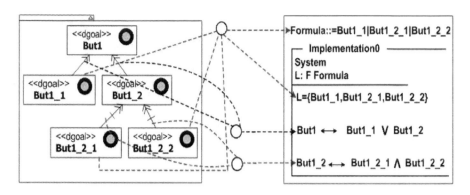

Fig. 8. Translation of the cooperation strategy definition model

Implementation0 schema includes *System* schema and contains declaration of variable L having the type $\mathbb{F}$ *Formula* (L is the set of the local goals) and the goals decomposition.

In addition, we generate the *CoopStrategy* theorem which guarantees that the common objective can be derived from the local goals (these concepts are described in [12]).

The translation of the cooperation strategy definition model of Fig. 4 leads to the following *Formula* type and *Implementation0* schema:

Formula ::=
... | *detectConflict*⟨⟨*Plane* × *Plane*⟩⟩
| *solConf*⟨⟨*Plane* × *Plane*⟩⟩
| *negoWith1*⟨⟨*Plane* × *Plane*⟩⟩
| *negoWith2*⟨⟨*Plane* × *Plane*⟩⟩

$$
\begin{array}{|l}
\underline{\quad Implementation0 \quad\quad\quad\quad\quad\quad\quad\quad}\\
System \\
L : \mathbb{F}\ Formula \\
\hline
L = \{\,detectConflict(av1, av2),\\
\quad negoWith1(init, part), ...\} \\
Eval(solveConflict(av1, av2)) = T \\
\Leftrightarrow Eval(detectConflict(av1, av2)) = T \\
\wedge Eval(resConflict(av1, av2)) = T \\
...
\end{array}
$$

5.3   Translation of the Organization Structure Definition Model

As seen in the last section, the construction of the organization structure definition model requires four steps. After each step, we have to translate the corresponding part of the obtained model in order to prove the adequate theorem.

– Translation of the roles instances: this translation is done after the identification and the instantiation of roles. As depicted in Fig. 9, it leads to the generation of *Implementation1* schema. *Implementation1* schema describes the roles in terms of their local goals. It includes the *System* schema and contains the declaration of variable R typed $\mathbb{F}$ *Role* representing the system

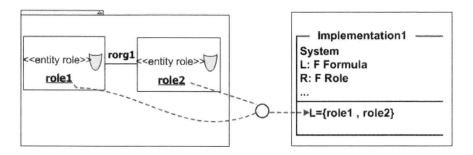

Fig. 9. Translation of the roles instances

set of roles. Moreover, this translation allows the generation of *Completeness* theorem stating that each local goal belongs to a role, and the roles cover all local goals [12].

- Translation of the organization relations between roles: this translation is done after the creation of the organization relation between roles. As depicted in Fig. 10, it allows the generation of the *Implementation2* schema describing the organizational relations in term of their participant roles. *Implementation2* schema includes the *System* schema and contains the declaration of the variable *Rorg* typed $\mathbb{F}$ *OrgRelationship* representing the set of organizational relations. We can also generate the *RoleParticipant* theorem verifying that the organizational relation participants cover the set of roles.

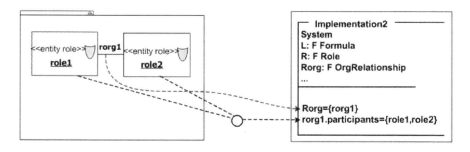

Fig. 10. Translation of the organization relations between roles

- Translation of the *play* links: this translation is done after the role assignment step. As depicted in Fig. 11, it leads to the generation of the *Implementation3* schema describing the roles of each agent.
  The *RoleAssignement* theorem is also generated in order to verify that each role was assigned at least to one agent.
- Translation of the organization link between agents: this translation is depicted in Fig. 12 and is done after dressing the complete organization structure definition model. It allows the generation of the *Implementation4* schema. *Implementation4* schema describes the organizational links between

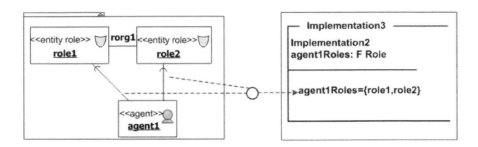

Fig. 11. Translation of the *play* links

agents. It includes the *System* schema and contains the declaration of the variable *organizationLink* typed $\mathbb{F}$ *OrganizationLink* representing the organizational links set.

The *Instantiation1* and *Instantiation2* theorems are also generated stating that every organizational link instantiates an organizational relationship and that every organizational relationship is instantiated by an organizational link.

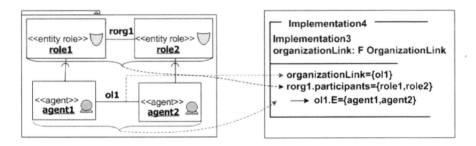

Fig. 12. Translation of the organization link between agents

5.4 Translation of the Collective and Individual Behavior Definition Model

The translation of these models to $\mathcal{T}_{emporal}\mathcal{Z}$ is done according to the following rules:

- Translation of the messages payloads: a message payload allows the description of a message exchanged between agents. It is characterized by a performative representing the message name and a list of attributes representing the transmitted objects. As depicted in Fig. 13, the translation of the messages payloads leads to the creation of a new type called *Message* whose values are the messages payloads performatives.
- Translation of the behavior fragments: the behavior fragments describe the actions performed by an agent. Each behavior fragment is characterized by

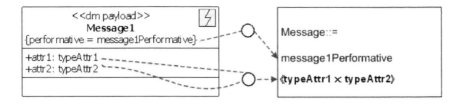

Fig. 13. Translation of the messages payloads

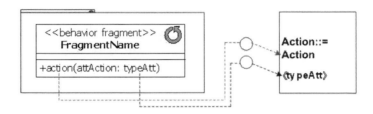

Fig. 14. Translation of the behavior fragments

a name and the set of actions. The behavior fragments lead to the definition of a new type called *Action* whose values are the actions existing in these behavior fragments. This translation is illustrated by Fig. 14.

The translation of the individual behavior definition model of Fig. 7 leads to the following definitions of *Message* and *Action* type.

$Message ::= propose \langle\!\langle Solution \rangle\!\rangle \mid accept \langle\!\langle Solution \rangle\!\rangle \mid$
$reject \langle\!\langle Solution \rangle\!\rangle \mid counterProposition \langle\!\langle Solution \rangle\!\rangle$

$Action ::= send \langle\!\langle Plane \times Plane \times Message \rangle\!\rangle \mid$
$receive \langle\!\langle Plane \times Plane \times Message \rangle\!\rangle \mid$
$perceive \mid performSolution \langle\!\langle Solution \rangle\!\rangle \mid evaluateSolution \langle\!\langle Solution \rangle\!\rangle$

– Translation of temporal constraints: this translation concerns the temporal constraints attached to the lifelines in the collective behavior definition model. It consists in inserting these constraints into the *Implementation6* schema. Applying this translation to the model of Fig. 6, we obtain the following *Implementation6* schema:

$$
\begin{array}{|l}
\_\,Implementation6 \_\!\!\!\_\!\!\!\_\!\!\!\_\!\!\!\_\!\!\!\_\!\!\!\_\!\!\!\_\!\!\!\_\!\!\!\_\!\!\!\_ \\
\quad Implementation5 \\
\hline
Eval(Now(send(pl1, pl2, propose(solution)))) = T \\
\Rightarrow Eval(Eventually(Now(evaluateSolution(sol)))) = T \\
... \\
\end{array}
$$

We also generate the *VerifSpec* theorem verifying that the obtained specification allows the achievement of the initial common objective.

6 $\mathcal{F}_{or}\mathcal{MAAD}$ Tools

StarUML [1] is a UML modeling framework supporting the MDA approach. This framework is characterized by its flexibility and its functionality extensibility. Thus, *StarUML* allows adding new functions in order to satisfy the user's requirements.

In order to be adapted to the $\mathcal{F}_{or}\mathcal{MAAD}$ approach, we propose to extend *StarUML* by (1) the insertion of a new approach in the approach part of *StarUML* called *ForMAAD approach* that integrates the presented models and that can be selected when launching *StarUML* ; (2) the extension of the UML profile part by creating a new profile called $\mathcal{F}_{or}\mathcal{MAAD}$ that is a part of the AML profile allowing the modification of the tool palette content for each diagram of the $\mathcal{F}_{or}\mathcal{MAAD}$ *approach*; the addition of some *JScript* scripts allowing the automatization of the model generation; (3) the addition of the $Add - In\ COM$ object developed under the *NetBeans* environment and allowing the transformation of the generated models into LaTeX; and (4) the insertion of a new panel called $\mathcal{F}_{or}\mathcal{MAAD}$ (Fig. 15) integrating some commands assisting the user to move from one $\mathcal{F}_{or}\mathcal{MAAD}$'s step to another and translating the resulting models into $\mathcal{T}_{emporal}\mathcal{Z}$.

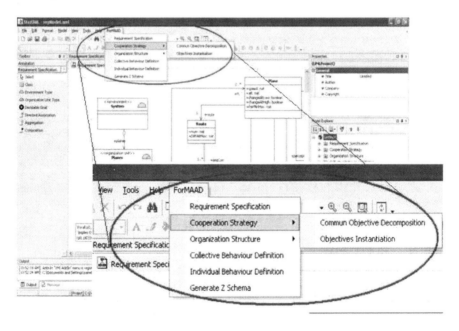

Fig. 15. $\mathcal{F}_{or}\mathcal{MAAD}$ menu

The generation of a LaTeX file from the $\mathcal{F}_{or}\mathcal{MAAD}$ models follows two steps. The first step allows the creation of a *UML XMI* file using the transformation tool

---

[1] `http://staruml/sourceforge.net`

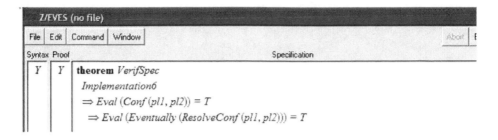

Fig. 16. The proof of the VerifSpec theorem

proposed by *StarUML*. The second step, consists on the application of a set of transformations of the *UML XMI* file in order to generate the LaTeX file. These transformations implement the translation rules presented in the previous section using some *XSLT* (eXtensible Styles Language Transformation) programs. Thus, the LaTeX file presenting a formal specification of the designed application, can be imported by the *Z/EVES* tool in order to prove the necessary theorems and to guarantee the requirement satisfaction.

Figure 16 shows the *VerifSpec* theorem in the case of the air traffic control. This theorem guarantees that the proposed solution satisfies the initial requirements. It is proven using the *Z/EVES* tool.

7 Conclusion

In this paper, we proposed a reformulation of the $\mathcal{F}_{or}\mathcal{MAAD}$ methodology in terms of the MDA paradigm. Our main contribution consists in providing a set of methodological hints which guide the design process and stressing the correctness of the obtained design with respect to the requirements specification. Thus, we defined two ground designs: in the *foreground design*, we present a model oriented representation using AML and in the *background design*, we propose the translation of each model of the *foreground design* into a formal language called $\mathcal{T}_{emporal}\mathcal{Z}$ ([10]) that consists in the introduction of a temporal operators in the Z schemas enabled us to make use of Z supporting tools, like *Z/EVES* [11], for syntax and type checking, as well as reasoning about the correctness of refinement steps.

As an example, we cited the air traffic control problem that allowed an illustration of the proposed method. Indeed, we designed a decentralized agent-based solution for conflict control in air traffic. The solution models a plane as an autonomous agent able to detect potential conflicts. The effective resolution of a conflict is the result of a negotiation process between planes.

The presented design process is supported by extending the *StarUML* tool in order to define a $\mathcal{F}_{or}\mathcal{MAAD}$ profile and to integrate the proposed approach with the five models. In this tool, we implemented the necessary rules allowing the transition into $\mathcal{T}_{emporal}\mathcal{Z}$ and the generation of the required theorems in order to be proved with the *Z/EVES* tool.

It is necessary to point out that these results, though original and promising, constitute a first step in the development process of MAS. Thus, our perspective consists in the pursuit of the proposed process in order to define a complete model oriented approach allowing the code generation of the designed system starting from the verified abstract specifications generated by $\mathcal{F}_{or}\mathcal{MAAD}$.

References

1. Luck, M., d'Inverno, M.: A conceptual framework for agent definition and development. The Computer Journal 44(1), 1–20 (2001)
2. Weyns, D., Haesevoets, R., Helleboogh, A.: The MACODO organization model for context-driven dynamic agent organizations. ACM Transaction on Autonomous and Adaptive Systems (2010), http://www.cs.kuleuven.be/~danny/papers/2010TAAS-model.pdf
3. Brasier, M.T., Jonker, M., Treur, J.: Principals of compositional multi-agent system development. In: Proceedings of the 15th IFIP World Computer Congress, WCC 1998, Conference on Information Technology and Knowledge Systems, IT&KNOWS 1998, Vienna and Budapest, pp. 347–360 (1998)
4. Pavon, J., Gomez-Sanz, J.J., Fuentes, R.: The INGENIAS Methodology and Tools. In: Agent-Oriented Methodologies, pp. 236–276. Idea Group Publishing, USA (2005)
5. Jarraya, T., Guessoum, Z.: Towards a Model Driven Process for Multi-Agent System. In: Burkhard, H.-D., Lindemann, G., Verbrugge, R., Varga, L.Z. (eds.) CEEMAS 2007. LNCS (LNAI), vol. 4696, pp. 256–265. Springer, Heidelberg (2007)
6. Perini, A., Susi, A.: Automating model transformations in agent-oriented modelling. In: Müller, J.P., Zambonelli, F. (eds.) AOSE 2005. LNCS, vol. 3950, pp. 167–178. Springer, Heidelberg (2006)
7. Rougemaille, S., Migeon, F., Maurel, C., Gleizes, M.P.: Model Driven Engineering for Designing Adaptive Multi-Agent Systems. In: Artikis, A., O'Hare, G.M.P., Stathis, K., Vouros, G.A. (eds.) ESAW 2007. LNCS (LNAI), vol. 4995, pp. 318–332. Springer, Heidelberg (2008)
8. Cervenka, R., Trencansky, I.: Agent Modeling Language: Language Specification. Version 0.9. Technical Report, Whitestein Technologies (2004)
9. Trencansky, I., Cervenka, R.: Agent Modeling Language (AML): A Comprehensive Approach to Modeling MAS. Informatica 29(4), 391–400 (2005)
10. Regayeg, A., Hadj-Kacem, A., Jmaiel, M.: Specification and Verification of Multi-Agent Applications using Temporal Z. In: 2004 IEEE/WIC/ACM International Conference on Intelligent Agent Technology (IAT 2004), September 20-24, 2004, pp. 260–266. IEEE Computer Society, Beijing (2004)
11. Meisels, I., Saaltink, M.: The Z/EVES 2.0 Reference Manual. Technical Report TR–99–5493–03e, ORA, Canada (1999)
12. Hadj-Kacem, A., Regayeg, A., Jmaiel, M.: ForMAAD: A Formal Method for Agent-Based Application Design. Journal of Web Intelligence and Agent Systems 5(4), 216–334 (2007)
13. Regayeg, A.: Approche Formelle de Développement de Systèmes Multi-Agents: de la Spécification à la Conception. PhD thesis (2009)
14. Regayeg, A., Kallel, S., Hadj-Kacem, A., Jmaiel, M.: ForMAAD Method: An Experimental Design for Air Traffic Control. International Transactions on Systems Science and Applications 1(4), 327–334 (2006)

An Architectural Perspective on Multiagent Societies*

Juan Manuel Serrano and Sergio Saugar

University Rey Juan Carlos
Madrid, Spain
{juanmanuel.serrano,sergio.saugar}@urjc.es

Abstract. This paper attempts to provide an architectural foundation
to multiagent societies through a systematic application of the notion of
software connector. It shows that multiagent societies can be explained
as a Component & Connector architectural style, made up of high-level
connectors defined in terms of common normative, communicative and
organizational abstractions. This is expected to yield a better alignment
of agent technology with mainstream software engineering practice and
conventional architectural styles. Moreover, we show that connectors are
a powerful metaphor for the design of organizational and communicative
abstractions. Last, the paper challenges a common architectural assumption, namely the application-independence of software connectors.

1 Introduction

Multiagent societies are particular types of distributed systems made up of a collection of autonomous and heterogeneous components, so-called agents, which
are situated in an open social environment that mediates their interactions and
provide them with access to different types of resources. Arguably, the most
salient and distinctive feature of multiagent societies is represented by the *social environment*, which plays a role akin to the one played by middleware in
mainstream software engineering [18]. Unlike conventional, object-oriented (e.g.
CORBA) or messaging (e.g. AMQP) middleware, however, the social environment stands as a first-class design abstraction for application developers [20].
Thus, the development of a multiagent society does not only encompass the design of software components, but in large part the design of its environment. This
latter part particularly accrues to open systems, where the precise specification
of component interconnections is vital to guarantee successful interoperation of
a dynamic population of autonomous and heterogeneous components [14].

Software architecture is a mature software engineering discipline [2] that also
places significant importance to the separation of concerns between interaction
and computation. In fact, component interactions are embodied in first-class abstractions, namely *software connectors* [6]. These software elements feature on a

---

* Research sponsored by the Spanish Ministry of Science and Innovation, project
TIN2009-14562-C05-05.

D. Weyns and M.-P. Gleizes (Eds.): AOSE 2010, LNCS 6788, pp. 165–176, 2011.

par with software components in the foundational definitions of software architecture [8,13] and are crucial in the satisfaction of software qualities of the system. Moreover, the definition of architectural styles largely builds upon the types of connectors supported by those styles. Although multiagent systems have already been approached from an architectural perspective [16,14], the notion of software connector has not been exploited as fully as possible. This paper attempts to alleviate this omission by providing a connector-based account of social environments. Moreover, it also introduces an UML profile for the design of social connector types which make up the social environment of particular applications.

This architectural approach to multiagent societies rivals other organizational metamodels such as MOISE+ [5], which alternatively builds upon *coordination artifacts* [7] as a foundational metaphor. Software connectors, however, are expected to yield a better alignment of agent technology with mainstream software engineering practice and conventional architectural styles. Moreover, we will show that connectors are a powerful design metaphor for the definition of new kinds of organizational abstractions. Last, we also expect to bring some benefits to software architecture research by considering the complex types of connectors that occur in multiagent systems.

The paper is structured as follows. Section 2 introduces the major notions of software architecture which pertain to this research, mainly architectural views, connectors and middleware. Sections 3 and 4 propose a collection of social connectors for multiagent societies and briefly sketches the major features of an UML profile to customize social connectors for particular applications. Finally, we conclude with a discussion on related and future work.

2   Software Architectural Concepts

According to the viewtype catalogue proposed in [1], a software system can be described from the perspectives defined by the *modular* and *component & connector* (C&C) viewtypes. Modular structures focus on the implementation units of the system and their relationships (functional dependencies, inheritance, part-of relations, etc.). C&C structures describe the structure of the system from a runtime perspective, thus focusing on the units of execution (components) and interaction (connectors). For each each viewtype, *architectural styles* can be defined which further refine the types of elements and relationships identified by the viewtype. In general, styles of the C&C viewtype such as client-server, pipe-and-filter, publish-subscribe, etc., identify different types of components and connectors, and hence characterise different kinds of computational models. Thus, they provide a useful framework for analysing new computational paradigms (e.g. multiagent societies), and comparing its features with other styles.

The definition of a new C&C style encompasses the identification of the corresponding types of components and connectors, as well as possible constraints in their configuration (or *topology*). Component types characterise particular classes of processing units or data stores, which communicate with the environment through specific points of interaction called *ports* (or simply, interfaces [1]).

For instance, *filters* are components which receive data from its input port, and deliver them through the output port after a transformation process. Connectors, on the other hand, are computational elements which mediate the interactions among components. According to the taxonomy of connectors proposed in [6], connectors provide services that belong to at least one of four different categories: *communication, coordination, conversion* and *facilitation*. The first two kinds of services essentially consists of the transmission of data and control, respectively, among the participating components. Conversion services allow to transform the interaction required by one participant to that provided by another. Last, facilitation connectors facilitate and streamline component interaction through different mechanisms (e.g. security, persistence, transactions, etc.).

The definition of a new type of connector requires identifying which services its instances will provide and how they are realized. For instance, both event channels and procedure calls provide communication and coordination services, although through different means. A connector type is also characterised by the different types of *roles* which can be played by components participating in the interaction. For instance, filters interacting through a *pipe* can play the *reader* or *writer* roles. Last, a new connector type has to specify its *protocol*, i.e. the rules that govern the initiation and finishing of the interaction, the behaviour of its participants, etc.

A particular class of connectors, particularly relevant for the purpose of this paper, is represented by middleware infrastructures. Indeed, the primary goal of middleware is to mediate interactions among distributed components. From a connector perspective, middleware infrastructures are *composite connectors* made up from different subconnectors which are offered to distributed components as basic interaction mechanisms. For instance, CORBA-based middleware offers several variants of method calls: synchronous, deferred synchronous, one-way requests, etc. Besides the basic control and data transfer services provided by atomic connectors, middleware also offers a number of facilitation and conversion services. Last, being connectors, middleware infrastructures are also characterised by a number of roles. For instance, in object-oriented middleware, the major role played by interacting components is that of *object*. Thus, a CORBA software component (e.g. programmed in Prolog) is not an object due to certain intrinsic properties that it possesses, but because it is attached to an ORB to provide the services specified by its IDL specification. Therefore, in a distributed setting objects are essentially roles, not components.

3   C&C Architecture of Multiagent Societies

Multiagent societies are distributed systems made up of a collection of autonomous, heterogeneous, situated and social components called agents. Autonomy means that agents exert full control on their runtime state and behaviour [15]. Heterogeneity amounts to independence of design, which does not only encompass implementation matters (e.g. programming language of choice) but also decision making policies [14]. Situatedness refer to the environment where agents are deployed, which plays a role akin to the role of middleware in traditional software engineering [18]. Last, sociability calls for a particular kind of middleware, namely *social middleware* (e.g. AMELI [3]), which represents the responsible infrastructure for managing the institutional state of the society.

Since multiagent societies are distributed systems, the C&C perspective leads us to explicate the nature of these kinds of systems in terms of the types of components and connectors supported by social middleware and the roles played by software components interacting through them. Figure 1 shows a schematic C&C view of the proposed structure for multiagent societies. According to this figure, components interacting through a social middleware can play two kinds of roles: *Agents* and *Resources*; moreover, four types of connectors are postulated: *SpeechActs*, *Observations*, *Invocations* and *SocialInteractions*. The following subsections describe the common structure and dynamics of these social connectors and middleware roles.

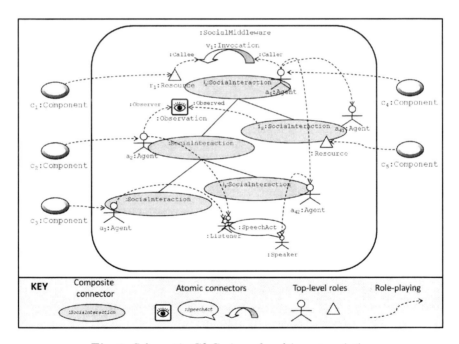

Fig. 1. Schematic C&C view of multiagent societies

3.1 Social Components

Agent. In accordance with section 2, a component is an agent if, and only if, it is attached to a social middleware as player of some *agent role*. The expression "agent component" is used to denote the component which plays some agent role within the society. Agent roles are represented in figure 1 as stick figures; thus, the only agent components are c_2, c_3 and c_4. Agent roles are characterised by a given *purpose*, viz. a public goal that they purport to achieve, and hold an event *mailbox* which stores any notification addressed to them by the environment.

The port (i.e. interface) implemented by agent components to interact with the social middleware includes the external actions *attempt* and *retrieve*. The former one allows the agent component to act within the society (as described in section 3.2), whereas the latter one allows the component to retrieve the events stored in its agent mailbox.

This role-based notion of agenthood impacts the standard attributes of autonomy and heterogeneity in two major ways. First, autonomy has to be regarded as a relative, rather than absolute property of agent components. In essence, this means that autonomy of agents is preserved only in their interactions through the social middleware. If the software component is approached through other mechanisms (e.g. from its user interface), the component may not be regarded as autonomous. Second, a complete decoupling of agent components and the social middleware is facilitated, thus enhancing autonomy. In fact, the social middleware infrastructure does not need to keep track of the agent component population; it just manages their social identity (i.e. the roles they play)[1]. Also, multiple components may access the same agent role, from different locations. Hence, modifiability and deployment flexibility (i.e. mobility) of agent components is also enhanced.

Resource. The agent environment is commonly regarded not only as the medium for agent-to-agent interaction, but also as a layer which mediates the access of agents to resources of different kinds [20]. Accordingly, *resources* represent the second type of role which a software component may play within a social middleware. Figure 1 shows two resource roles, depicted through triangle icons, played by components c_1 and c_5. Unlike agents, resources are non-autonomous, and provide different computational or informational (e.g. virtualization [18]) services to the multiagent society where they are attached. Like agents, resources are heterogeneous and its deployment may be decoupled from the social middleware, e.g. a resource may be fulfilled by a web service deployed in an arbitrary location. Unlike agents, however, the middleware infrastructure needs to know the precise location of the resource component (e.g. to enact one of the provided services upon invocation of another resource or agent).

3.2   Social Connectors

The sociability of agents commonly refers to the use of high-level normative (permissions, commitments, empowerment, etc.), organizational (institutions, groups, teams, etc.) and communicative (speech acts, dialogue games, conversations, etc.) abstractions in the coordination of agent components. In essence, these abstractions do not concern the components of the system but rather the interactions (i.e. connectors) in which components engage through the social middleware. We show in the following paragraphs how the chosen social connectors are shaped out of these abstractions, in accordance with the general model of connector described in section 3. Table 1 summarizes the major features of each kind of connector.

---

[1] In contrast, CORBA-based middleware and most agent-based middleware (e.g. JADE) are tightly coupled with their registered components.

Table 1. Summary of social connector features

Social Connector	Services			Roles	Protocol
	Communication	*Coordination*	*Facilitation*		
Social-Interaction	X		X	Agent/Resource	Initiation & Finishing & Purpose & Monitoring rules
SpeechAct	X		X	Speaker/Listener	Empowerment & Permission & Synchronization rules
Invocation	X	X		Caller/Callee	
Observation	X			Observer/Observee	

SocialInteraction. Social connectors of this type represent social processes of different kinds and scales (e.g. conversations, teams, groups, organizations, etc.). Social interactions can be decomposed into lower-level subinteractions, so that the whole interaction space of the multiagent society is structured in terms of a tree of social interactions. The root of this tree represents the multiagent society itself, and the leafs atomic interaction mechanisms (speech acts, invocations and observations) or social interactions which are not further decomposed. Thus, this type of connector essentially provide a *facilitation* service, namely structuring the atomic interactions of components through the middleware.

Every component which attaches to the social middleware (either as agent or resource), does it so within the context of a given social interaction. Thus, *agents* and *resources* represent the two types of roles of this type of social connector. In figure 1, roles of social interaction i_1 are represented by agent a_4 and resource r_1. Besides the social interaction hierarchy, the topology of the multiagent society also consists of role-playing agent hierarchies. These run-time structures represent the decomposition of the agent activity according to the different contexts in which it participates. Thus, the activity of agent a_4 within the context of social interactions i_2 and i_3 is represented by agents a_{41} and a_{42}, respectively.

The protocol of a particular type of social interaction specifies the rules which govern the initiation and finishing of interactions of that type, as well as the purposes of its member agent roles. Also, the social interaction protocol includes monitoring rules which specify the subscriptions of agents to events of the social environment. In this way, social interactions also serve a communication purpose. Finally, the protocol may include constraints on the decomposition of the interaction into lower-level subinteractions, and the role-playing hierarchies of its member agents.

SpeechAct. Agent communication is commonly conceptualised in terms of speech acts, i.e. actions performed in saying something. For instance, *requesting* or *promising* someone to do something, *informing* someone that something holds, etc. The successful performance of these particular actions results in the communication of some mental attitude (intentions and beliefs, respectively), so that speech acts connectors may serve a *communication* purpose. Also, the performance of other types of speech acts, such as declarations, may creates new institutional facts so that speech acts may also serve a *facilitation* purpose. For instance, the speech acts *SetUp* and *Close* allow agents to declare the initiation and finishing, respectively, of a social interaction. These speech acts thus provide an alternative mechanism to the initiation and finishing rules of social interactions protocols.

The agents interacting through speech acts may play two kinds of roles: *speaker* and *listener*. The initiation of speech acts is governed by *empowerment* rules. In particular, a speech act is created when some component *attempts* its empowered agent to say something. If the agent is not empowered, the speech act will not be created and the institutional state will not be affected at all. Once the speech act is created, the empowered agent becomes its *speaker*. Figure 1 shows agent a_{41} saying something to agents a_2 and a_3. Note that the speaker role of speech acts is not played directly by software components, but by agent roles. Agents and resources, so-called *top roles*, are the only roles of the social middleware directly played by components.

Immediately after its creation, *permission* rules govern the execution of the speech act. If permission is granted, institutional facts are brought about (in case of declarations) and addressees are notified through their corresponding mailboxes, etc. If permission is not granted, then the speech act is prohibited and its execution canceled. Last, it may also happen that the rules of the society allow to infer neither than the action is permitted nor prohibited. In this case, the speech act is left pending for execution [11].

Once addressees are notified, they may become *listeners* of the speech act if the speaker initiated the speech act in a *synchronous* mode. By listening, agents acknowledge the receipt of the message. An asynchronous speech act finishes as soon as permission is granted; a synchronous one requires every addressee to listen to it; moreover, a synchronous speech act blocks the behaviour of the agent (role) until it is finished. Of course, the agent component itself is only blocked as far as its activity within the multiagent society is concerned. Figure 1 shows that agents a_2 and a_3 has listened to the speech act.

Invocation. This type of connector allows agents and resources to access the services provided by other environmental resources. For instance, a *clock* resource may provide an *alarm* service. The invocation of a service commonly needs to specify certain information, such as the time and date for the alarm service. Thus, invocation connectors provide both *coordination* and *communication* services. Similarly to speech acts, they can be initiated in a synchronous or asynchronous mode, and its life-cycle (i.e. initiation and execution) is governed by empowerment and permission rules. The agent or resource which initiates the invocation acts as *caller*. Invocations are finished as soon as the resource providing the service, i.e. the *callee*, fulfills the service or signals some problem. Figure 1 shows agent a_4 requesting some service provided by resource r_1.

Observation. This type of interaction allows agents to observe a given social entity (namely, another agent, resource, social interaction, speech act, etc.), subject to the agent being empowered to see that entity and permission for execution is granted. Thus, it is a pure *communication* connector. Two roles characterise this interaction mechanism: the *observer* agent and the social entity being *observed*. For instance, figure 1 shows agent a_2 observing a social interaction. The observer may specify a particular attribute of the social entity being observed. In that case, the observer agent is just notified of the value held by that attribute; otherwise, the connector notifies the agent about the whole state of the social entity. In any case, the notification is deliver to the mailbox of the observer agent.

4   UML Profile for Social Connectors Types

Taking into account section 3, programming the social environment amounts to declaring the types of social connectors which implement the functional requirements of the application domain – as far as interaction is concerned. For instance, *ProgramCommittee*, *Submission*, *ReviewingTeam*, etc., are common social interaction types of a conference management application; *Submit* a paper and *Notify* its acceptance or rejection are among its characteristic speech act types; last, *ObserveReview* is a common type of observation which is characterised by specific empowerment and permission rules (e.g. permission is granted to authors during the rebuttal stage)[2]. Note that some social connector types may be largely generic and, hence, reusable across many applications. For instance, the design of the reviewing team may profit from customizing a generic *DiscussionGroup* social interaction type.

The definition of social connector types requires a metamodel which identifies the programmable features of social interaction, speech act, observation and invocation connectors. These features can be classified according to the different dimensions of software connectors: services, roles, subconnectors and protocol rules (e.g. life-cycle rules). The next subsection briefly describes a light-weight implementation of this metamodel in terms of an UML Profile. Due to lack of space, we only deal with social interaction types. This version of the metamodel actually represents a visual and informal surface syntax of the metamodel presented in [12], where the C+ action language is used as the formal underlying technique. The UML profile is illustrated in figure 2, which shows a partial specification of the social interaction space for a conference management application. Note that this UML diagram actually represent a *modular* view of the application, in contrast with the C&C view shown in figure 1.

4.1   Social Interaction Types

As figure 2 shows, social interaction types are defined by stereotyped *use cases*. This is in accordance with the UML standard [4, cap. 16], which defines use cases

---

[2] These types can be regarded as specialisations of the corresponding generic types introduced in section 3. Thus, the social interaction type *Program Committee* is an specialisation of the generic social interaction type *SocialInteraction*; the speech act type *Submit* is an specialisation of the generic speech act type *SpeechAct*, etc.

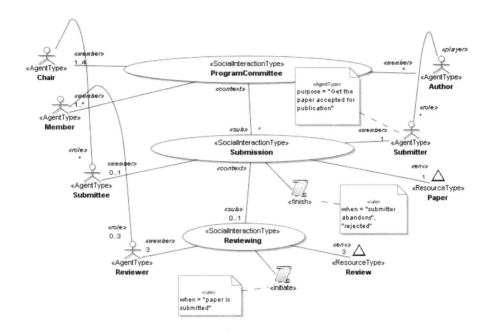

Fig. 2. Social interaction types of the conference management application

as types of behaviour or functionality that the system offers to its users. Indeed, social interaction types can be regarded as units of functionality offered by the social middleware (the system) to its external software components (the users). The stereotypes and tagged values which specialise the use case metamodel for representing social interaction types are introduced in the next paragraphs.

Subinteractions. The definition of a new type of social interaction may include a number of constraints on the types of subinteractions in which its activity is decomposed, and the social interaction context to which it belongs. For instance, *submissions* can only take place within the context of a program committee, and its only subinteraction can be a reviewing team. Neither the *extend* nor the *include* relationships of the use case metamodel are good candidates for representing these constraints. Hence, these alternatives are discharged in favor of the ad-hoc stereotypes «context» and «sub» which are applied at the corresponding ends of a generic association between the corresponding use cases. The cardinality at the «sub» end indicates the number of possible instances of that type.

Connector Roles. Another constraint which may be part of the definition of a social interaction type concerns its types of member agents and environmental resources. For instance, only two agents may be members of a submission: the *submitter* and a *submittee*, and only one resource is part of its environment: the *paper* to be submitted. As figure 2 shows, types of agents are represented as stereotyped UML actors. The representation of resource types is also carried out through actors, although in this case a distinguishing icon is attached to the stereotype. This decision is consistent with the UML metamodel which defines actors as roles played by external entities in its interaction with the system. Agent and resource actors are associated to social interaction use cases through general associations whose actor end is stereotyped with the labels «member» and «env», respectively.

The specification of a type of agent may constrain the kinds of agents which can play roles of that type, as well as the types of roles which instances of that type may play. These constraints on the role-playing hierarchy of agents is not supported by the actor metamodel, so new stereotypes «role» and «player» are introduced for general association ends. Moreover, the specification of an agent type may also identify the particular purpose shared by agents of that type. For instance, submitters purport to get their papers accepted for publication. The tag **purpose** of the «AgentType» stereotype represents this feature.

Protocol Rules. Commonly the initiation and finishing rules of social interactions are specified by their particular type. These features are represented in UML with the class stereotypes «initiate» and «finish». These stereotypes specialise the «rule» stereotype which provide several multi-valued, string tags for representing rule bodies: `when`, `if`, `iff`, etc. For instance, figure 2 shows that reviewing teams are automatically initiated when the stage of the submission interaction changes to *submitted*. It also specifies that a submission is automatically finished when the paper is rejected or the submitter abandons the submission.

5   Discussion

Any kind of software can be described from a C&C perspective, and multiagent societies ought to be no exception. This paper has shown that it is indeed possible to explicate social middleware and their interaction mechanisms in reference to a C&C architectural style made up from *high-level* connector types, i.e. connectors which somehow refer to common normative, communicative and organizational abstractions. In so doing, this paper complements other architectural approaches to multiagent systems [17,19], which alternatively favour reference architectures, patterns and low-level connectors over high-level architectural styles.

The proposed architectural view on multiagent societies postulates four kinds of connectors, *social interactions*, *speech acts*, *invocations* and *observations*, which are specified in terms of their types of services, roles and protocol rules – as any type of software connector is specified. First, this ensures alignment with the common engineering practice in defining architectural styles and connector types [1,6], and facilitates comparison with conventional connectors. For instance, the atomic social connectors differ from common message passing, data access and procedure call connectors in the rules which govern their life-cycle, viz. empowerment and permission rules, the social interaction context within which they are executed, etc. Second, significant features of the resulting interaction mechanisms directly derive from the application of a connector perspective to these abstractions, thus showing connectors as a powerful design metaphor. In particular, the synchronization and possibility of pending executions of speech acts are only possible because speech acts are not considered as low-level transient messages, i.e. events, but connectors, i.e. stateful entities. Similarly, the accompanying *role-based* notion of agenthood comes directly from a connector-based approach to social middleware. These features alone set our approach apart from other organizational metamodels, such as AMELI, MOISE, Madkit, etc.

These four kinds of connectors were identified in accordance with the target application domain of the architectural style, and three major design principles: generality, expressiveness and simplicity. First, multiagent societies represent a software paradigm which is aimed at the development of *social applications*, i.e. applications which are designed to support the activity of a group of people within a given social context. Now, in any social context people may *say* things to each other, *manipulate* resources of the environment, and *see* what happens. Hence, speech acts, invocations and observations can be regarded as *general-*purpose connectors, not tied to any particular subdomain. We can not dispense with any of them either, since that would negatively affect expressiveness. Regarding this later principle, it is also clearly needed some mechanism which allows structuring the activity of people. Social interactions provide a general and simple mechanism for this purpose. Last, simplicity comes into play to avoid the unnecessary proliferation of structuring abstractions (e.g. conversations, groups, organizations, institutions, teams, etc.).

This paper has also sketched a social connector metamodel which allows designers to define the particular types of social interactions, speech acts, etc., which actually specialise the generic architectural style according to the requirements of the social application domain. This part of the paper is important for two major reasons: first, it gives an architectural reading of the expression "the agent environment as a first-class design abstraction" [20]; second, it challenges the common view in the software architecture community which regards connectors as application-independent architectural elements [6]. This paper has also shown how the UML use case metamodel can be customised to account for a light-weight version of this social connector metamodel.

The work reported in this paper represents a first step towards the architectural foundation of SPEECH, an interaction-oriented language for programming social applications[3]. The runtime semantics [10,11] and type system [12] of the language provide further details on the social connector semantics and metamodel introduced in this paper. Concerning implementation matters, we are currently working in the mapping between the proposed architectural style and REST, which will result in a Web-based social middleware infrastructure for the SPEECH language [9].

References

1. Bass, L., Clements, P., Kazman, R.: Software Architecture in Practice, 2nd edn. Addison Wesley, Reading (2003)
2. Clements, P.C., Shaw, M.: "the golden age of software architecture" revisited. IEEE Software 26(4), 70–72 (2009)

---

[3] http://www.speechlang.org

3. Esteva, M., Rosell, B., Rodríguez-Aguilar, J.A., Arcos, J.L.: AMELI: An agent-based middleware for electronic institutions. In: Kudenko, D., Kazakov, D., Alonso, E. (eds.) AAMAS 2004. LNCS (LNAI), vol. 3394, pp. 236–243. Springer, Heidelberg (2005)
4. Object Management Group. OMG Unified Modeling Language™ (OMG UML), Superstructure. Version 2.2. OMG (2009)
5. Hübner, J.F., Sichman, J.S., Boissier, O.: Developing organised multi-agent systems using the moise+ model: Programming issues at the system and agent levels. IJAOSE 1(3/4), 370–395 (2007)
6. Mehta, N.R., Medvidovic, N., Phadke, S.: Towards a taxonomy of software connectors. In: ICSE, pp. 178–187. ACM Press, New York (2000)
7. Omicini, A., Ricci, A., Viroli, M.: Artifacts in the a&a meta-model for multi-agent systems. JAAMAS 17(3), 432–456 (2008)
8. Perry, D., Wolf, A.: Foundations for the study of software architecture. ACM SIG-SOFT Software Engineering Notes 17(4), 40–52 (1992)
9. Saugar, S., Serrano, J.M.: A web-based virtual machine for developing computational societies. In: Klusch, M., Pěchouček, M., Polleres, A. (eds.) CIA 2008. LNCS (LNAI), vol. 5180, pp. 162–176. Springer, Heidelberg (2008)
10. Serrano, J.M., Saugar, S.: Run-time semantics of a language for programming social processes. In: Fisher, M., Sadri, F., Thielscher, M. (eds.) CLIMA IX. LNCS (LNAI), vol. 5405, pp. 37–56. Springer, Heidelberg (2009)
11. Serrano, J.M., Saugar, S.: Dealing with incomplete normative states. In: Padget, J., Artikis, A., Vasconcelos, W., Stathis, K., da Silva, V.T., Matson, E., Polleres, A. (eds.) COIN@AAMAS 2009. LNCS (LNAI), vol. 6069. Springer, Heidelberg (2010)
12. Serrano, J.M., Saugar, S.: Programming social middleware through social interaction types. In: Dastani, M., El Fallah Segrouchni, A., Leite, J., Torroni, P. (eds.) LADS 2009. LNCS (LNAI), vol. 6039. Springer, Heidelberg (2010)
13. Shaw, M., Garlan, D.: Software Architecture: Perspectives on an Emerging Discipline. Prentice Hall, Englewood Cliffs (1996)
14. Singh, M.P., Chopra, A.K.: Programming multiagent systems without programming agents. In: Proc. of the AAMAS ProMAS Workshop (2009)
15. Singh, M.P., Huhns, M.N.: Service-Oriented Computing. Semantics, Processes, Agents. John Wiley & Sons, Ltd., Chichester (2005)
16. Weyns, D.: Special issue on multiagent systems and software architecture. IJAOSE 2(1) (2008)
17. Weyns, D.: A pattern language for multi-agent systems. In: WICSA/ECSA 2009, pp. 191–200. IEEE, Los Alamitos (2009)
18. Weyns, D., Helleboogh, A., Holvoet, T., Schumacher, M.: The agent environment in multi-agent systems: A middleware perspective. Multiagent and Grid Systems 5(1), 93–108 (2009)
19. Weyns, D., Holvoet, T.: A reference architecture for situated multiagent systems. In: Weyns, D., Van Dyke Parunak, H., Michel, F. (eds.) E4MAS 2006. LNCS (LNAI), vol. 4389, pp. 1–40. Springer, Heidelberg (2007)
20. Weyns, D., Omicini, A., Odell, J.: Environment as a first class abstraction in multiagent systems. JAAMAS 14(1), 5–30 (2007)

A Methodology for Developing
an Agent Systems Reference Architecture

Duc N. Nguyen[1], Kyle Usbeck[1], William M. Mongan[1], Christopher T. Cannon[1],
Robert N. Lass[1], Jeff Salvage[1], William C. Regli[1], Israel Mayk[2], and Todd Urness[2]

[1] Applied Communications and Information Networking Institute, Drexel University
{dn53,kfu22,wmm24,ctc82,urlass,jks29,regli}@drexel.edu
[2] Communications-Electronics Research, Development and Engineering Center, US Army

Abstract. The slow adoption of agent-oriented methodologies as a paradigm
for developing industry systems is due in part to their lack of integration and
general-purpose use. There exists a need to define common patterns, relationships
between components, and structural qualities that a reference architecture for
agent-based systems would solve. However, there is little, if any, consensus on
how to create a reference architecture for agent-based systems. This paper presents
a methodology for developing a reference architecture that documents agent-
based systems from different system viewpoints. Rather than the traditional approach of studying existing systems, the documentation methodology relies on
forensic software analysis of agent frameworks (*i.e.*, APIs and libraries for constructing agent systems). We demonstrate the methodology by describing the process used to create the Agent System Reference Architecture.

1   Introduction

Using agent-based approaches for constructing large complex distributed systems can
provide advantages over traditional methods [5]. Unfortunately, industry has been slow
to adopt this agent-oriented paradigm. One reason for this slow adoption is the lack of
integration and general-purpose technologies [13]. Standards bodies such as the Foundation for Intelligent Physical Agents (FIPA)[1] are leading efforts to standardize protocols and formats of an agent-based system. However, there is a need to construct
a reference *architecture* that defines the relationships between standardized terms and
concepts of an agent-based system. Furthermore, such an architecture would give a set
of architectural blueprints and best practices to aid in developing new agent frameworks
and systems. To this end, a reference architecture for agent-based systems would speed
other standardization efforts and adoption as a viable systems engineering perspective.

This paper describes a documentation methodology for creating the Agent Systems
Reference Architecture (ASRA) for agent frameworks. Rather than studying agent systems across unrelated application domains, this work studies the agent frameworks used
to construct software systems composed of agents. The ASRA builds upon the Agent
Systems Reference Model (ASRM) [11] by identifying and documenting the interactions between ASRM functional concepts typically found in an agent system.

---

[1] http://www.fipa.org

D. Weyns and M.-P. Gleizes (Eds.): AOSE 2010, LNCS 6788, pp. 177–188, 2011.

Our approach to creating the ASRA for agent frameworks combines *static* and *dynamic* software analysis tools with a regimented documenting process 4+1 View Model [6] to existing agent framework implementations creating five architectural views. The process for creating the ASRA is as follows:

1. For every ASRM functional concept, the ASRM definiton of each functional concept comprises the Scenario view of the 4+1 Model.
2. For each agent framework implementation under analysis, implement a basic application that exercises the functional concept. Execute this application within an application profiler to generate runtime data to build the Process view.
3. Perform static analysis on the source code of the agent system functional concept to build the Implementation view.
4. Finally, abstract the package decompositions into the Logical view.

The main contribution of this paper is a novel methodology for creating reference architectures for a class of systems based on a domain reference model. Previous approaches rely on studying classes of existing systems and constructing reference architecture documents. Moreover, we believe this methodology is general enough to apply to other software system domains.

The rest of this paper is organized as follows: Section 2 defines the terms *architecture*, *reference architecture* in the context of agent systems and agent frameworks. Section 2.2 describes the Agent Systems Reference *Model* and its basis for creating the ASRA. Section 3 provides a description of the 4+1 Model and how it will be applied to agent frameworks followed by an application of the process to create a portion of the ASRA in Section 4. Section 5 provides a summary of related efforts in reference architectures for agent-based systems. Finally, we conclude with related efforts and a roadmap of this continuing work for developing a reference architecture for agent systems.

2   Background

This section defines a reference model and a reference architecture. We use these definitions to further define a reference architecture for agent systems.

2.1   What Is a Reference Model and Architecture?

A **reference model** describes the abstract functional elements of a system. A reference model does not impose specific design decisions. APIs, protocols, encodings, and other standards are not included within a reference model, but can be use concurrently. A reference model does not explicitly define an architecture, but rather can drive the implementation of multiple architectures. The novelty of a reference model is that it provides a common ontology, innovative and practical system engineering techniques, and software development guidance [11].

A software architecture is an abstract representation of a software system. It is composed of structures and components of the system, their properties, and the relationships between them [2]. A **reference architecture** has many definitions, but the most commonly used in the software engineering literature is that a reference architecture consists of standardized diagrams (*e.g.*, UML, ADL, *etc.*) that describe the architecture from different viewpoints to cover the concerns of the stakeholders of a system. These standardized diagrams are used to abstract the implementation details of a system and illustrate the relationships between the components of a system [14].

2.2   A Reference Model for Agent Systems

The basis for the ASRA is the Agent Systems Reference Model (ASRM) [11]. The ASRM provides a model for software systems composed of agents. It establishes terms, concepts, and definitions required to compare agent systems.

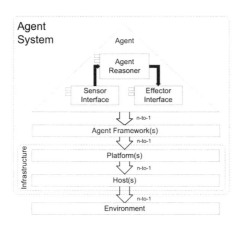

Fig. 1. Anatomy of an agent and its role in an agent system

The ASRM defines an intelligent agent—or simply agent—as *situated* computational processes that embody one or more of the following qualities: autonomy, proactivity, interactivity, continuous, sociality, and/or mobility. The ASRM also formalizes concepts and layers of organization in an agent-based system. The layers (shown in Figure 1) are: *agents*, *frameworks*, *platforms*, *hosts*, and *environments*. An agent-based system is the set of frameworks, the agents that execute in them, the platform (other software) that supports them and the hosts (hardware) upon which they execute.

The ASRM describes an agent system as a set of abstract functional concepts that support overall system execution. The functional concepts represent the complex interactions between software and hardware located at different layers of the agent system. The functional concepts are as follows:

- **Agent Administration** facilitates and enables command and control of agents and allocates resources to those agents as needed.
- **Security and Survivability** prevents execution of undesirable actions within an agent system while allowing execution of desirable actions.
- **Mobility** facilitates and enables the migration of agents among framework instances (typically, but not necessarily, on different hosts)
- **Conflict Management** facilitates and enables the management of interdependencies between agents activities and decisions.
- **Messaging** facilitates and enables information and data transfer among agents in the system.
- **Logging** facilitates and enables information about events to be recorded occurring during system execution for subsequent inspection.
- **Directory Services** facilitates and enables the locating and accessing of shared resources.

The functional concepts are necessary in developing the ASRA as they are the starting point for the analysis process.

2.3   The Agent Systems Reference Architecture

The Agent Systems Reference Architecture (ASRA) is an elaboration of the ASRM. It establishes relationships between the ASRM functional concepts in agent frameworks and defines patterns for these concepts. The ASRA does not address implementation specifics but rather describes possible interactions between functional concepts. A reference architecture for agent systems can be defined from the standpoint of the individual agent functionality, the agent framework, the group and agent societies, or the system-to-system interaction viewpoints. In this work, we focus on the agent frameworks because the functional concepts defined in the ASRM are largely implemented in these frameworks.

3   Serial Approach to Constructing the ASRA

We construct the ASRA by applying reverse engineering methods on sample applications built using existing open source agent frameworks. We systematically build multiple view models by analyzing popular agent framework implementations: **JADE**[2], **Cougaar**[3] and **AGLOBE**[4]. These agent frameworks were chosen for analysis because of their popularity in the agent system community and the availability of their source code and documentation.

Agent systems have a broad definition and have many applicable domains, studying a particular fielded system or class of systems may not cover all the architectural variations of a reference architecture. Therefore, we study agent frameworks rather than fielded systems or specific domains. This approach avoids the endless debate of the exact definition of an agent and *intelligence* and simply addresses the systems composed of *agents*.

Adapting the Rational/4+1 View Model.   The Rational/4+1 View Model [6,7] creates different architectural descriptions, or *views*, of software systems for different interested parties (*e.g.* system developers, business-persons, customers). Each view identifies and describes the relationships between components and concepts. Interested parties will view these relationships with different weights and significance. The views in the 4+1 Model are as follows:

– **The Logical View** describes the static structural layout of the software system from the perspective of a software developer.
– **The Process View** describes the runtime behavior of the system, including concurrency relationships and ordered tasks carried out by components of the system from the perspective of a workflow designer or manager.

---

[2] http://jade.tilab.com
[3] http://www.cougaar.org
[4] http://agents.felk.cvut.cz/aglobe

- **The Implementation View** describes the package layout of the system from the perspective of the system architect.
- **Deployment View** describes the hardware-software configurations at a platform-level as viewed by system administrators or deployment teams.
- **Scenario View** is the "+1" view that spans the other four views. This crosscutting view is composed of narrative use cases to provide an executive level view of the architecture.

The ASRA is documented using the Scenario, Process, Logical, and Implementation Views. Each ASRM functional concept is documented with these four views to cover the needs of agent system architects, developers, agent framework designers, and system users. The ASRA does not present the Deployment view because this view addresses the needs for system administrators and deployment teams.

The Serial Approach. The goal of the serial approach is to produce overlapping series of documents and diagrams detailing many views of a system from different perspectives. We document the most abstract views first and augment each with software analysis data and domain knowledge to create the next view. We mine for software architecture data by performing static and dynamic analysis of multi-agent frameworks [10].

For each functional concept defined in the ASRM apply the following process:

1. Construct the Scenario View for a functional concept. The scenario view consists of functional concept definitions from the ASRM including possible interactions with other functional concepts. The scenario view for each functional concept consists of UML use-case diagrams and/or descriptions depicting the use, role, and functionality of the concept.
2. Construct the Process View from the Scenario View. We implement a snippet of code exercising the functional concept for each agent framework. Execute this snippet of code and use the dynamic runtime analysis framework, Enterprise Java Profiler (EJP)[5], to generate trace data. With this trace data, construct a UML process diagram to illustrate a concrete architecture for the functional concept for a particular agent framework. After constructing process diagrams for each agent framework, create a new process diagram from the common features across the agent framework implementations while documenting differences as points of variation. This abstract architecture for the functional concept and the points for variation comprise the Process View.
3. Construct the Implementation View using the static analysis tools, BAT [4] to identify data flow and package/class dependencies of each functional concept. We use these software tools on the agent frameworks and code snippets from Step 2. Focusing on the code snippets allows us to bypass extraneous information such as dead code and common library dependencies. We construct a UML component diagram for each agent framework. Components represent the modules and packages and connectors represent interdependencies. Next we construct an abstract architectural package representation by identifying similar packages and modules from the concrete architectures. Different packages are documented as points of variabilion.

[5] http://ejp.sourceforge.net

4. Construct the Logical View using the Bunch clustering system [9] and the static analysis data from the previous step. The Logical View consists of UML package diagrams of a functional concept. This abstract architectural representation of a functional concept is created from the concrete architectural views of the agent frameworks. The clustered data, represented as a graph, illustrates interdependencies between components (edges) and modules (nodes) within the agent framework implementation. Highly connected modules indicate components and subsystems within an agent framework implementation. UML package diagrams depict the the concrete logical architecture of each agent framework implementation where packages are the modules and the connectors are interdependencies. Packages within other packages represent interdependencies that do not travel outside the enclosing package. From the concrete logical architectures of the agent framworks, we create an abstraction noting similarities and differences. The differences are documented as points of variation.

The result yields the agent systems reference architecture consisting of four documents for each ASRM functional concept.

4   Application of the Serial Approach

To demonstrate the serial approach, we step through the documentation process for the mobility functional concept by analyzing agent framework implementations: Jade, AGLOBE, and Cougaar.

4.1   The Scenario View for Agent Mobility

The Scenario View of the ASRA, based on the 4+1 View Model, contains scenarios and use cases of a system's architecturally significant behavior.

Mobility Definition. Mobility is the process by which an agent migrates from one executing platform instance to another. The functional concept use cases (ellipses) are depicted in a UML use-case diagram (Fig. 2). The *move agent* (moving an agent from one container to another) and the *clone agent* (making a copy of an agent in another container) use cases are invoked by the container (represented by an actor). Note, this figure also illustrates interactions between the Agent Administration and Directory Services functional concepts. For example, the clone agent use case *uses* the create agent, modify agent state use case.

4.2   The Process View for Agent Mobility

The Process view documents the runtime behavior of a functional concept based on a code snippets for each agent framework. Executing EJP on code snippets yield runtime traces. The runtime trace illustrates the percentage of time spent in methods during execution. The runtime trace (Fig. 3(a)) shows a temporal view of the mobility functional concept and illustrates the invocation points of the agent mobility functional concept. From the runtime trace, we create a UML activity diagram (Fig. 3(b)).

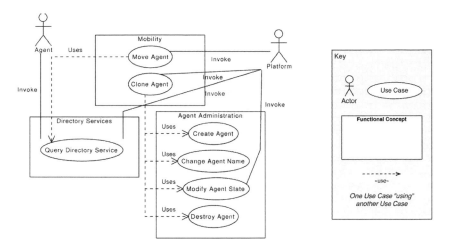

Fig. 2. The Mobility functional concept use case diagram and the interactions with the Agent Administration and Directory Services functional concept

Mobility Process View Patterns. We repeat this process for AGLOBE and Cougaar to construct similar Process diagrams. Comparing the diagrams, two patterns for agent mobility emerge. Jade and AGLOBE exhibit *Serialization mobility* (Fig. 3(c)) in which an agent's execution is paused, converted into a transferable form, transmitted to a target platform, converted into an executable form, and resuming agent's execution. Cougaar exhibits *shared-object mobility* in which agents are shared between platform containers and the agent's state is synchronized across platforms during execution. Agent mobility is achieved by changing the shared state to the new platform location.

4.3   The Implementation View for Agent Mobility

The Implementation view is the static view of the agent system derived through static code analysis tools and temporal data from the process view. UML component diagrams depict the high-level components of a functional concept and their interactions with other components and functional concepts.

Mobility Implementation View Patterns. The two patterns for Mobility from the Implementation view (Fig. 4): *serialization mobility* and *ticketing mobility*.

Jade and AGLOBE mobility follow a serialization mobility pattern (Fig. 4(a)). The Platform Discovery component uses Directory Services to find the destination platform. The Agent Encapsulation component creates a representation of the mobile agent for transport. The Messaging component delivers the mobile agent to the destination platform. Finally, the Agent Extraction component receives the mobile agent, loads it in the platform, and resumes its execution.

Cougaar mobility follows a ticketing system pattern (Fig. 4(b)). The Platform Discovery component uses the Directory Services component to find the destination platform. A Mobility Factory component generates a ticket ID to identify the destination

(a) Runtime Trace for Jade Mobility.

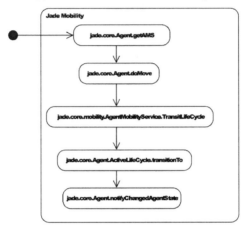

(b) Activity Diagram for Jade Mobility.

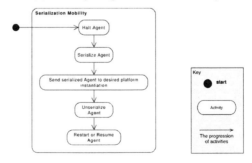

(c) Mobility Process View: Serialization Pattern.

Fig. 3. Jade Mobility runtime trace and resulting concrete architecture Process view diagram. Comparing architecture diagrams for each agent framework leads to an abstract architecture for the mobility functional concept.

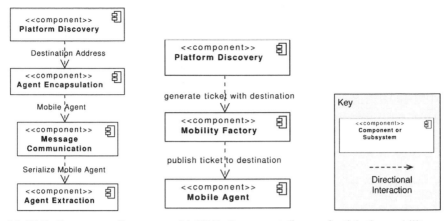

(a) UML Component diagram for serialization mobility

(b) UML Component diagram for ticketing mobility

Fig. 4. Implementation View: Two Patterns for Mobility

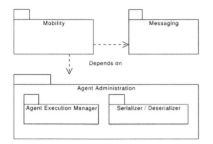

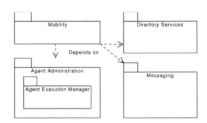

(a) Serialization paradigm: The migration component depends on the agent execution manager and serialization components of the agent controller component and the messaging component.

(b) Shared Object paradigm: The migration component depends on the directory services component, the agent controller component, and the messaging component.

Fig. 5. The Logical View: two paradigms for Mobility

platform of the mobile agent. Finally, the Mobile Agent component uses messaging functional concept to publish the ticket to the other hosts.

4.4 The Logical View for Agent Mobility

The Logical Views express the high level packages and interacting components existing in an agent system. The Logical View is constructed by observing the clustered runtime data generated from EJP and BAT and organizing the major objects into packages. This organization is represented with UML package diagrams.

Mobility Logical View Patterns. The Logical view for Mobility depicts two patterns: *Serialization Mobility* and *Shared Object Mobility*.

Jade and AGLOBE follow the serialization pattern in which the agent is converted to a transferable form before migrating the agent to its destination. The Mobility functionality (Fig. 5(a)) depends on the agent administration to pause and start the agent and messaging components to transmit the agent.

Cougaar follows the shared object mobility pattern in which the agent representation is shared among platforms. Agent mobility involves synchronizing the state of the agent then halting the agent on the source platform and initializing and executing the agent on the target instance. Shared object mobility (Fig. 5(b)) depends on the agent administration component for halting and initializing the agents, the messaging component for synchronizing the state, and directory services for finding the target platform.

5   Related Work

In developing the methodology for creating the ASRA, we studied two related areas of research: approaches and methodologies for creating a reference architecture, and reference architecture related to agent-based systems.

The multiple view presentation for the ASRA is adopted from the ISO/IEEE1471 [1] recommendation for architecture documentation. Another example of presenting a reference architecture in multiple views is the Reference Architecture Foundation for Service Oriented Architectures (RAF-SOA) [8] from the OASIS foundation. The RAF-SOA presents a reference architecture for SOA systems. Moreover, similar to the ASRA, the RAF-SOA is based on the definitions, layered OASIS reference model for service oriented architectures.

The process for creating a reference architecture for systems in a regimented manner is often addressed through analyzing existing and deployed systems. The Product Line Software Engineering, Domain-Specific Software Architecture (PuLSE-DSSA) [3] is a process for creating reference architectures in an iterative fashion. PuLSE-DSSA still depends on instantiated architectures. Architecture Structure Description Language (ASDL) also depends on existing systems to find commonalities to abstract a reference architecture. This process is does not directly aid in constructing new agent frameworks.

Reference architectures for agent-based systems has been studied to a limited extent. The FIPA Abstract Architecture Specification[6] discusses agent system architecture in an effort to promote interoperability and reusability. FIPA provides a generic view on agent systems and describes how specific functionality should interact. FIPA provides low-level details such as mechanisms for how agents perform service look-ups. The ASRA also focuses on identifying architectural paradigms and patterns in agent frameworks but focuses on the higher level, implementation-agnostic interactions.

Weyns and Holvoet [12] developed a Reference Architecture for Situated Multiagent Systems. This reference architecture focuses on the agent operating in an application environment. This architecture was developed through an interative process of analysis and validation studying different agent-based systems. In their reference architecture, the authors constructed multiple documents from different views: the module

---

[6] http://www.fipa.org/specs/fipa00001

decomposition, the shared data, and the communicating processes views. This reference architecture approach focuses on the agent in the environment whereas the ASRA address the infrastructure of the environment.

6 Conclusion and Future Work

The Agent Systems Reference Architecture (ASRA) is an ongoing effort to create a reference architecture for agent-based systems. The primary contribution of this work is the serial process for creating a reference architecture for an agent systems. This process begins with functional concepts defined by the ASRM and serially applies dynamic and static software analysis of agent framework implementations. The resulting architecture is a set of architectural views depicting relationships and structural qualities among instantiated functional components.

In future work, we will apply this process on the rest of the ASRM functional concepts to present a full architecture for agent frameworks. Moreover, we intend to extend this process to include a Deployment view of agent systems. The Deployment view presents the architecture of an agent system as it would be situated in the physical environment. Addressing how conceptual components of an agent system is beneficial to agent system architects, developers, and system integrators in identifying real-world issues in system engineering. Furthermore, we intend to address the paradigms of how agent systems interoperate with external systems (*e.g.* agents integrated with web services).

References

1. ANSI/IEEE. Recommended practice for architectural description of software-intensive systems (2009), http://www.iso-architecture.org/ieee-1471
2. Bass, L., Clements, P., Kazman, R.: Software Architecture in Practice. Addison-Wesley Professional, Reading (2003)
3. DeBaud, J.-M., Flege, O., Knauber, P.: PuLSE-DSSA – a method for the development of software reference architectures. In: ISAW 1998: Proceedings of the Third International Workshop on Software Architecture, pp. 25–28. ACM Press, New York (1998)
4. Eichberg, M.: BAT2XML: XML-based java bytecode representation. Electronic Notes in Theoretical Computer Science 141(1), 93–107 (2005); Proceedings of the First Workshop on Bytecode Semantics, Verification, Analysis and Transformation (Bytecode 2005)
5. Jennings, N.R.: An agent-based approach for building complex software systems. Commun. ACM 44(4), 35–41 (2001)
6. Kruchten, P.: Architectural blueprints—The "4+1" view model of software architecture. IEEE Software 12(6), 42–50 (1995)
7. Kruchten, P.: The rational unified process: an introduction, 3rd edn. Addison-Wesley Longman Publishing Co., Inc., Amsterdam (2003)
8. Laskey, K., Estefan, J.A., McCabe, F.G., Thornton, D.: Reference architecture foundation for service oriented architecture. Technical report, OASIS (2009), http://docs.oasis-open.org/soa-rm/soa-ra/v1.0/soa-ra.html
9. Mancoridis, S., Mitchell, B.S., Chen, Y., Gansner, E.R.: Bunch: A clustering tool for the recovery and maintenance of software system structures (August 1999)

10. Mongan, W.M., Dugan, C.J., Lass, R.N., Hight, A.K., Salvage, J., Regli, W.C., Modi, P.J.: Dynamic analysis of agent frameworks in support of a multiagent systems reference model. In: IADIS International Conference Intelligent Systems and Agents (2007)
11. Regli, W.C., Mayk, I., Dugan, C.J., Kopena, J.B., Lass, R.N., Modi, P.J., Mongan, W.M., Salvage, J.K., Sultanik, E.A.: Development and specification of a reference model for agent-based systems. IEEE Trans. On Systems, Man, and Cybernetics, Part C 39(5), 572–596 (2009)
12. Weyns, D., Holvoet, T.: A reference architecture for situated multiagent systems. In: Weyns, D., Van Dyke Parunak, H., Michel, F. (eds.) E4MAS 2006. LNCS (LNAI), vol. 4389, pp. 1–40. Springer, Heidelberg (2007)
13. Weyns, D., Parunak, H.V.D., Shehory, O.: The future of software engineering and multi-agent systems. Special Issue on Future of Software Engineering and Multi-Agent Systems, International Journal of Agent-Oriented Software Engineering, IJAOSE (2008)
14. Zhou, Y., Chen, Y., Lu, H.: UML-based systems integration modeling technique for the design and development of intelligent transportation management system. In: Proceedings of the 2004 IEEE International Conference on Systems, Man and Cybernetics. IEEE, The Hague (2004)

A Middleware Model in Alloy
for Supply Chain-Wide Agent Interactions

Robrecht Haesevoets, Danny Weyns, Mario Henrique Cruz Torres,
Alexander Helleboogh, Tom Holvoet, and Wouter Joosen

Distrinet, Katholieke Universiteit Leuven, 3001 Leuven, Belgium
robrecht.haesevoets@cs.kuleuven.be

Abstract. To support the complex coordination activities involved in
supply chain management, more and more companies have autonomous
software agents acting on their behalf. Due to confidentiality concerns,
such as hiding sensitive information from competitors, agents typically
only have a local view on the supply chain. In many situations, however,
companies would like to expand the view of their agents to share valuable
information such as transportation tracking and service delays. Non of
the participating companies, however, has enough knowledge or authority
to realize such interactions in a controlled manner.

In this paper, we present an organization middleware that offers a collaboration platform and enables agents to interact across the boundary
of local interactions. Policies and laws enable companies to define the
scope of interactions of their agents and the restrictions on their exposed
information. Using Alloy, we formally define the relation between the
interactions offered by the middleware, the exposed information and the
provided policies and laws. This allows us to guarantee a number properties which are of particular interest to companies using the middleware.

Keywords: Organisations and institutions; Social and organizational
structure; Verification of MAS.

1   Introduction

In today's competitive and globalized market, streamlined collaborations between business entities are a necessity. In the DiCoMas project[1], a joint research
effort with academic and industrial partners, we have been studying the use of
agents for managing collaborations between business entities in the domain of
supply chain management. A key objective of this project is to improve integration and collaboration among supply chain partners.

Due to company-specific restrictions, such as hiding sensitive data from competitors or having clients exchange pricing info with subcontractors, companies
typically only allow their agents to participate in local supply chain interactions [14]. As a result, agents only have a local view on the supply chain. Nevertheless, in many situations companies would like to extend the view of their

---

[1] DiCoMas: Distributed Collaboration using Multi-agent System Architectures:
http://distrinet.cs.kuleuven.be/projects/dicomas/index.html

D. Weyns and M.-P. Gleizes (Eds.): AOSE 2010, LNCS 6788, pp. 189–204, 2011.

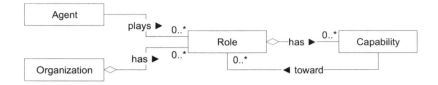

Fig. 1. A visual representation of the organization model

agents and allow them to participate in supply chain-wide interactions in a controlled manner. Examples are tracking containers throughout the supply chain or monitoring problems such as delays outside the local view of agents.

A typical way to structure such interactions between agents is by means of roles and organizations [9,1]. In previous work [17], we have presented an organization model for collaborative multi-agent systems. Although the model is relatively simple, it is powerful enough to model controlled supply chain-wide interactions. A subset of the model is shown in Fig. 1. The core abstractions of the model are organization, role, and capability. Organizations, defined as a set of roles, specify the boundaries in which controlled interactions can take place. A role represents a concrete participation in the organization. It defines the agents that have access to the organization, and it defines the capabilities these agents have in the organization. Each capability represents a concrete interaction ability relative to another role in the organization.

Realizing organizations and managing their dynamics in a heterogeneous and distributed supply chain setting is a very complex task, for which none of the participating companies has enough authority or knowledge. Additionally, companies want guarantees before exposing confidential information or allowing their agents to collaborate with external parties.

To address these challenges we present an organization middleware approach. The middleware offers organizations and roles as a set of reusable programming abstractions to application developers. At run-time, the middleware realizes a collaboration platform. Agents provide the middleware with local information on the supply chain, and in return, the middleware offers managed organizations that enable agents to engage in supply-wide interactions in a controlled way. Companies can specify interaction laws to define the desired scope of interactions for their agents and a set of policies to restrict the information they expose, in order to deal with confidentiality concerns. These laws and policies will then be enforced by the middleware.

The use of organizational abstractions together with a middleware has a number of key benefits: (1) it allows to represent and structure supply chain-wide interactions at a high-level of abstraction; (2) it allows to separate the management of dynamic supply chain-wide interactions, performed by the middleware, from the actual functionality, provided by agents participating in the interactions; (3) it allows to accurately restrict the interactions between agents according to provided policies in terms of capabilities.

The contributions of this paper are:

1. We motivate and specify a set of concrete requirements for supply chain-wide interactions in the domain of logistics for supply chain management.
2. We present a formal model in the Alloy specification language [8] of an organization middleware supporting supply chain-wide interactions. The model formally defines the relation between supply chain-wide interactions enabled by the organizations offered by the middleware and the local supply chain information exposed by the agents and the provided policies.
3. We assert a number of relevant properties offering companies formal guarantees in terms of confidentiality using the model and the Alloy Analyzer.

Overview of this paper. Section 2 introduces a running example together with a set of requirements for supply chain-wide interactions. The organization middleware is presented in Sect. 3 and illustrated in the running example. Section 4 presents the middleware model in Alloy and shows how the Alloy Analyzer can be used to assert a number of properties. Finally, related work is discussed in Sect. 5, and Sect. 6 concludes and reflects on future work.

2 Logistics in Supply Chain Management

In the domain of supply chain management, companies usually outsource their logistic activities to one or more specialized third-party logistics providers (3PL). To integrate and streamline the operations of different 3PLs, an extra level of outsourcing can be introduced, called fourth-party logistics providers (4PL). Figure 2 shows an example of a hierarchical outsourcing structure in a supply chain, used as a running example in this paper. In the example, several companies collaborate to realize the logistic needs of company 0. Company 0 has an outsourcing contract with company 1, which as acts as a 4PL and integrates the services of two 3PLs, company 2 and 3. Company 2, in turn, has two additional subcontractors, company 4 and 5. In the example, company 3 is currently carrying a container of company 0, and company 4 and 5 are expecting a delay.

Due to confidentiality concerns, companies only allow their agents to participate in local interactions corresponding to active outsourcing contracts. As a result, agents only have a local view on the supply chain. Typical supply chain flows, such as information and services, are propagated through the supply chain

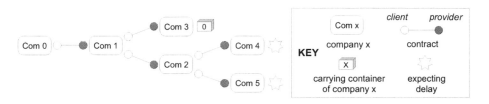

Fig. 2. Supply chain collaborations

based on local interactions. In the DiCoMas project, we aim to enhance the integration and collaboration of the supply chain partners to improve information sharing and responsiveness. To realize this, agents acting on behalf of companies need extended views on the supply chain and have to interact across the supply chain in a controlled way. We give a number of concrete stakeholder requirements that motivate the need for supply chain-wide interactions. For clarity, the requirements are explained in the context of the running example.

Collaborative Planning. To create a planning in correspondence with the individual goals of each stakeholder, company 1 wants to use a collaborative planning approach. This requires agents of both clients, such as company 0, and subcontractors, such as company 2 and 3, to participate in coordinated planning and negotiation activities, while company 1 maintains a supervising position and can enforce the necessary restrictions on the involved interactions.

Traceability. Company 0 wants to track the location and status of its containers throughout the supply chain. Instead of having to contact its service provider, company 1, who in turn has to contact other service providers, company 2 or 3, and so on, company 0 requires it agents to directly interact with the agents of the current carriers of its containers, increasing responsiveness and reducing overhead. Using policies, intermediate companies such as company 1 should be able to restrict the information that can be exposed to company 0.

Improved Responsiveness in Case of Problems. As a 4PL, Company 1 wants its agents to be directly informed by agents managing third-party resources when serious problems occur, such as delays or decommitment. This enables company 1 to anticipate future problems at a supply chain-wide level and offer its clients a higher quality of service. Intermediate companies should be able to restrict the information exposed by their subcontractors.

3   The Organization Middleware

The previous section introduced a number of stakeholder requirements that underpin the need for supply chain-wide interactions. Such interactions can be modeled and coordinated using organizational abstractions we introduced in [17]. In this section we present an organization middleware that offers such organizations and roles as a set of reusable programming abstractions to application developers. At runtime, the middleware provides a collaboration platform and takes the responsibility of managing organizations and their dynamics, for which non of the partners in a supply chain has enough authority or knowledge.

Figure 3 gives a high-level overview of the approach. To participate, agents of supply chain companies have to provide the middleware with context information and a set of interaction laws. In return, the middleware offers agents a broader view on the supply chain and support for supply chain-wide interactions, while taking the responsibility of managing the interactions and their dynamics. Using a middleware allows us to separate the management of the organizations from the agents, who can now focus on realizing the functionality in organizations.

Fig. 3. High-level overview of the approach

Internally the middleware can be realized using different technologies including agents. Agents using the middleware have to conform to certain communication standards, which are outside the scope of the current model.

In the remainder of this section we first explain the notions of context and interaction laws in more detail. We then show how context and laws can be used by the middleware to offer organizations that enable controlled supply chain-wide interactions in the running example.

3.1 Context Information and Interaction Laws

Agents have to provide the middleware with local information on the supply chain, consisting of context and interaction laws. The completeness of the context depends on the amount of information exposed by the agents on behalf of the companies. Context includes information on companies, their dynamic properties, such as containers currently carried or expected delays, the current outsourcing contracts between companies, and a set of flow policies. Flow policies define the allowed supply chain flows between agents of particular companies. We currently consider two types of flows: information flow and service flow. These allow companies to specify which information exchange and which concrete service provision can take place between which specific companies. Flow policies are specified at the level of outsourcing contracts as allowed flows within outsourcing contracts as well as between different contracts. An example is shown in Fig. 4, illustrating how flow policies of different companies create a graph-like structure defining the allowed information and service flows at a supply chain-wide level.

Interaction laws allow companies to define in a declarative way the desired scope of the supply chain-wide interactions for their agents. In particular, an interaction law specifies a desired set of interaction partners whose agents should be allowed to participate in the interaction, such as "all providers of a company" or "all companies carrying a specific container", as well as the supply chain flows the interaction should enable between these partners.

3.2 Realizing Supply Chain-Wide Interactions

The middleware uses the interaction laws together with the current context to provide a set of organizations supporting the desired supply chain-wide interactions. Each organizations enables a set of interactions, defined by the capabilities of its role and each capability enables a specific supply chain flow toward another role in the organization in correspondence with the current flow policies. As context or laws change, the middleware adapts the organizations accordingly.

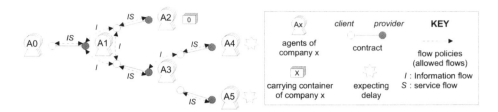

Fig. 4. Context consisting of flow policies and outsourcing contracts

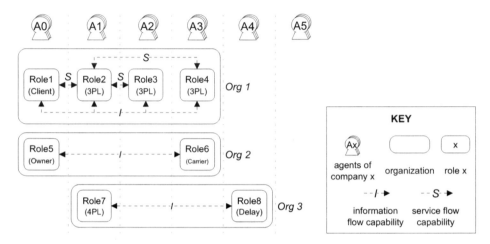

Fig. 5. Examples of organizations and roles realizing supply chain-wide interactions

Figure 5 illustrates a set of organizations realizing the requirements for supply chain-wide interactions introduced in Sect. 2 for the running example. Organization 1 illustrates collaborative planning, enabling the agents of client 0 to exchange planning information with the agents of subcontractors 2 and 3. Role capabilities, compliant with the flow policies, show that company 1, as a 4PL, remains in a supervising position, ensuring clients have no capabilities to make any direct service requests to subcontractors. Organization 2 shows the tracking of a container throughout the supply chain, enabling the agents of company 0 to interact with the carrier of their container, the agents of company 3. Improved responsiveness is exemplified by organization 3, allowing agents of company 1 to interact with the agents of company 4, which is expecting a delay. Because company 2 wants to hide its internal outsourcing strategy, it does not allow any flows between company 5 and other parties, as illustrated in Fig. 4. As a result, company 5 is excluded from organization 3, although it is also expecting a delay.

4   Middleware Model in Alloy

In this section we give a formal model of the middleware abstractions using the Alloy specification language. Alloy [8] is a structural modeling language based on first-order logic for expressing complex structural constraints and behavior in software systems. The Alloy Analyzer[2] is a constraint solver, supporting automatic simulation and checking of Alloy models within a specific scope. Simulation consists of finding instances satisfying a specification, while checking consists of finding counter examples violating certain assumptions about a model. The Alloy analysis is based on the notion of *small scope hypothesis* [8], assuming that assertions checked within a well-chosen scope will also hold for larger scopes. However, with a well-chosen scope and model, it can even be possible to do a complete analysis for a specific setting.

The purpose of our formal model in Alloy is threefold: (1) present a rigorous specification of the main concepts of the organization middleware; (2) formally define which supply chain-wide interactions the middleware can and should provide, given the context and a set of interaction laws; (3) show how this model can be used together with the Alloy analyzer to guarantee a number of properties in terms of confidentiality constraints.

4.1   Middleware Model

The middleware model is shown in Spec. 1. Some parts of the model are omitted, but can be found in Appendix A. An executable version of the model is also available for download[3]. Every concepts is represented by *signature*. In Alloy, a signature introduces a new set of atoms in the universe (*univ*) of the model (the universal set *univ* contains all atoms of the model).

Context Information. Context information consists of information on companies, their dynamic properties and their flow policies. We start by defining the signatures *Company* and *Contract* to represent companies and their outsourcing contracts. *Company* has one *field*, named *properties*, mapping each company to a set of properties, defined by the signature *Property*. *Contract* has three fields, two disjunct companies representing the client and provider in the contract, and a field *flows* mapping each contract to the set of supply chain flows that are allowed to take place within the contract. Supply chain flows are defined by the signature *Flow*. Subtypes *Info* and *Service* represent some of the typical supply chain flows, but more expressive subtypes can be introduced.

On line 11 the signature *context* defines the context of the middleware as a set of companies, contracts and flow policies. Flow policies are defined on line 14[4] as ternary relations which specify the allowed flows between different contracts. For example, `Info->c1->c2` represents a flow policy allowing information to flow from contract `c1` to contract `c2`. A signature fact on line 16[5] introduces an additional constraint to ensure companies can only define flow policies between

---

[2] Alloy Analyzer 4 - `http://alloy.mit.edu/alloy4/`

[3] `http://people.cs.kuleuven.be/~robrecht.haesevoets/AOSE2010/`

[4] The field *flowPolicies* can refer to multiple flow policies. The Alloy syntax does not require the *set* keyword for relations.

[5] The *box join* `a[b]` is the equivalent of the relational join `b.a`. The `+` sign represents the union of two sets while the `&` sign represents the intersection.

Specification 1. Middleware Model (partial)

```
1  sig Company{
2    properties:set Property
3  }
4  sig Contract{
5    disj client,provider:Company,
6    flows:set Flow
7  }
8  sig Property{}
9  abstract sig Flow{}
10 one sig Info,Service extends Flow{}
11 sig Context{
12   companies:set Company,
13   contracts:set Contract,
14   flowPolicies:Flow->contracts->contracts
15 }{
16   all c1,c2:Contract | c1->c2 in flowPolicies[univ] implies
17     some c1.(client+provider) & c2.(client+provider)
18 }
19 fun allowedFlows[context:Context]:Flow->Company->Company{
20   {flow:Flow,com1,com2:Company | some c1,c2:context.contracts |
21     flow in c1.flows & c2.flows and
22     com1+com2 in (c1+c2).(client+provider) and
23     c2 in c1.*(flows.flow<:context.flowPolicies[flow].>flows.flow)}
24 }
25 sig Law{
26   scope:Flow->Company->Company
27 }
28 fun propertyBasedSelection[p:Property, vp:Company, context:Context]:set Company{
29   {c:Company | p in c.properties and Info->c->vp in allowedFlows[context]}
30 }
31 sig Role{
32   company:Company,
33   capabilities:Role->Flow
34 }
35 sig Organization{
36   roles:set Role
37 }
38 fun enabledFlows[org:Organization]:Flow->Company->Company{
39   {flow:Flow,com1,com2:Company | some r1,r2:org.roles |
40     r1.company = com1 and r2.company = com2 and r2->flow in r1.capabilities}
41 }
42 sig MiddlewareModel{
43   context:Context,
44   laws:set Law,
45   orgs:set Organization
46 }{
47   enabledFlows[orgs] = laws.scope & allowedFlows[context]
48 }
```

their own contracts. We also define a help function *allowedFlows* on line 19^6 which returns the supply chain flows that are allowed between companies by the contracts and flow policies in the given context.

Example: Specification 2 shows an example of context corresponding to the setting shown in Fig. 4. There are six companies and five contracts between these companies. All contracts allow information and service flows. *Company2* is carrying a container of *Company0* and both *Company4* and *Company5* are expecting a delay. The context also specifies a set of flow policies that allow information to flow between *Contract01* and *Contract12*, *Contract01* and *Contract13*, *Contract12* and *Contract13*, and *Contract13* and *Contract34*.

Specification 2. An example of context specified in the middleware model

```
1
2    ...
3    one sig Context1 extends Context{
4    }{
5       companies = Company0 + Company1 + Company2 + Company3 + Company4 +
6                   Company5
7       contracts = Contract01 + Contract12 + Contract13 + Contract34 +
8                   Contract35
9       Contract01.client = Company0 and Contract01.provider = Company1
10      Contract12.client = Company1 and Contract12.provider = Company2
11      ...
12      Contract01.flows = Info + Service
13      Contract12.flows = Info + Service
14      ...
15      Company2.properties = CarryingContainerOfCompany0
16      Company4.properties = ExpectingDelay
17      Company5.properties = ExpectingDelay
18      flowPolicies = Info->Contract01->Contract12 +
19                     Info->Contract12->Contract01 +
20                     Info->Contract01->Contract13 +
21                     Info->Contract13->Contract01 +
22                     Info->Contract13->Contract34 +
23                     Info->Contract34->Contract13
24   }
```

Interaction Laws. Interaction laws are represented by the signature *Law* on line 25. The field *scope* specifies the desired scope of interaction, as the set of supply chain-wide flows the interaction should enable between companies. To represent a meaningful scope of interaction, functions can be used which use the

---

[6] The set comprehension {a: A | constraint} returns all elements of *A* satisfying the given constraint. *a represents the reflexive transitive closure. <: and :> represent the domain and range restriction of a relation.

current context as input. An example is the property-based selection function on line 28, which returns all companies having a given property p and that are visible from the given viewpoint vp.

Example: Specification 3 shows an example of three laws, corresponding to the organizations shown in Fig. 5. *Law1* specifies an interaction scope between *Company0*, *Company1*, *Company2* and *Company3*. *Law2* uses the property-based selection function to specify an interaction scope between *Company0* and the companies carrying its containers. *Law3* specifies an interaction scope between *Company1* and the companies expecting a delay.

Specification 3. An example of interaction laws specified in the middleware model

```
1   ...
2   one sig Law1 extends Law{
3   }{
4     scope = (Info+Service)->Company0->Company1 +
5             (Info+Service)->Company1->Company0 +
6             Info->Company0->Company2 +
7             ...
8   }
9   one sig Law2 extends Law{
10  }{
11    scope = Info->propertyBasedSelection[CarryingContainer,
12                                          Company0,
13                                          Context1]->Company0 +
14            ...
15  }
16  one sig Law1 extends Law{
17  }{
18    scope = Info->propertyBasedSelection[ExpectingDelay,
19                                          Company1,
20                                          Context1]->Company1 +
21            ...
22  }
```

Roles and Organizations. Roles and organizations are defined on lines 31 and 35. Each role has a field *company*, mapping the role to the company whose agents are allowed to play the role, and a field *capabilities*, representing the capabilities of the role in terms of supply chain flows allowed toward other roles in the organization. Organizations contain the field *roles* representing the current roles of the organization. We also define a help function *enabledFlows* which returns the flows between companies that are enabled by a given organization.

Example: Specification 4 shows a specification of the organizations in Fig. 5. Each role has a company and a set of capabilities. For example, *Role1* is played by *Company1* and has capabilities for information and service flow with *Role2*, and capabilities for information flow with *Role3* and *Role4*.

Specification 4. An example of organizations in the middleware model

```
 1  one sig Role1 extends Role{
 2  }{
 3    company = Company0
 4    capabilities = Role2->(Info+Service) +
 5                   (Role3+Role4)->Info
 6  }
 7  ...
 8  one sig Org1 extends Organization{
 9  }{
10    roles = Role1 + Role2 + Role3 + Role4
11  }
12  one sig Org2 extends Organization{
13  }{
14    roles = Role5 + Role6
15  }
16  one sig Org3 extends Organization{
17  }{
18    roles = Role7 + Role8
19  }
20
```

Middleware Model. The state of the middleware is represented by the signature *MiddlewareModel* on line 42. This state is defined as the current context and interaction laws, and the organizations offered by the middleware. A signature fact on line 47 uses the two help functions, we defined earlier, to specify the relation between the organizations offered by the middleware and the current context and interaction laws. The fact specifies that organizations offered by the middleware should enable those, and only those, supply chain flows between companies that are both defined by the scope of the interaction laws and allowed within the current context and its flow policies.

Example: Specification 5 the specification of a middleware model with the context and laws we specified in the previous examples. The application of the laws to the context results in a set of organizations (Org1 + Org2 + Org3), which were illustrated in the previous example.

Specification 5. An example of a specific middleware model

```
 1  one sig MiddlewareModel1 extends MiddlewareModel{
 2  }{
 3    context = Context1
 4    laws = Law1 + Law2 + Law3
 5  }
```

4.2   Asserting Properties

Using the Alloy Analyzer, we can check a number of useful properties of our model. We focus on two relevant properties: (1) asserting that the middleware only offers organizations compliant with the current context; (2) asserting that companies *can* put forward a number of confidentiality constraints, by restricting the supply chain flows in the outsourcing hierarchy. The Alloy specification of these properties is shown in Spec. 6[7]. Both properties have been checked by the Alloy analyzer within a scope of 6 atoms for each type. Although this scope is limited, it covers more than all the possibilities in our running example.

The first property states that companies always need some direct or indirect contractual link, known to the middleware, before their agents can participate in any supply chain-wide interaction. The second property states that a company (*com3*) can restrict all supply chain-wide interactions between any two companies (*com1* and *com2*) that do not have a direct or indirect contractual link with each other independent from the restricting company (*com3*). This property ensures, for example, that 3PLs, such as company 2 in Fig. 4, can restrict the information their subcontractors can expose, such as company 4 and 5. In the example, company 2 allows company 4 to expose information in supply chain-wide interactions, but restricts this for company 5. As a result, the agents of company 1 can participate in an interaction with the agents of company 4, expecting a delay, but not with the agents of company 5, also expecting a delay.

Specification 6. Properties

```
1  check property1{
2    all mw:MiddlewareModel, disj com1,com2:Company |
3      !contractPath[com1,com2,mw.context] implies
4      no role1,role2:mw.orgs.roles | role1.company = com1 and
5      role2.company = com2 and role2 in role1.capabilities.univ
6  } for 6
7  check property2{
8    all mw:MiddlewareModel, disj com1,com2,com3:Company |
9      !indepContractPath[com1,com2,com3,mw.context] and
10     (all c1,c2:(client+provider).com3 |
11       no Flow->c1->c2 & mw.context.flowPolicies) implies
12     no r1,r2:mw.orgs.roles | some r2->Flow & r1.capabilities
13       and r1.company = com1 and r2.company = com2
14 } for 6
```

---

[7] contractPath[com1,com2,context] returns true if a path from com1 to com2 exists in the contractual structure of the given context. indepContract-Path[com1,com2,com3,context] returns true if a path exists independent from com3.

5   Related Work

The approach presented in this paper intersects with several domains of related work. We focus on a number of representative approaches for business to business (B2B) integration in supply chain management, roles and organizations, organization middleware and formal methods for organizations in multi-agent systems.

B2B Integration in Supply Chain Management. Several approaches have been proposed to address the integration of business processes in supply chain management. Preist et al. [13] recognize the problems of setting up interactions between agents of different supply chain partners, and propose a Web service architecture providing automated B2B integration. Stefansson [15] stresses the importance of automated information sharing in supply chains, but also states the lack of scientific research covering the management of information flows within supply chains. Projects, such as CrossFlow [5], have explored the integration of business process between outsourcing partners using cross-organizational workflow management and virtual organizations. In contrast to the work presented in this paper, these approaches typically focus on the local integration of business processes, lacking explicit support for setting up and managing supply chain-wide interactions.

Roles and Organizations. Roles and organizations are generally acknowledged as valuable abstractions to structure complex interactions [9,1]. Two particular lines of related research are electronic institutions [4] and Law-Governed Interactions [10]. Both approaches use laws, norms or policies to govern interactions among agents. Most of the existing approaches, however, put the responsibility of managing organizations with the agents, such as AGRE [3] and TuCSoN [11]. The organization middleware presented in this paper encapsulates the management of organizations as a reusable service. This greatly enhances the portability of our approach and can reduce the complexity of developing and maintaining the agents themselves. An interesting approach to support the development of the organization middleware is the A&A meta-model proposed by Omicini et al. [12].

Organization Middleware. A number of approaches propose middleware-supported organizations and interactions, such as AMELI [2], S-moise+ and ORA4MAS [7], and Law-Governed Interactions [10]. However, most other approaches take an agent-centric perspective in which agents are responsible for performing the functions in organization and managing life cycle of organizations. Novelty toward e-institutions and norm-based approaches is two-folded: (1) Flow policies can specify *local restrictions* on agent interactions. E-institutions and norm-based approaches typically use global norms rather than company-specific and context-aware restrictions. (2) Implementations of norm-based approaches often rely on central entities enforcing norms, e.g. managers in AMELI and S-Moise+. Our model could also support decentralized realizations [18].

Formal Methods for Organizations. Formalization is recognized as a foundation for analyzing properties such as structure and stability of organizations [1,16].

Most approaches focus on theoretical aspects of organizations, relying on heavy-weight formal methods. Grossi et al. [6], for example, represent organizations as multi-graphs. By adding formal semantics to the graphs, different organizational structures can be compared in terms of performance, flexibility and efficiency. In this paper, we presented a model in Alloy and focused on the management of organizations and domain specific concerns, such as confidentiality. Because Alloy is limited, both in terms of expressiveness and the ability to analyze complex models, alternative approaches such as temporal logic and Petri nets may be more appropriate to explore run-time issues of organizations or complex interaction protocols.

6   Conclusions and Future Work

We have made the case for using an organization middleware to support supply chain-wide interactions in the domain of supply chain management. The organization middleware realizes a collaboration platform and offers organization and role as reusable abstractions to enhance the integration of different business processes. Although we applied our approach to a specific case in logistics management, we have shown how a limited set of organizational abstractions and a light-weight formal modeling language can be used to offer formal guarantees in terms of confidentiality constraints, such as the ability of companies to restrict the interactions between their subcontractors. These guarantees can contribute in establishing the trust of companies in such a middleware approach.

The organizational abstractions, used by the middleware, have proved powerful enough to structure supply chain-wide interactions at a high-level, and enable the separation of managing the interactions and their dynamics from providing the actual functionality provided in the interactions itself. But most importantly, they allow to accurately restrict the interactions among agents, according to company-specific confidentiality constraints.

A prototype implementation of the middleware is also available on the web[8], showing a visual representation of the approach within a controlled setting. Using a web-based GUI, users are able to set up a number of supply chain-wide interactions and dynamically alter the context, flow policies and laws.

Future work. A number of concerns are not addressed by our current model such as dealing with incomplete and incorrect information, security and authentication, and explicit support for interaction protocols, such as automated auctions. Other interesting future directions include a domain specific policy language and integrating the model into a development process.

Acknowledgement

This research is supported by the Foundation for Scientific Research in Flanders (FWO-Vlaanderen), the Interuniversity Attraction Poles Programme Belgian State, Belgian Science Policy, and the Research Fund K.U.Leuven.

---

[8] http://people.cs.kuleuven.be/~robrecht.haesevoets/AOSE2010/

References

1. Dignum, V.: Handbook of Research on Multi-Agent Systems: Semantics and Dynamics of Organizational Models. Information Science Reference (2009)
2. Esteva, M., Rosell, B., Rodriguez-Aguilar, J., Arcos, J.: Ameli: An Agent-Based Middleware for Electronic Institutions. In: AAMAS 2004, pp. 236–243. IEEE Computer Society, Washington, DC (2004)
3. Ferber, J., Michel, F., Baez, J.: AGRE: Integrating environments with organizations. In: Weyns, D., Van Dyke Parunak, H., Michel, F. (eds.) E4MAS 2004. LNCS (LNAI), vol. 3374, pp. 48–56. Springer, Heidelberg (2005)
4. Garcia-Camino, A., Noriega, P., Rodrguez-Aguilar, J.: Implementing norms in electronic institutions. In: AAMAS 2005, pp. 667–673. ACM Press, New York (2005)
5. Grefen, P., Aberer, K., Hoffner, Y., Ludwig, H.: CrossFlow: Cross-organizational workflow management in dynamic virtual enterprises. Computer Systems Science and Engineering 15(5), 277–290 (2000)
6. Grossi, D., Dignum, F., Dignum, V., Dastani, M., Royakkers, L.: Structural aspects of the evaluation of agent organizations. In: Noriega, P., Vázquez-Salceda, J., Boella, G., Boissier, O., Dignum, V., Fornara, N., Matson, E. (eds.) COIN 2006. LNCS (LNAI), vol. 4386, pp. 3–18. Springer, Heidelberg (2007)
7. Hübner, J.F., Boissier, O., Kitio, R., Ricci, A.: Instrumenting Multi-Agent Organisations with Organisational Artifacts and Agents. Autonomous Agents and Multi-Agent Systems, 1–32
8. Jackson, D.: Software Abstractions: logic, language, and analysis. The MIT Press, Cambridge (2006)
9. Jennings, N.R.: On agent-based software engineering. Artificial Intelligence 177(2), 277–296 (2000)
10. Minsky, N., Ungureanu, V.: Law-Governed Interaction: A Coordination and Control Mechanism for Heterogeneous Distributed Systems. ACM TOSEM 9(3) (2000)
11. Omicini, A., Ricci, A.: Reasoning about organisation: Shaping the infrastructure. AI* IA Notizie 16(2), 7–16 (2003)
12. Omicini, A., Ricci, A., Viroli, M.: Artifacts in the A&A Meta-Model for Multi-Agent Systems. Autonomous Agents and Multi-Agent Systems 17(3), 432–456 (2008)
13. Preist, C., Esplugas-Cuadrado, J., Battle, S., Grimm, S., Williams, S.: Automated business-to-business integration of a logistics supply chain using semantic web services technology. In: Gil, Y., Motta, E., Benjamins, V.R., Musen, M.A. (eds.) ISWC 2005. LNCS, vol. 3729, pp. 987–1001. Springer, Heidelberg (2005)
14. Stadtler, H.: Supply chain management and advanced planning: basics, overview and challenges. European Journal of Operational Research 163(3), 575–588 (2005)
15. Stefansson, G.: Business-to-business data sharing: A source for integration of supply chains. International Journal of Production Economics 75(1-2), 135–146 (2002)
16. Van Den Broek, E., Jonker, C., Sharpanskykh, A., Treur, J., Yolum, P.: Formal modeling and analysis of organizations. In: Boissier, O., Padget, J., Dignum, V., Lindemann, G., Matson, E., Ossowski, S., Sichman, J.S., Vázquez-Salceda, J. (eds.) ANIREM 2005 and OOOP 2005. LNCS (LNAI), vol. 3913, pp. 18–34. Springer, Heidelberg (2006)
17. Weyns, D., Haesevoets, R., Helleboogh, A., Holvoet: The macodo organization model for context-driven dynamic agent organzations. ACM Transaction on Autonomous and Adaptive Systems 6(4) (2010)

204   R. Haesevoets et al.

18. Weyns, D., Haesevoets, R., Helleboogh, A., Holvoet, T., Joosen, W.: The MACODO Middleware for Context-Driven Dynamic Agent Organzations. ACM Transaction on Autonomous and Adaptive Systems 5(1), 3:1–3:29 (2010)

A   Omitted Parts of the Middleware Model

```
1  fun contractualLinks[context:Context]:Company->Company{
2    {disj com1,com2:Company |
3      some c:context.contracts | com1+com2 in c.(client+provider)}
4  }
5
6  pred contractualPath[com1,com2:Company, context:Context]{
7    com2 in com1.*(contractualLinks[context])
8  }
9
10 pred indepContractualPath[c1,c2,dependence:Company,context:Context]{
11   let indepContractualLinks =
12     (Company-dependence)<:contractualLinks[context]:>(Company-dependence) |
13   c2 in c1.*indepContractualLinks
14 }
```

A Delegation-Based Architecture
for Collaborative Robotics*

Patrick Doherty, Fredrik Heintz, and David Landén

Linköping University
Dept. of Computer and Information Science
581 83 Linköping, Sweden
{patrick.doherty,fredrik.heintz}@liu.se

Abstract. Collaborative robotic systems have much to gain by leveraging results from the area of multi-agent systems and in particular agent-oriented software engineering. Agent-oriented software engineering has much to gain by using collaborative robotic systems as a testbed. In this article, we propose and specify a formally grounded generic collaborative system shell for robotic systems and human operated ground control systems. Collaboration is formalized in terms of the concept of delegation and delegation is instantiated as a speech act. Task Specification Trees are introduced as both a formal and pragmatic characterization of tasks and tasks are recursively delegated through a delegation process implemented in the collaborative system shell. The delegation speech act is formally grounded in the implementation using Task Specification Trees, task allocation via auctions and distributed constraint problem solving. The system is implemented as a prototype on Unmanned Aerial Vehicle systems and a case study targeting emergency service applications is presented.

1 Introduction

In the past decade, the Unmanned Aircraft Systems Technologies Lab[1] at the Department of Computer and Information Science, Linköping University, has been involved in the development of autonomous unmanned aerial vehicles (UAV's) and associated hardware and software technologies [14–16]. The size of our research platforms range from the RMAX helicopter system (100kg) [8, 17, 59, 66, 69] developed by Yamaha Motor Company, to smaller micro-size rotor based systems such as the LinkQuad[2] (1kg) and LinkMAV [28, 60] (500g) in addition to a fixed wing platform, the PingWing [9] (500g). These UAV platforms are shown in Figure 1.The latter three have been designed and developed by the Unmanned Aircraft Systems Technologies Lab. All four platforms are fully autonomous and have been deployed.

---

* This work is partially supported by grants from the Swedish Research Council (VR) Linnaeus Center CADICS, VR grant 90385701, the ELLIIT Excellence Center at Linköping-Lund for Information Technology, NFFP5-The Swedish National Aviation Engineering Research Program, and the Center for Industrial Information Technology CENIIT.

[1] www.ida.liu.se/divisions/aiics/
[2] www.uastech.com

D. Weyns and M.-P. Gleizes (Eds.): AOSE 2010, LNCS 6788, pp. 205–247, 2011.

Fig. 1. The UASTech RMAX (upper left), PingWing (upper right), LinkQuad (lower left) and LinkMAV (lower right)

Previous work has focused on the development of robust autonomous systems for UAV's which seamlessly integrate control, reactive and deliberative capabilities that meet the requirements of hard and soft realtime constraints [17, 55]. Additionally, we have focused on the development and integration of many high-level autonomous capabilities studied in the area of cognitive robotics such as task planners [18, 19], motion planners [66–68], execution monitors [21], and reasoning systems [20, 23, 54], in addition to novel middleware frameworks which support such integration [40, 42, 43]. Although research with individual high-level cognitive functionalities is quite advanced, robust integration of such capabilities in robotic systems which meet real-world constraints is less developed but essential to introduction of such robotic systems into society in the future. Consequently, our research has focused, not only on such high-level cognitive functionalities, but also on system integration issues.

More recently, our research efforts have transitioned toward the study of systems of UAV's. The accepted terminology for such systems is Unmanned Aircraft Systems (UAS's). A UAS may consist of one or more UAV's (possibly heterogenous) in addition to one or more ground operator systems (GOP's). We are interested in applications where UAV's are required to collaborate not only with each other but also with diverse human resources [22, 24, 25, 41, 52]. UAV's are now becoming technologically mature enough to be integrated into civil society. Principled interaction between UAV's and human resources is an essential component in the future uses of UAV's in complex emergency services or bluelight scenarios. Some specific target UAS scenario examples are search and rescue missions for inhabitants lost in wilderness regions and assistance in guiding them to a safe destination; assistance in search at sea scenarios; assistance in more devastating scenarios such as earthquakes, flooding or forest fires; and environmental monitoring.

As UAV's become more autonomous, mixed-initiative interaction between human operators and such systems will be central in mission planning and tasking. By mixed-initiative, we mean that interaction and negotiation between one or more UAV's and one or more humans will take advantage of each of their skills, capacities and knowledge in developing a mission plan, executing the plan and adapting to contingencies during the execution of the plan.

In the future, the practical use and acceptance of UAV's will have to be based on a verifiable, principled and well-defined interaction foundation between one or more human operators and one or more autonomous systems. In developing a principled framework for such complex interaction between UAV's and humans in complex scenarios, a great many interdependent conceptual and pragmatic issues arise and need clarification not only theoretically, but also pragmatically in the form of demonstrators. Additionally, an iterative research methodology is essential which combines foundational theory, systems building and empirical testing in real-world applications from the start.

The complexity of developing deployed architectures for realistic collaborative activities among robots that operate in the real world under time and space constraints is very high. We tackle this complexity by working both abstractly at a formal logical level and concretely at a systems building level. More importantly, the two approaches are related to each other by grounding the formal abstractions into actual software implementations. This guarantees the fidelity of the actual system to the formal specification. Bridging this conceptual gap robustly is an important area of research and given the complexity of the systems being built today demands new insights and techniques.

The conceptual basis for the proposed collaboration framework includes a triad of fundamental, interdependent conceptual issues: delegation, mixed-initiative interaction and adjustable autonomy (Figure 2). The concept of delegation is particularly important and in some sense provides a bridge between mixed-initiative interaction and adjustable autonomy.

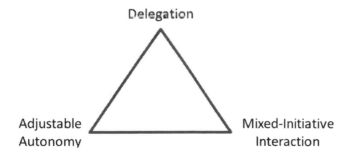

Fig. 2. A conceptual triad of concepts

Delegation – In any mixed-initiative interaction, humans may request help from robotic systems and robotic systems may request help from humans. One can abstract and concisely model such requests as a form of delegation, $Delegate(A, B, task, constraints)$, where A is the delegating agent, B is the contractor, $task$ is the task being delegated and consists of a goal and possibly a plan to achieve the goal, and $constraints$ represents a context in which the request is made and the task should be carried out. In our framework, delegation is formalized as a speech act and the delegation process invoked can be recursive.

Adjustable Autonomy – In solving tasks in a mixed-initiative setting, the robotic system involved will have a potentially wide spectrum of autonomy, yet should only use as much autonomy as is required for a task and should not violate the degree of autonomy mandated by a human operator unless agreement is made. One can begin to develop a principled means of adjusting autonomy through the use of the $task$ and $constraint$ parameters in $Delegate(A, B, task, constraints)$. A task delegated with only a goal and no plan, with few constraints, allows the robot to use much of its autonomy in solving the task, whereas a task specified as a sequence of actions and many constraints allows only limited autonomy. It may even be the case that the delegator does not allow the contractor to recursively delegate.

Mixed-Initiative Interaction – By mixed-initiative, we mean that interaction and negotiation between a robotic system, such as a UAV and a human, will take advantage of each of their skills, capacities and knowledge in developing a mission plan, executing the plan and adapting to contingencies during the execution of the plan. Mixed-initiative interaction involves a very broad set of issues, both theoretical and pragmatic. One central part of such interaction is the ability of a ground operator (GOP) to be able to delegate tasks to a UAV, $Delegate(GOP, UAV, task, constraints)$ and in a symmetric manner, the ability of a UAV to be able to delegate tasks to a GOP, $Delegate(UAV, GOP, task, constraints)$. Issues pertaining to safety, security, trust, etc., have to be dealt with in the interaction process and can be formalized as particular types of constraints associated with a delegated task.

This article is intended to provide a description of a relatively mature iteration of a principled framework for collaborative robotic systems based on these concepts which combines both formal theories and specifications with an agent-based software architecture which is guided by the formal framework. As a test case, the framework and architecture will be instantiated using a UAS involved in an emergency services application. A prototype software system has been implemented and has been used and tested both in simulation and on UAV systems.

1.1   Outline

In Section 2, we propose and specify a formal logical characterization of delegation in the form of a speech act. This speech act will be grounded in the software architecture proposed. In Section 3, an overview of the software architecture used to support collaboration via delegation is provided. It is an agent-based, service oriented architecture consisting of a generic shell that can be integrated with physical robotics systems. In Section 4, a formal characterization of tasks in the form of Task Specification Trees is proposed. Task Specification Trees are tightly coupled to the the Delegation speech act and to the actual software processes that instantiate the speech act in the software architecture. In Section 5, the important topic of allocating tasks in a Task Specification Tree to specific platforms is considered. Additionally, we show how the semantic characterization of Task Specification Trees is grounded in a distributed constraint problem whose solution drives the actual execution of the tasks in the tree. In Section 6,we turn our attention to describing the computational process that realizes the speech act on a robotic platform. In Section 7, we describe how that computational process is pragmatically realized in the software architecture by defining a number of agents, services and protocols which drive the process. In Section 8, we put the formal and pragmatic aspects of the approach together and show how the collaboration framework can be used in a relatively complex real-life emergency services scenario consisting of a number of UAV systems. In Section 9, we describe some of the representative related work and in Section 10 we conclude with a summary and future work.

2 Delegation as a Speech Act

Delegation is central to the conceptual and architectural framework we propose. Consequently, formulating an abstraction of the concept with a formal specification amenable to pragmatic grounding and implementation in a software system is paramount. As a starting point, in [5, 31], Falcone & Castelfranchi provide an illuminating, but informal discussion about delegation as a concept from a social perspective. Their approach to delegation builds on a BDI model of agents, that is, agents having beliefs, goals, intentions, and plans [6]. However, their specification lacks a formal semantics for the operators used. Based on intuitions from their work, we have previously provided a formal characterization of their concept of strong delegation using a communicative speech act with pre- and post-conditions which update the belief states associated with the delegator and contractor, respectively [25]. In order to formally characterize the operators used in the definition of the speech act, we use KARO [48] to provide a formal semantics. The KARO formalism is an amalgam of dynamic logic and epistemic/doxastic logic, augmented with several additional modal operators in order to deal with the motivational aspects of agents.

The target for delegation is a *task*. A dictionary definition of a task is "a usually assigned piece of work often to be finished within a certain time".[3] Assigning a piece of work to someone by someone is in fact what delegation is about. In computer science, a *piece of work* in this context is generally represented as a composite action. There is also often a purpose to assigning a piece of work to be done. This purpose is generally represented as a *goal*, where the intended meaning is that a task is a means of achieving a goal. We will require both a formal specification of a task at a high-level of abstraction in addition to a more data-structural specification flexible enough to be used pragmatically in an implementation.

For the formal specification, the definition provided by Falcone & Castelfranchi will be used. For the data-structure specification used in the implementation, task specification trees (TST's) will be defined in a Section 4. Falcone & Castelfranchi define a task as a pair $\tau = (\alpha, \phi)$ consisting of a goal ϕ, and a plan α for that goal, or rather, a plan

---

[3] Merriam-Webster free on-line dictionary. m-w.com

and the goal associated with that plan. Conceptually, a plan is a composite action. We extend the definition of a task to a tuple $\tau = (\alpha, \phi, cons)$, where $cons$ represents additional constraints associated with the plan α, such as timing and resource constraints. At this level of abstraction, the definition of a task is purposely left general but will be dealt with in explicit detail in the implementation using TST's and constraints.

From the perspective of adjustable autonomy, the task definition is quite flexible. If α is a single elementary action with the goal ϕ implicit and correlated with the post-condition of the action, the contractor has little flexibility as to how the task will be achieved. On the other hand, if the goal ϕ is specified and the plan α is not provided, then the contractor has a great deal of flexibility in achieving the goal. There are many variations between these two extremes and these variations capture the different levels of autonomy and trust exchanged between two agents. These extremes loosely follow Falcone & Castelfranchi's notions of closed and open delegation described below.

Using KARO to formalize aspects of Falcone & Castelfranchi 's work, we consider a notion of *strong delegation* represented by a speech act Delegate(A, B, τ) of A delegating a task $\tau = (\alpha, \phi, cons)$ to B, where α is a possible plan, ϕ is a goal, and $cons$ is a set of constraints associated with the plan ϕ. Strong delegation means that the delegation is explicit, an agent explicitly delegates a task to another agent. It is specified as follows:

S-Delegate(A, B, τ), where $\tau = (\alpha, \phi, cons)$

Preconditions:

(1) $Goal_A(\phi)$
(2) $Bel_A Can_B(\tau)$ (Note that this implies $Bel_A Bel_B(Can_B(\tau))$)
(3) $Bel_A(Dependent(A, B, \tau))$
(4) $Bel_B Can_B(\tau)$

Postconditions:

(1) $Goal_B(\phi)$ and $Bel_B Goal_B(\phi)$
(2) $Committed_B(\alpha)$ (also written $Committed_B(\tau)$)
(3) $Bel_B Goal_A(\phi)$
(4) $Can_B(\tau)$ (and hence $Bel_B Can_B(\tau)$, and by (1) also $Intend_B(\tau)$)
(5) $Intend_A(do_B(\alpha))$
(6) $MutualBel_{AB}$("the statements above" $\wedge$ $SociallyCommitted(B, A, \tau))$[4]

Informally speaking this expresses the following: the preconditions of the delegate act of A delegating task τ to B are that (1) ϕ is a goal of delegator A (2) A believes that B can (is able to) perform the task τ (which implies that A believes that B itself believes that it can do the task) (3) A believes that with respect to the task τ it is dependent on B. The speech act S-Delegate is a communication command and can be viewed as a request for a synchronization (a "handshake") between sender and receiver. Of course, this can only be successful if the receiver also believes it can do the task, which is expressed by (4).

---

[4] A discussion pertaining to the semantics of all non-KARO modal operators may be found in [25].

The postconditions of the strong delegation act mean: (1) B has ϕ as its goal and is aware of this (2) it is committed to the task τ (3) B believes that A has the goal ϕ (4) B can do the task τ (and hence believes it can do it, and furthermore it holds that B intends to do the task, which was a separate condition in Falcone & Castelfranchi's formalization), (5) A intends that B performs α (so we have formalized the notion of a goal to have an acheivement in Falcone & Castelfranchi's informal theory to an intention to perform a task) and (6) there is a mutual belief between A and B that all preconditions and other postconditions mentioned hold, as well as that there is a contract between A and B, i.e. B is socially committed to A to achieve τ for A. In this situation we will call agent A the *delegator* and B the *contractor*.

Typically a social commitment (contract) between two agents induces obligations to the partners involved, depending on how the task is specified in the delegation action. This dimension has to be added in order to consider how the contract affects the autonomy of the agents, in particular the contractor's autonomy. Falcone & Castelfranchi discuss the following variants:

- Closed delegation: the task is completely specified and both the goal and the plan should be adhered to.
- Open delegation: the task is not completely specified, either only the goal has to be adhered to while the plan may be chosen by the contractor, or the specified plan contains abstract actions that need further elaboration (a sub-plan) to be dealt with by the contractor.

In open delegation the contractor may have some freedom in how to perform the delegated task, and thus it provides a large degree of flexibility in multi-agent planning and allows for truly distributed planning.

The specification of the delegation act above is based on closed delegation. In case of open delegation, α in the postconditions can be replaced by an α', and τ by $\tau' = (\alpha', \phi, cons')$. Note that the fourth clause, $Can_B(\tau')$, now implies that α' is indeed believed to be an alternative for achieving ϕ, since it implies that $Bel_B[\alpha']\phi$ (B believes that ϕ is true after α' is executed). Of course, in the delegation process, A must agree that α', together with constraints $cons'$, is indeed viable. This would depend on what degree of autonomy is allowed.

This particular specification of delegation follows Falcone & Castelfranchi closely. One can easily foresee other constraints one might add or relax in respect to the basic specification resulting in other variants of delegation [7, 11, 27]. It is important to keep in mind that this formal characterization of delegation is not completely hierarchical. There is interaction between both the delegators and contractors as to how goals can best be achieved given the constraints of the agents involved. This is implicit in the formal characterization of open delegation above, although the process is not made explicit. This aspect of the process will become much clearer when the implementation is described.

There are many directions one can take in attempting to close the gap between this abstract formal specification and grounding it in implementation. One such direction taken in [25] is to correlate the delegate speech act with plan generation rules in 2APL [10], which is an agent programming language with a formal semantics. In this article, a different direction is taken which attempts to ground the important aspects of the speech act specification in the actual processes used in our robotic systems. Intuitions will become much clearer when the architectural details are provided, but let us describe the approach informally based on what we have formally specified.

If a UAV system A has a goal ϕ which it is required to achieve, it first introspects and determines whether it is capable of achieving ϕ given its inherent capabilities and current resources in the context it is in, or will be in, when the goal has to be achieved. It will do this by accessing its capability specification (assumed) and determine whether it believes it can achieve ϕ, either through use of a planning and constraint solving system (assumed) or a repertoire of stored actions. If not, then the fundamental preconditions in the S-Delegate speech act are the second, $Bel_A Can_B(\tau)$ and the fourth, $Bel_B Can_B(\tau)$. Agent A must find another agent it believes *can* achieve the goal ϕ implicit in τ. Additionally, B must also believe it can achieve the the goal ϕ implicit in τ. Clearly, if A can not achieve ϕ itself and finds an agent B that it believes can achieve ϕ and B believes it can achieve ϕ, then it is dependent on B to do that (precondition 3: $Bel_A(Dependent(A, B, \alpha))$). Consequently, all preconditions are satisfied and the delegation can take place.

From a pragmatic perspective, determining (in an efficient manner) whether an agent B *can* achieve a task τ (in an efficient) manner, is the fundamental problem that has to be not only implemented efficiently, but also grounded in some formal sense. The formal aspect is important because delegation is a recursive process which may involve many agents, automated planning and reasoning about resources, all in the context of temporal and spatial constraints. One has to have some means of validating this complex set of processes relative to a highly abstract formal specification which is convincing enough to trust that the collaborative system is in fact doing what it is formally intended to do.

The pragmatic aspects of the software architecture through which we ground the formal specification include the following:

- An agent layer based on the FIPA Abstract Architecture will be added on top of existing platform specific legacy systems such as our UAV's. This agent layer allows for the realization of the delegation process using speech acts and protocols from the FIPA Agent Communication Language.
- The formal specification of tasks will be instantiated pragmatically as Task Specification Trees (TST's), which provide a versatile data structure for mapping goals to plans and plans to complex tasks. Additionally, the formal semantics of tasks is defined in terms of a predicate Can which can be directly grounded above to the semantics of the S-Delegate speech act and below to a constraint solving system.
- Finding a set of agents who together can achieve a complex task with time, space and resource constraints through recursive delegation can be defined as a very complex distributed task allocation problem. Explicit representation of time, space and resource constraints will be used in the delegation process and modeled as a distributed constraint satisfaction problem (DCSP). This allows us to apply existing DCSP solvers to check the consistency of partial task assignments in the delegation process and to formally ground the process. Consequently, the Can predicate used in the precondition to the S-Delegate speech act is both formally and pragmatically grounded into the implementation.

3 Delegation-Based Software Architecture Overview

Before going into details regarding the implementation of the delegation process and its grounding in the proposed software architecture, we provide an overview of the architecture itself.

Our RMAX helicopters use a CORBA-based distributed architecture [17]. For our experimentation with collaborative UAV's, we view this as a legacy system which provides sophisticated functionality ranging from control modes to reactive processes, in addition to deliberative capabilities such as automated planners, GIS systems, constraint solvers, etc. Legacy robotic architectures generally lack instantiations of an agent metaphor although implicitly one often views such systems as agents. Rather than redesign the legacy system from scratch, the approach we take is to agentify the existing legacy system in a straightforward manner by adding an additional agent layer which interfaces to the legacy system. The agent layer for a robotic system consists of one or more agents which offer specific functionalities or services. These agents can communicate with each other internally and leverage existing legacy system functionality. Agents from different robotic systems can also communicate with each other if required.

Our collaborative architectural specification is based on the use of the FIPA (Foundation for Intelligent Physical Agents) Abstract Architecture [32]. The FIPA Abstract Architecture provides the basic components for the development of a multi-agent system. Our prototype implementation is based on the FIPA compliant Java Agent Development Framework (JADE) [29, 62] which implements the abstract architecture. "JADE (Java Agent Development Framework) is a software environment to build agent systems for the management of networked information resources in compliance with the FIPA specifications for interoperable multi-agent systems." [30].

The FIPA Abstract Architecture provides the following fundamental modules:

- An Agent Directory module keeps track of the agents in the system.
- A Directory Facilitator keeps track of the services provided by those agents.
- A Message Transport System module allows agents to communicate using the FIPA Agent Communication Language (FIPA ACL) [33].

The relevant concepts in the FIPA Abstract Architecture are agents, services and protocols. All communication between agents is based on exchanging messages which represent speech acts encoded in an agent communication language (FIPA ACL). Services provide functional support for agents. There are a number of standard global services including agent-directory services, message-transport services and a service-directory service. A protocol is a related set of messages between agents that are logically related by some interaction pattern.

JADE provides base classes for agents, message transportation, and a behavior model for describing the content of agent control loops. Using the behavior model, different agent behaviors can be constructed, such as cyclic, one-shot (executed once), sequential, and parallel behavior. More complex behaviors can be constructed using the basic behaviors as building blocks.

From our perspective, each JADE *agent* has associated with it a set of *services*. Services are accessed through the Directory Facilitator and are generally implemented as behaviors. In our case, the communication language used by agents will be FIPA ACL which is speech act based. New protocols will be defined in Section 7 to support the delegation and other processes.

The purpose of the Agent Layer is to provide a common interface for collaboration. This interface should allow the delegation and task execution processes to be implemented without regard to the actual realization of elementary tasks, capabilities and resources which are specific to the legacy platforms.

We are currently using four agents in the agent layer:

1. **Interface agent** - This agent is the clearinghouse for communication. All requests for delegation and other types of communication pass through this agent. Externally, it provides the interface to a specific robotic system or ground control station.
2. **Delegation agent**- The delegation agent coordinates delegation requests to and from other UAV systems and ground control stations, with the Executor, Resource and Interface agents. It does this essentially by verifying that the pre-conditions to a $Delegate()$ request are satisfied.
3. **Execution agent** - After a task is contracted to a particular UAV or ground station operator, it must eventually execute that task relative to the constraints associated with it. The Executor agent coordinates this execution process.
4. **Resource agent** - The Resource agent determines whether the UAV or ground station of which it is part has the resources and ability to actually do a task as a potential contractor. Such a determination may include the invocation of schedulers, planners and constraint solvers in order to determine this.

Figure 3 provides an overview of an agentified robotic or ground operator system.

The FIPA Abstract Architecture will be extended to support delegation and collaboration by defining an additional set of services and a set of related protocols. The interface agent, resource agent and delegation agent will have an interface service, resource service and delegation service associated with it, respectively, on each individual robotic or ground station platform. The executor service is implemented as a non-JADE agent that understands FIPA protocols and works as a gateway to a platform's legacy system. Additionally, three protocols, the Capability-Lookup, Delegation and Auction protocols, will be defined and used to drive the delegation process.

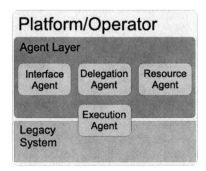

Fig. 3. Overview of an agentified platform or ground control station

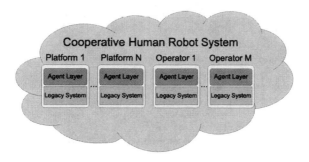

Fig. 4. An overview of the collaborative human robot system

Human operators interacting with robotic systems are treated similarly by extending the control station or user interface functionality in the same way. In this case, the control station is the legacy system and an agent layer is added to this. The result is a collaborative human robot system consisting of a number of human operators and robotic platforms each having both a legact system and an agent layer as shown in Figure 4.

The reason for using the FIPA Abstract Architecture and JADE is pragmatic. The focus of our research is not to develop new agent middleware, but to develop a formally grounded generic collaborative system shell for robotic systems. Our formal characterization of the *Delegate()* operator is as a speech act. We also use speech acts as an agent communication language and JADE provides a straightforward means for integrating the FIPA ACL language which supports speech acts with our existing systems.

Further details as to how the delegation and related processes will be implemented based on additional services and protocols will be described in Section 7. Before doing this, the processes themselves will be specified in Section 6. We begin by providing a formal characterization of Tasks in the form of Task Specification Trees.

4   Task Specification Trees

Both the declarative and procedural representation and semantics of tasks are central to the delegation process. The relation between the two representations is also essential if one has the goal of formally grounding the delegation process in the system implementation. A task was previously defined abstractly as a tuple $(\alpha, \phi, cons)$ consisting of a composite action α, a goal ϕ and a set of constraints $cons$, associated with α. In this section, we introduce a formal task specification language which allows us to represent tasks as *Task Specification Trees* (TST's). The task specification trees map directly to procedural representations in our proposed system implementation.

For our purposes, the task representation must be highly flexible, sharable, dynamically extendible, and distributed in nature. Tasks need to be delegated at varying levels of abstraction and also expanded and modified because parts of complex tasks can be recursively delegated to different robotic agents which are in turn expanded or modified. Consequently, the structure must also be distributable. Additionally, a task structure is a form of compromise between an explicit plan in a plan library at one end of the spectrum and a plan generated through an automated planner [51] at the other end of the spectrum. The task representation and semantics must seamlessly accommodate plan representations and their compilation into the task structure. Finally, the task representation should support the adjustment of autonomy through the addition of constraints or parameters by agents and human resources.

The flexibility allows for the use of both central and distributed planning, and also to move along the scale between these two extremes. At one extreme, the operator plans everything, creating a central plan, while at the other extreme the agents are delegated goals and generate parts of the distributed plan themselves. Sometimes neither completely centralized nor completely distributed planning is appropriate. In those cases the operator would like to retain some control of how the work is done while leaving the details to the agents. Task Specification Trees provide a formalism that captures the scale from one extreme to the next. This allows the operator to specify the task at the point which fits the current mission and environment.

The task specification formalism should allow for the specification of various types of task compositions, including sequential and concurrent, in addition to more general constructs such as loops and conditionals. The task specification should also provide a clear separation between tasks and platform specific details for handling the tasks. The specification should focus on what should be done and hide the details about how it could be done by different platforms.

In the general case, A TST is a declarative representation of a complex multi-agent task. In the architecture realizing the delegation framework a TST is also a distributed data structure. Each node in a TST corresponds to a task that should be performed. There are six types of nodes: sequence, concurrent, loop, select, goal, and elementary action. All nodes are directly executable except goal nodes which require some form of expansion or planning to generate a plan for achieving the goal.

Each node has a *node interface* containing a set of parameters, called *node parameters*, that can be specified for the node. The node interface always contains a platform assignment parameter and parameters for the start and end times of the task, usually denoted P, T_S and T_E, respectively. These parameters can be part of the constraints associated with the node called *node constraints*. A TST also has *tree constraints*, expressing precedence and organizational relations between the nodes in the TST. Together the constraints form a constraint network covering the TST. In fact, the node parameters function as constraint variables in a constraint network, and setting the value of a node parameter constrains not only the network, but implicitly, the degree of autonomy of an agent.

4.1   TST Syntax

The syntax of a TST specification has the following BNF:

SPEC ::= TST
TST ::= NAME ('(' VARS ')')? '=' (**with** VARS)? TASK (**where** CONS)?
TSTS ::= TST | TST ';' TSTS

TASK ::= ACTION | GOAL | (NAME '=')? NAME ('(' ARGS ')')? |
       while COND TST | **if** COND **then** TST **else** TST |
       sequence TSTS | **concurrent** TSTS
VAR ::= <variable name> | <variable name> '.' <variable name>
VARS ::= VAR | VAR ',' VARS
CONSTRAINT ::= <constraint>
CONS ::= CONSTRAINT | CONSTRAINT **and** CONS
ARG ::= VAR | VALUE
ARGS ::= ARG | ARG ',' ARGS
VALUE ::= <value>
NAME ::= <node name>
COND ::= <ACL query>
GOAL ::= <goal statement>
ACTION ::= <elementary action>

Where

- <ACL query> is a FIPA ACL query message requesting the value of a boolean expression.
- <elementary action> is an elementary action $name(p_0, ..., p_N)$, where $p_0, ..., p_N$ are parameters.
- <goal statement> is a goal $name(p_0, ..., p_N)$, where $p_0, ..., p_N$ are parameters.

The TST clause in the BNF introduces the main recursive pattern in the specification language. The right hand side of the equality provides the general pattern of providing a variable context for a task (using **with**) and a set of constraints (using **where**) which may include the variables previously introduced.

Example. Consider a small scenario where the mission is to first scan Area$_A$ and Area$_B$, and then fly to Dest$_4$ (Figure 5). A TST describing this mission is shown in Figure 6.

Fig. 5. Example mission of first scanning Area$_A$ and Area$_B$, and then fly to Dest$_4$

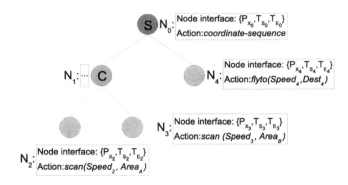

Fig. 6. A TST for the mission in Figure 5

Nodes N_0 and N_1 are composite action nodes, sequential and concurrent, respectively. Nodes N_2, N_3 and N_4 are elementary action nodes. Each node specifies a task and has a node interface containing node parameters and a platform assignment variable. In this case only temporal parameters are shown representing the respective intervals a task should be completed in.

In the TST depicted in Figure 6. The nodes N_0 to N_4 have the task names τ_0 to τ_4 associated with them respectively. This TST contains two composite actions, *sequence* (τ_0) and *concurrent* (τ_1) and three elementary actions *scan* (τ_2, τ_3) and *flyto* (τ_4). The resulting TST specification is:

$\tau_0(T_{S_0}, T_{E_0}) =$
  with $T_{S_1}, T_{E_1}, T_{S_4}, T_{E_4}$ **sequence**
    $\tau_1(T_{S_1}, T_{E_1}) =$
      with $T_{S_2}, T_{E_2}, T_{S_3}, T_{E_3}$ **concurrent**
        $\tau_2(T_{S_2}, T_{E_2}) = \mathrm{scan}(T_{S_2}, T_{E_2}, Speed_2, Area_A);$
        $\tau_3(T_{S_3}, T_{E_3}) = \mathrm{scan}(T_{S_3}, T_{E_3}, Speed_3, Area_B)$
      where $cons_{\tau_1}$;
    $\tau_4(T_{S_4}, T_{E_4}) = \mathrm{flyto}(T_{S_4}, T_{E_4}, Speed_4, Dest_4)$
  where $cons_{\tau_0}$

$cons_{\tau_0} = \{T_{S_0} \leq T_{S_1} \wedge T_{S_1} \leq T_{E_1} \wedge T_{E_1} \leq T_{S_4} \wedge T_{S_4} \leq T_{E_4} \wedge T_{E_4} \leq T_{E_0}\}$
$cons_{\tau_1} = \{T_{S_1} \leq T_{S_2} \wedge T_{S_2} \leq T_{E_2} \wedge T_{E_2} \leq T_{E_1} \wedge T_{S_1} \leq T_{S_3} \wedge T_{S_3} \leq T_{E_3} \wedge T_{E_3} \leq T_{E_1}\}$

4.2 TST Semantics

A TST specifies a complex task (composite action) under a set of tree-specific and node-specific constraints which together are intended to represent the context in which a task should be executed in order to meet the task's intrinsic requirements, in addition to contingent requirements demanded by a particular mission. The leaf nodes of a TST represent elementary actions used in the definition of the composite action the TST represents and the non-leaf nodes essentially represent control structures for the ordering and execution of the elementary actions. The semantic meaning of non-leaf nodes is essentially application independent, whereas the semantic meaning of the leaf nodes are highly domain dependent. They represent the specific actions or processes that an agent will in fact execute. The procedural correlate of a TST is a program.

During the delegation process, a TST is either provided or generated to achieve a specific set of goals, and if the delegation process is successful, each node is associated with an agent responsible for the execution of that node.

Informally, the semantics of a TST node will be characterized in terms of whether an agent believes it *can* successfully execute the task associated with the node in a given context represented by constraints, given its capabilities and resources. This can only be a belief because the task will be executed in the future and even under the best of conditions, real-world contingencies may arise which prevent the agent from successfully completing the task. The semantics of a TST will be the aggregation of the semantics for each individual node in the tree.

The formal semantics for TST nodes will be given in terms of the logical predicate $Can()$ which we have used previously in the formal definition of the S-Delegate speech act, although in this case, we will add additional arguments. This is not a coincidence since our goal is to ground the formal specification of the S-Delegate speech act into the implementation in a very direct manner.

Recall that in the formal semantics for the speech act S-Delegate described in Section 2, the logical predicate $Can_X(\tau)$ is used to state that an agent X has the capabilities and resources to achieve task τ.

An important precondition for the successful application of the speech act is that the delegator (A) believes in the contractor's (B) ability to achieve the task τ, (2): $Bel_A Can_B(\tau)$. Additionally, an important result of the successful application of the speech act is that the contractor actually has the capabilities and resources to achieve the task τ, (4): $Can_B(\tau)$. In order to directly couple the semantic characterization of the S-Delegate speech act to the semantic characterization of TST's, we will assume that a task $\tau = (\alpha, \phi, cons)$ in the speech act characterization corresponds to a TST. Additionally, the TST semantics will be characterized in terms of a Can predicate with additional parameters to incorporate constraints explicitly.

In this case, the Can predicate is extended to include as arguments a list $[p_1, \ldots, p_k]$ denoting all node parameters in the node interface together with other parameters provided in the (**with** VARS) construct[5] and an argument for an additional constraint set $cons$ provided in the (**where** CONS) construct.[6] Observe that $cons$ can be formed incrementally and may in fact contain constraints inherited or passed to it through a recursive delegation process. The formula $Can(B, \tau, [t_s, t_e, \ldots], cons)$[7] then asserts that an agent B has the capabilities and resources for achieving task τ if $cons$, which also

---

[5] For reasons of clarity, we only list the node parameters for the start and end times for a task, $[t_s, t_e, \ldots]$, in this article.

[6] For pedagogical expediency, we can assume that there is a constraint language which is reified in the logic and is used in the CONS constructs.

[7] Note that we originally defined $\tau = (\alpha, \phi, cons)$ as a tuple consisting of a plan, a goal and a set of constraints for reasons of abstraction when defining the delegation speech act. Since we now want to explicitly use $cons$ as an argument to the Can predicate in the implementation, we revert to defining $\tau = (\alpha, \phi)$ as a pair instead, where the constraints $cons$ are lifted up as an argument to Can.

contains node constraints for τ, is consistent. The temporal variables t_s and t_e associated with the task τ are part of the node interface which may also contain other variables which are often related to the constraints in $cons$.

Determining whether a fully instantiated TST satisfies its specification, will now be equivalent to the successful solution of a constraint problem in the formal logical sense. The constraint problem in fact provides the formal semantics for a TST. Constraints associated with a TST are derived from a reduction process associated with the $Can()$ predicate for each node in the TST. The generation and solution of constraints will occur on-line during the delegation process. Let us provide some more specific details. In particular, we will show the very tight coupling between the TST's and their logical semantics.

The basic structure of a Task Specification Tree is:

$$\text{TST} ::= \text{NAME ('(' VARS}_1\text{ ')')? '=' (\textbf{with} VARS}_2\text{)? TASK (\textbf{where} CONS)?}$$

where VARS$_1$ denotes node parameters, VARS$_2$ denotes additional variables used in the constraint context for a TST node, and CONS denotes the constraints associated with a TST node. Additionally, TASK denotes the specific type of TST node. In specifying a logical semantics for a TST node, we would like to map these arguments directly over to arguments of the predicate $Can()$. Informally, an abstraction of the mapping is

$$Can(agent_1, TASK, VARS_1 \cup VARS_2, CONS) \tag{1}$$

The idea is that for any fully allocated TST, the meaning of each allocated TST node in the tree is the meaning of the associated $Can()$ predicate instantiated with the TST specific parameters and constraints. The meaning of the instantiated $CAN()$ predicate can then be associated with an equivalent constraint satisfaction problem (CSP) which turns out to be true or false dependent upon whether that CSP can be satisfied or not. The meaning of the fully allocated TST is then the aggregation of the meanings of each individual TST node associated with the TST, in other words, a conjunction of CSP's.

One would also like to capture the meaning of partial TST's. The idea is that as the delegation process unfolds, a TST is incrementally expanded with additional TST nodes. At each step, a partial TST may contain a number of fully expanded and allocated nodes in addition to other nodes which remain to be delegated. In order to capture this process semantically, one extends the semantics by providing meaning for an unallocated TST node in terms of both a $Can()$ predicate and a $Delegate()$ predicate:

$$\exists agent_2\, Delegate(agent_1, agent_2, TASK, VARS_1 \cup VARS_2, CONS) \tag{2}$$

Either $agent_1$ can achieve a task, or (exclusively) it can find an agent, $agent_2$, to which the task can be delegated. In fact, it may need to find one or more agents if the task to be delegated is a composite action.

Given the $S\text{-}Delegate(agent_1, agent_2, TASK)$ speech act semantics, we know that if delegation is successful then as one of the postconditions of the speech act, $agent_2$ can in fact achieve $TASK$ (assuming no additional contingencies):

$$Delegate(agent_1, \text{agent}_2, TASK, VARS_1 \cup VARS_2, CONS) \tag{3}$$
$$\rightarrow Can(\text{agent}_2, TASK, VARS_1 \cup VARS_2, CONS)$$

Consequently, during the computational process associated with delegation, as the TST expands through delegation where previously unallocated nodes become allocated, each instance of the $Delegate()$ predicate associated with an unallocated node is replaced with an instance of the $Can()$ predicate. This recursive process preserves the meaning of a TST as a conjunction of instances of the $Can()$ predicate which in turn are compiled into a (interdependent) set of CSPs and which are checked for satisfaction using distributed constraint solving algorithms.

Sequence Node

- In a *sequence node*, the child nodes should be executed in sequence (from left to right) during the execution time of the sequence node.
- $Can(B, S(\alpha_1, ..., \alpha_n), [t_s, t_e, ...], cons) \leftrightarrow$
  $\exists t_1, ..., t_{2n}, ... \bigwedge_{k=1}^{n} [(Can(B, \alpha_k, [t_{2k-1}, t_{2k}, ...], cons_k)$
  $\vee \exists a_k Delegate(B, a_k, \alpha_k, [t_{2k-1}, t_{2k}, ...], cons_k))]$
  $\wedge consistent(cons)^8$
- $cons = \{t_s \leq t_1 \wedge (\bigwedge_{i=1}^{n} t_{2i-1} < t_{2i}) \wedge (\bigwedge_{i=1}^{n-1} t_{2i} \leq t_{2i+1}) \wedge t_{2n} \leq t_e\} \cup cons'^9$

Concurrent Node

- In a *concurrent node* each child node should be executed during the time interval of the concurrent node.
- $Can(B, C(\alpha_1, ..., \alpha_n), [t_s, t_e, ...], cons) \leftrightarrow$
  $\exists t_1, ..., t_{2n}, ... \bigwedge_{k=1}^{n} [(Can(B, \alpha_k, [t_{2k-1}, t_{2k}, ...], cons_k)$
  $\vee \exists a_k Delegate(B, a_k, \alpha_k, [t_{2k-1}, t_{2k}, ...], cons_k))]$
  $\wedge consistent(cons)$
- $cons = \{\bigwedge_{i=1}^{n} t_s \leq t_{2i-1} < t_{2i} \leq t_e\} \cup cons'$

Selector Node

- Compared to a sequence or concurrent node, only one of the *selector node*'s children will be executed, which one is determined by a test condition in the selector node. The child node should be executed during the time interval of the selector node. A selector node is used to postpone a choice which can not be known when the TST is specified. When expanded at runtime, the net result can be any of the legal node types.

Loop Node

- A *loop node* will add a child node for each iteration the loop condition allows. In this way the loop node works as a sequence node but with an increasing number of child nodes which are dynamically added. Loop nodes are similar to selector nodes, they describe additions to the TST that can not be known when the TST is specified. When expanded at runtime, the net result is a sequence node.

[8] The predicate $consistent()$ has the standard logical meaning and checking for consistency would be done through a call to a constraint solver which is part of the architecture.

[9] In addition to the temporal constraints, other constraints may be passed recursively during the delegation process. $cons'$ represents these constraints.

Goal

- A *goal node* is a leaf node which can not be directly executed. Instead it has to be expanded by using an automated planner or related planning functionality. After expansion, a TST branch representing the generated plan is added to the original TST.
- $Can(B, Goal(\phi), [t_s, t_e, \ldots], cons) \leftrightarrow$
  $\exists \alpha \, (GeneratePlan(B, \alpha, \phi, [t_s, t_e, \ldots], cons) \wedge Can(B, \alpha, [t_s, t_e, \ldots], cons))$
  $\wedge \, consistent(cons)$

Observe that the agent B can generate a partial or complete plan α and then further delegate execution or completion of the plan recursively via the $Can()$ statement in the second conjunct.

Elementary Action Node

- An *elementary action node* specifies a domain-dependent action. An elementary action node is a leaf node.
- $Can(B, \tau, [t_s, t_e, \ldots], cons) \leftrightarrow$
  $Capabilities(B, \tau, [t_s, t_e, \ldots], cons) \wedge Resources(B, \tau, [t_s, t_e, \ldots], cons)$
  $\wedge \, consistent(cons)$

There are two parts to the definition of Can for an elementary action node. These are defined in terms of a *platform specification* which is assumed to exist for each agent potentially involved in a collaborative mission. The platform specification has two components.

The first, specified by the predicate $Capabilities(B, \tau, [t_s, t_e], cons)$ is intended to characterize all static capabilities associated with platform B that are required as capabilities for the successful execution of τ. These will include a list of tasks and/or services the platform is capable of carrying out. If platform B has the necessary static capabilities for executing task τ in the interval $[t_s, t_e]$ with constraints $cons$, then this predicate will be true.

The second, specified by the predicate $Resources(B, \tau, [t_s, t_e], cons)$ are intended to characterize dynamic resources such as fuel and battery power, which are consumable, or cameras and other sensors which are borrowable. Since resources generally vary through time, the semantic meaning of the predicate is temporally dependent.

Resources for an agent are represented as a set of parameterized resource constraint predicates, one per task. The parameters to the predicate are the task's parameters, in addition to the start time and the end time for the task. For example, assume there is a task $flyto(dest, speed)$. The resource constraint predicate for this task would be $flyto(t_s, t_e, dest, speed)$. The resource constraint predicate is defined as a conjunction of constraints, in the logical sense. The general pattern for this conjunction is:

$t_e = t_s + F, C_1, ..., C_N$, where
- F is a function of the resource constraint parameters and possibly local resource variables and
- $C_1, \ldots, C_N$ is a possibly empty set of additional constraints related to the resource model associated with the task.

Example. As an example, consider the task $flyto(dest, speed)$ with the corresponding resource constraint predicate $flyto(t_s, t_e, dest, speed)$. The constraint model associated with the task for a particular platform P_1 might be:

$$t_e = t_s + \frac{distance(pos(t_s, P_1), dest)}{speed} \wedge (Speed_{Min} \leq speed \leq Speed_{Max})$$

Depending on the platform, this constraint model may be different for the same task. In that sense, it is platform dependent.

5   Allocating Tasks in a TST to Platforms

Given a TST representing a complex task, an important problem is to find a set of platforms that can execute these tasks according to the TST specification. The problem is to allocate tasks to platforms and assign values to parameters such that each task can be carried out by its assigned platform and all the constraints of the TST are satisfied.

For a platform to be able to carry out a task, it must have the capabilities and the resources required for the task as described in the previous section. A platform that can be assigned a task in a TST is called a *candidate* and a set of candidates is a *candidate group*. The capabilities of a platform are fixed while the available resources will vary depending on its commitments, including the tasks it has already been allocated. These commitments are generally represented in the constraint stores and schedulers of the platforms in question. The resources and the commitments are modeled with constraints. Resources are represented by variables and commitments by constraints. These constraints are local to the platform and different platforms may have different constraints for the same action. Figure 7 shows the constraints for the scan action for platform P_1.

When a platform is assigned an action node in a TST, the constraints associated with that action are instantiated and added to the constraint store of the platform. The platform constraints defined in the constraint model for the task are connected to the constraint problem defined by the TST via the node parameters in the node interface for the action node. Figure 8 shows the constraint network after allocating node N_2 from the TST in Figure 6 (on page 218) to platform P_1.

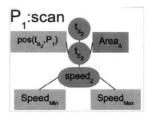

Fig. 7. The parameterized platform constraints for the scan action. The red/dark variables represent node parameters in the node interface. The gray variables represent local variables associated with the platform P1's constraint model for the scan action. These are connected through dependencies.

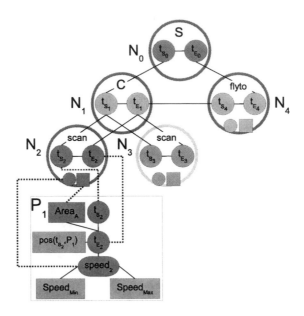

Fig. 8. The combined constraint problem after allocating node N_2 to platform P_1

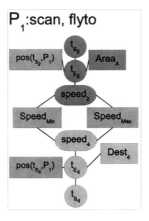

Fig. 9. The parameter constraints of platform P_1 when allocated node N_2 and N_4

A platform can be allocated to more than one node. This may introduce implicit dependencies between actions since each allocation adds constraints to the constraint store of the platform. For example, there could be a shared resource that both actions use. Figure 9 shows the constraint network of platform P_1 after it has been allocated nodes N_2 and N_4 from the example TST. In this example the position of the platform is implicitly shared since the first action will change the location of the platform.

A *complete allocation* is an allocation which allocates every node in a TST to a platform. A completely allocated TST defines a constraint problem that represents all the constraints for this particular allocation of the TST. As the constraints are distributed among the platforms it is in effect a distributed constraint problem. If a consistent solution for this constraint problem is found then a *valid allocation* has been found and verified. Each such solution can be seen as a potential execution schedule of the TST. The consistency of an allocation can be checked by a distributed constraint satisfaction problem (DCSP) solver such as the Asynchronous Weak Commitment Search (AWCS) algorithm [70] or ADOPT [56].

Example. The constraint problem for a TST is derived by recursively reducing the Can predicate statements associated with each task node with formally equivalent expressions, beginning with the top-node τ_0 until the logical statements reduce to a constraint network. Below, we show the reduction of the TST from Figure 6 (on page 218) when there are three platforms, P_0, P_1 and P_2, with the appropriate capabilities. P_0 has been delegated the composite actions τ_0 and τ_1. P_0 has recursively delegated parts of these tasks to P_1 (τ_2 and τ_4) and $P_2(\tau_3)$.

$$Can(P_0, \alpha_0, [t_{s_0}, t_{e_0}], cons) = Can(P_0, S(\alpha_1, \alpha_4), [t_{s_0}, t_{e_0}], cons) \leftrightarrow$$
$$\exists t_{s_1}, t_{e_1}, t_{s_4}, t_{e_4}(Can(P_0, \alpha_1, [t_{s_1}, t_{e_1}], cons_{P_0})$$
$$\vee \exists a_1 Delegate(P_0, a_1, \alpha_1, [t_{s_1}, t_{e_1}], cons_{P_0}))$$
$$\wedge (Can(P_0, \alpha_4, [t_{s_4}, t_{e_4}], cons_{P_0})$$
$$\vee \exists a_2 Delegate(P_0, a_2, \alpha_4, [t_{s_4}, t_{e_4}], cons_{P_0}))$$

Let's continue with a reduction of the 1st element in the sequence α_1 (the 1st conjunct in the previous formula on the right-hand side of the biconditional):

$$Can(P_0, \alpha_1, [t_{s_1}, t_{e_1}], cons_{P_0})$$
$$\vee \exists a_1(Delegate(P_0, a_1, \alpha_1, [t_{s_1}, t_{e_1}], cons_{P_0}))$$

Since P_0 has been allocated α_1, the 2nd disjunct is false.

$$Can(P_0, \alpha_1, [t_{s_1}, t_{e_1}], cons_{P_0}) =$$
$$Can(P_0, C(\alpha_2, \alpha_3), [t_{s_1}, t_{e_1}], cons_{P_0}) \leftrightarrow$$
$$\exists t_{s_2}, t_{e_2}, t_{s_3}, t_{e_3} ((Can(P_0, \alpha_2, [t_{s_2}, t_{e_2}], cons_{P_0}) \vee$$
$$\exists a_1 Delegate(P_0, a_1, \alpha_2, [t_{s_2}, t_{e_2}], cons_{P_0})) \wedge$$
$$(Can(P_0, \alpha_3, [t_{s_3}, t_{e_3}], cons_{P_0}) \vee$$
$$\exists a_2 Delegate(P_0, a_2, \alpha_3, [t_{s_3}, t_{e_3}], cons_{P_0})))$$

The node constraints for τ_0 and τ_1 are then added to P_0's constraint store. What remains to be done is a reduction of tasks τ_2 and τ_4 associated with P_1 and τ_3 associated with P_2. We can assume that P_1 has been delegated α_2 and P_2 has been delegated α_3 as specified. Consequently, we can reduce to

$$Can(P_0, \alpha_1, [t_{s_1}, t_{e_1}], cons_{P_0}) =$$
$$Can(P_0, C(\alpha_2, \alpha_3), [t_{s_1}, t_{e_1}], cons_{P_0}) \leftrightarrow$$
$$\exists t_{s_2}, t_{e_2}, t_{s_3}, t_{e_3} (Can(P_1, \alpha_2, [t_{s_2}, t_{e_2}], cons_{P_0}) \wedge$$
$$Can(P_2, \alpha_3, [t_{s_3}, t_{e_3}], cons_{P_0}))$$

Since P_0 has recursively delegated α_4 to P_1 (the 2nd conjunct in the original formula on the right-hand side of the biconditional) we can complete the reduction and end up with the following:

$$Can(P_0, \alpha_0, [t_{s_0}, t_{e_0}], cons) = Can(P_0, S(C(\alpha_2, \alpha_3), \alpha_4), [t_{s_0}, t_{e_0}], cons) \leftrightarrow$$
$$\exists t_{s_1}, t_{e_1}, t_{s_4}, t_{e_4}$$
$$\exists t_{s_2}, t_{e_2}, t_{s_3}, t_{e_3} Can(P_1, \alpha_2, [t_{s_2}, t_{e_2}], cons_{P_1}) \wedge Can(P_2, \alpha_3, [t_{s_3}, t_{e_3}], cons_{P_2})$$
$$\wedge Can(P_1, \alpha_4, [t_{s_4}, t_{e_4}], cons_{P_1})$$

These remaining tasks are elementary actions and consequently the definitions of Can for these action nodes are platform dependent. When a platform is assigned to an elementary action node a local constraint problem is created on the platform and then connected to the global constraint problem through the node parameters of the assigned node's node interface. In this case, the node parameters only include temporal constraints and these are coupled to the internal constraint variables associated with the elementary actions. The completely allocated and reduced TST is shown in Figure 10. The reduction of Can for an elementary action node contains no further Can predicates, since an elementary action only depends on the platform itself. All remaining Can predicates in the recursion are replaced with constraint sub-networks associated with specific platforms as shown in Figure 10.

In summary, the delegation process, if successful, provides a TST that is both valid and completely allocated. During this process, a network of distributed constraints is

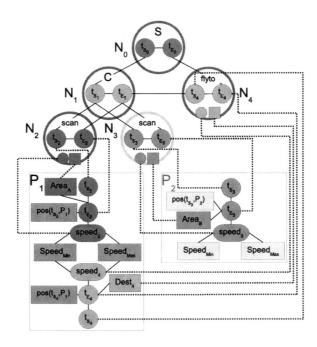

Fig. 10. The completely allocated and reduced TST showing the interaction between the TST constraints and the platform dependent constraints

generated which if solved, guarantees the validity of the multi-agent solution to the original problem, provided that additional contingencies do not arise when the TST is actually executed in a distributed manner by the different agents involved in the collaborative solution. This approach is intended to ground the original formal specification of the S-Delegate speech act with the actual processes of delegation used in the implementation. Although the process is pragmatic in the sense that it is a computational process, it in effect strongly grounds this process formally, due to the reduction of the collaboration to a distributed constraint network which is in effect a formal representation. This results in real-world grounding of the semantics of the Delegation speech act via the Can predicate.

6   The Delegation Process

Now that the S-Delegate speech act, the Task Specification Tree representation, and the formal relation between them has been considered, we turn our attention to describing the computational process that realizes the speech act in a robotic platform.

According to the semantics of the Delegate(A,B,$\tau = (\alpha, \phi)$) speech act the delegator A must have ϕ as a goal, believe that there is an agent B that is able to achieve τ, and believe that it is dependent on B for the achievement of τ via action α. In the following, we assume that the agent A already has ϕ as a goal and that it is dependent on some other agent to achieve the task. Consequently, the main issue is to find an agent B that is able to achieve the task τ.

This could be done in at least two ways. Agent A could have a knowledge base encoding all its knowledge about what other agents can and can not do and then reason about which agents could achieve τ. This would be very similar to a centralized form of multi-agent planning since the assumption is that τ is a complex task. This is problematic because it would be difficult to keep such a knowledge base up-to-date and it would be quite complex given the heterogeneous nature of the platforms involved. Additionally, the pool of platforms accessible for any given mission at a given time is not known since platforms come and go.

As an alternative, the process of finding agents to achieve tasks will be done in a more distributed manner through communication among agents and an assumption that elementary actions are platform dependent and the details of such actions are not required in finding appropriate agents to achieve the tasks at hand.

The following process takes as input a complex task represented as a TST. The TST is intended to describe a complex mission. The process will find an appropriate agent or set of agents capable of achieving the mission possibly through the use of recursive delegation. If the allocation of agents in the TST is approved by the delegators recursively, then the mission can then be executed. Note that the mission schedule will be distributed among the group of agents that have been allocated tasks and the mission may not necessarily start immediately. This will depend on the temporal constraints used in the TST specification. But commitments to the mission will have been made in the form of constraints in the constraint stores and schedulers of the individual platforms. Note also, that the original TST given as input does not have to be completely specified. It may contain goal nodes which require expansion of the TST with additional nodes.

The process is as follows:

1. Allocate the complex task through an iterative and recursive process which finds a platform to whom the task can be delegated to. This process expands goals into tasks, assigns platforms to tasks, and assigns values to task parameters. The input is a TST and the output is a fully expanded, assigned and parameterized TST.
2. Approve the mission or request the next consistent instantiation. Repeat 1 until approved or no more instantiations.
3. If no approved instantiated mission is found then fail.
4. Otherwise, execute the approved mission until finished or until constraints associated with the mission are violated during execution. While executing the mission, constraints are monitored and their parameterization might be changed to avoid violations on the fly.
5. If constraints are violated and can not be locally repaired goto 1 and begin a recursive repair process.

The first step of the process corresponds to finding a set of platforms that satisfy the preconditions of the S-Delegate speech act for all delegations in the TST. The approval corresponds to actually executing the speech act where the postconditions are implicitly represented in the constraint stores and schedulers of the platforms. During the execution step, the contractors are committed to the constraints agreed upon during the approval of the tasks. They do have limited autonomy during execution in the form of being able to modify internal parameters associated with the tasks as long as they do not violate those constraints externally agreed upon in the delegation process.

6.1   An Algorithm for Allocating Complex Tasks Specified by TSTs

The most important part of the Delegation Process is to find a platform that satisfies the preconditions of the S-Delegate speech act. This is equivalent to finding a platform which is able to achieve the task either itself of through recursive delegation. This can be viewed as a task allocation problem where each task in the TST should be allocated to an agent.

Multi-robot task allocation (MRTA) is an important problem in the multi-agent community [38, 39, 53, 63, 71, 72]. It deals with the complexities involved in taking a description of a set of tasks and deciding which of the available robots should do what. Often the problem also involves maximizing some utility function or minimizing a cost function. Important aspects of the problem are what types of tasks and robots can be described, what type of optimization is being done, and how computationally expensive the allocation is.

This section presents a heuristic search algorithm for allocating a fully expanded TST to a set of platforms. A successful allocation allocates each node to a platform and assigns values to parameters such that each task can be carried out by its assigned platform and all the constraints of the TST are satisfied. During the allocation, temporal variables will be instantiated resulting in a schedule for executing the TST.

The algorithm starts with an empty allocation and extends it one node at a time in a depth-first order over the TST. To extend the allocation, the algorithm takes the current allocation, finds a consistent allocation of the next node, and then recursively allocates the rest of the TST. Since a partial allocation corresponds to a distributed constraint satisfaction problem, a DCSP solver is used to check whether the constraints are consistent. If all possible allocations of the next node violate the constraints, then the algorithm uses backtracking with backjumping to find the next allocation.

The algorithm is both sound and complete. It is sound since the consistency of the corresponding constraint problem is verified in each step and it is complete since every possible allocation is eventually tested. Since the algorithm is recursive the search can be distributed among multiple platforms.

To improve the search, a heuristic function is used to determine the order platforms are tested. The heuristic function is constructed by auctioning out the node to all platforms with the required capabilities. The bid is the marginal cost for the platform to accept the task relative to the current partial allocation. The cost could for example be the total time required to execute all tasks allocated to the platform.

To increase the efficiency of the backtracking, the algorithm uses backjumping to find the latest partial allocation which has a consistent allocation of the current node. This preserves the soundness as only partial allocations that are guaranteed to violate the constraints are skipped.

AllocateTST. The AllocateTST algorithm takes a TST rooted in the node N as input and finds a valid allocation of the TST if possible. To check whether a node N can be allocated to a specific platform P the TryAllocateTST algorithm is used. It tries to allocate the top node N to P and then tries to recursively find an allocation of the sub-TSTs.

AllocateTST(Node N)

1. Find the set of candidates C for N.
2. Run an auction for N among the candidates in C and order C according to the bids.
3. For each candidate c in the ordered set C:
   (a) If TryAllocateTST(c, N) then return success.
4. Return failure.

TryAllocateTST(Platform P, Node N)

1. AllocateTST P to N.
2. If the allocation is inconsistent then undo the allocation and return false.
3. For each sub-TST n of N do
   (a) If AllocateTST(n) fails then undo the allocation and do a backjump.
4. An allocation has been found, return true.

Node Auctions. Broadcasting for candidates for a node N only returns platforms with the required capabilities for the node. There is no information about the usefulness or cost of allocating the node to the candidate. Blindly testing candidates for a node is an obvious source of inefficiency. Instead, the node is auctioned out to the candidates. Each bidding platform bids its marginal cost for executing the node. I.e., taking into account all previous tasks the platform has been allocated, how much more would it cost the platform to take on the extra task. The cost could for example be the total time needed to complete all tasks. To be efficient, it is important that the cost can be computed by the platform locally. We are currently only evaluating the cost of the current node, not the sub-TST rooted in the node. This leaves room for interesting extensions. Low bids are favorable and the candidates are sorted according to their bids. The bids are used as a heuristic function that increases the chance of finding a suitable platform early in the search.

7 Extending the FIPA Abstract Architecture for Delegation

In Section 3, we provided an overview of the software architecture being used to support the delegation-based collaborative system. It consists of an agent layer added to a legacy system. There are four agents in this layer with particular responsibilities, the Interface Agent, the Resource Agent, the Delegation Agent and the Executor Agent. In previous sections, we described the delegation process which includes recursive delegation, the generation of TSTs, allocation of tasks in TST's to agents, and the use of distributed constraint solving in order to guarantee the validity of an allocation and solution of a TST. This complex set of processes will be implemented in the software architecture by extending the FIPA Abstract Architecture with a number of application dependent services and protocols:

- We will define a Interface Service, Resource Service, Delegation Service and Executor Service, associated with each Interface, Resource, Delegation, and Executor Agent, respectively, on each platform. These services are local to agents and not global.
- We will also define three interaction protocols, the Capability Lookup Protocol, Auction Protocol, and Delegation Protocol. These protocols will be used by the agents to guide the interaction between them as the delegation process unfolds.

7.1 Services

To implement the Delegation Process the Directory Facilitator and four new services are needed. The *Delegation Service* is responsible for coordinating delegations. The Delegation Service uses the *Interface Service* to communicate with other platforms, the Directory Facilitator to find platforms with appropriate capabilities, the *Resource Service* to keep track of local resources and the *Executor Service* to execute tasks using the legacy system.

Directory Facilitator. The Directory Facilitator (DF) is part of the FIPA Abstract Architecture. It provides a registry over services where a service name is associated with an agent providing that service. In the collaborative architecture the DF is used to keep track of the capabilities of platforms. Every platform should register the names of the tasks that it has the capability to achieve. This provides a mechanism to find all platforms that have the appropriate capabilities for a particular task. To check that a platform also has the necessary resources a more elaborate procedure is needed which is provided by the Resource Service. The Directory Facilitator also implements the Capability Lookup protocol described below.

The Interface Service. The Interface Service, implemented by an Interface Agent, is a clearinghouse for communication. All requests for delegation and other types of communication pass through this service. Externally, it provides the interface to a specific robotic system. The Interface Service does not implement any protocols, rather it forwards approved messages to the right internal service.

The Resource Service. The Resource Service, implemented by a Resource Agent, is responsible for keeping track of the local resources of a platform. It determines whether the platform has the resources to achieve a particular task with a particular set of constraints. It also keeps track of the bookings of resources that are required by the tasks the platform has committed to. When a resource is booked a *booking constraint* is added to the local constraint store. During the execution of a complex task the Resource Service is responsible for monitoring the resource constraints of the task and detecting violations as soon as possible. Since resources are modeled using constraints this reasoning is mainly a constraint satisfaction problem (CSP) which is solved using local solvers that are part of the service.

In the prototype implementation, constraints are expressed in ESSENCE' which is a sub-set of the ESSENCE high-level language for specifying constraint problems [35]. The idea behind ESSENCE is to provide a high-level, solver independent, language which can be translated or compiled into solver specific languages. This opens up the possibility for different platforms to use different local solvers. We use the translator Tailor [37] which can compile ESSENCE' problems into either Minion [36] or ECLiPSe [65]. We currently use Minion as the local CSP solver. The Resource Service implements the Auction protocol described below.

The Delegation Service. The Delegation Service, implemented by a Delegation Agent, coordinates delegation requests to and from the platform using the Executor, Resource and Interface Services. It does this by implementing the Delegation Process described in Section 6. The Delegation Service implements the Delegation Protocol described below.

The Executor Service. The Executor Service, implemented by a Executor Agent, is responsible for executing tasks using the legacy system on the platform. In the simplest case this corresponds to calling a single function in the legacy system while in more complicated cases the Executor Service might have to call local planners to generate a local plan to achieve a task with a particular set of constraints.

7.2 Protocols

This section describes the three main protocols used in the collaboration framework: the Capability Lookup Protocol, the Auction Protocol, and the Delegation Protocol. An overview of the agents involved in the protocols is shown in Figure 11.

The Capability Lookup Protocol. The Capability Lookup Protocol is based on the FIPA Request Protocol. This protocol is used to find all platforms that have the

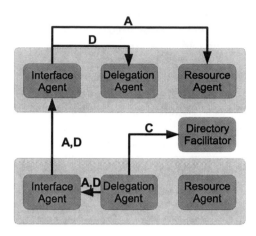

Fig. 11. An overview of the agents involved in the Auction (A), Capability Lookup (C), and Delegation (D) protocols

capabilities for a certain task. The content of the *request* message is the name of the task. The reply is an *inform* message with the platforms that have the capabilities required for the task.

The Auction Protocol. The Auction Protocol is based on the FIPA Request Protocol. The protocol is used to request bids for tasks from platforms. The bid should reflect the cost for the platform to accept the task and is calculated by an *auction strategy*. An auction strategy could for instance be the marginal cost strategy where the bid is the marginal cost (in time) for a platform to take on the task. The content of the *request* message is the task that is being auctioned out. If the platform makes a bid, then the reply is an *inform* message containing the task and the bid. Otherwise, a *refuse* message is returned. One reason for not making a bid could be that the platform lacks the capabilities or resources for the task.

The Delegation Protocol. The Delegation Protocol, which is an extension of the FIPA Contract Net protocol [34, 61], implements the Delegation Process described in Section 6. The Delegation Protocol, like the Contract Net Protocol, has two phases, each containing the sending and receiving of a message. The first phase allocates platforms to tasks satisfying the preconditions of the S-Delegate speech act and the second phase executes the task satisfying the postconditions of the S-Delegate speech act.

In the first phase a *call-for-proposal* message is sent from the delegator, and a *propose* or *refuse* message is returned by the potential contractor. The content is a declarative representation of the task in the form of a TST and a set of constraints. When a potential contractor receives a *call-for-proposal* message, an instance of the Delegation Protocol is started. When the first phase is completed, if successful, the preconditions for the S-Delegate speech act are satisfied and all the sub-tasks in the TST have been allocated to platforms such that all the constraints are satisfied.

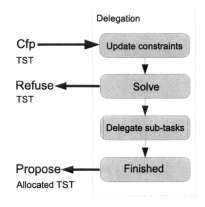

Fig. 12. An overview of the Delegation Protocol

In the second phase an *accept-proposal* is sent from the delegator to the contractor. This starts the execution of the task. If the execution is successful, then the contractor returns an *inform* message otherwise a *failure* message. Such failure messages will invoke repair processes that will not be described in this article.

An overview of the steps in the Delegate Protocol is shown in Figure 12. When a Delegation Agent receives a *call-for-proposal* message with a TST the platform becomes a potential contractor. To check if the platform can accept the delegation it first updates that part of the its constraint network representing all the constraints related to the TST. This is done by instantiating the platform specific resource constraints for the action associated with the top node of the TST. If the resulting constraint problem is inconsistent, then a *refuse* message is returned to the delegator. Otherwise, the resources required for the node are booked through the Resource Service and the sub-tasks of the TST are recursively delegated. When a platform books its resources, it places commitments in the form of constraints in its constraint stores and schedulers which reserve resources and schedule activities relative to the temporal constraints which are part of the TST solution.

For each sub-task of the TST the Delegation Protocol goes through the steps shown in Figure 13. First, it will use the Capability Lookup Protocol to find all the platforms that have the capabilities, but not necessarily the resources, to achieve the task. Then it will use the Auction Protocol to request bids from these platforms in parallel. The bids are used to decide the order in which the platforms are tried. The platform with the lowest bid, i.e. the lowest cost, will be allocated the task first. If that allocation fails, then the platform with the next lowest bid will be allocated the task. Allocating a task to a platform involves sending a *call-for-proposal* message with the task to the platform. This will trigger the Delegation Protocol on that platform. If an allocation fails, then backtracking starts. If backtracking has tested all the choices, then the potential contractor returns a *refuse* message to the delegator.

If all sub-tasks can either be allocated to the platform or delegated to some other platform, then a *propose* message with the allocated TST is returned to the delegator.

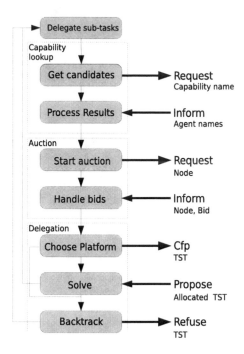

Fig. 13. An overview of the recursive delegation of sub-tasks part of the Delegation Protocol

8   A Collaborative UAS Case Study

On December 26, 2004, a devastating earthquake of high magnitude occurred off the west coast of Sumatra. This resulted in a tsunami which hit the coasts of India, Sri Lanka, Thailand, Indonesia, and many other islands. Both the earthquake and the tsunami caused great devastation. During the initial stages of the catastrophe, there was a great deal of confusion and chaos in setting into motion rescue operations in such wide geographic areas. The problem was exacerbated by a shortage of manpower, supplies, and machinery. The highest priorities in the initial stages of the disaster were searching for survivors in many isolated areas where road systems had become inaccessible and providing relief in the form of delivery of food, water, and medical supplies. Similar real-life scenarios have occurred more recently in China and Haiti where devastating earthquakes have caused tremendous material and human damage.

Let us assume that one has access to a fleet of autonomous unmanned helicopter systems with ground operation facilities. How could such a resource be used in the real-life scenario described?

A prerequisite for the successful operation would be the existence of a multi-agent software infrastructure for assisting emergency services. At the very least, one would require the system to allow mixed-initiative interaction with multiple platforms and ground operators in a robust, safe, and dependable manner. As far as the individual platforms are concerned, one would require a number of different capabilities, not necessarily shared by each individual platform, but by the fleet in total. These capabilities would include: the ability to scan and search for salient entities such as injured humans, building structures, or vehicles; the ability to monitor or survey these salient points of interest and continually collect and communicate information back to ground operators and other platforms to keep them situationally aware of current conditions; and the ability to deliver supplies or resources to these salient points of interest if required. For example, identified injured persons should immediately receive a relief package containing food, water, and medical supplies.

To be more specific in terms of the scenario, we can assume there are two separate legs or parts to the emergency relief scenario in the context sketched previously.

Leg I. In the first part of the scenario, it is essential that for specific geographic areas, the unmanned aircraft platforms cooperatively scan large regions in an attempt to identify injured persons. The result of such a cooperative scan would be a saliency map pinpointing potential victims and their geographical coordinates and associating sensory output such as high resolution photos and thermal images with the potential victims. The saliency map could then be used directly by emergency services or passed on to other unmanned aircrafts as a basis for additional tasks.

Leg II. In the second part of the scenario, the saliency map from Leg 1 would be used for generating and executing a plan for the UAS to deliver relief packages to the injured. This should also be done in a cooperative manner.

We will now consider a particular instance of the emergency services assistance scenario. In this instance there is a UAS consisting of two platforms (P_1 and P_2) and an operator (OP_1). In the first part of the scenario the UAS is given the task of searching two areas for victims. The main capability required by the platforms is to fly a search pattern scanning for people. In this scenario, both platforms have this capability. It is implemented by looking for salient features in the fused video streams from color and thermal cameras [59]. In the second part the UAS is given the task to deliver boxes with food and medical supplies to the identified victims. To transport a box it can either be carried directly by an unmanned aircraft or it can be loaded onto a carrier which is then transported to a key position from where the boxes are distributed to their final locations. In this scenario, both platforms have the capability to transport a single box while only platform P_1 has the capability to transport a carrier. Both platforms also have the capabilities to coordinate sequential and concurrent tasks.

8.1   Leg I: The Victim Search Case Study

The victim search case study covers the first part of the emergency services assistance scenario. In this particular scenario, see Figure 5 on page 217, the UAS should first scan Area$_A$ and Area$_B$ for survivors, and then fly to Dest$_4$ to be ready to load emergency supplies. The TST for this mission is shown in Figure 6 on page 218.

To carry out the mission, the operator needs to delegate the TST to one of the platforms. This is done by invoking the Delegation Protocol in the operator ground station.

Fig. 14. The schedule after assigning node N_0 to P_1

Fig. 15. The schedule after assigning node N_1 to P_1

The protocol will find a platform that can achieve the complex task and then give the operator the option to approve the choice. If the choice is approved, then the mission will be carried out.

The Delegation Agent of OP_1 starts the process of finding a platform that can achieve the TST by finding all platforms that have the capabilities for the top node N_0, which is both platforms. It then auctions out N_0 to both platforms to find the best initial choice. In this case, the marginal cost is the same for both platforms, so the first platform, P_1, is chosen. The Delegation Agent of OP_1 then sends a *call-for-proposal* message with the TST to the winner, P_1. This invokes the Delegation Protocol on P_1.

P_1 is now responsible for N_0 and for recursively delegating the nodes in the TST that it is not able to do itself. See Figure 14 for the schedule. The allocation algorithm traverses the TST in depth-first order. P_1 will first find a platform for node N_1. When the entire sub-TST rooted in N_1 is allocated then it will find an allocation for node N_4. Node N_1 is a composite action node which has the same marginal cost for all platforms. P_1 therefore allocates N_1 to itself. The extended schedule is shown in Figure 15. The constraints from nodes N_0–N_1 are added to the constraint network of P_1. The network is consistent because the composite action nodes describe a schedule without any restrictions.

Platform P_1 should now allocate the elementary action nodes N_2 and N_3. A capability lookup operation followed by an auction of node N_2 determines the candidates P_1 and P_2. A *call-for-proposal* message containing N_2 is sent to platform P_2.

P_2 receives the *call-for-proposal* message, loads and instantiates the platform's resource constraint for the *scan* action. The constraint network is connected to the constraint network of the TST. The network is then checked for consistency. Since the network is consistent, node N_2 is now allocated to platform P_2. P_2 returns a *propose* message to P_1. The constraint network now involves both platforms. Figure 16 shows the schedule.

Continuing with node N_3, platform P_1 searches for candidates for the node. The capability lookup and auctioning determines platform P_1 as a better choice than P_2 for the second scan node. P_1 delegates the node to itself since the extended constraint network is consistent. Figure 17 shows the extended schedule.

```
Node        11:00                              11:30      Platform
 0:         N0s ———————————————————— N0e         1:

 1:         N1s———————————— N1e                   1:

 2:         N2s ———N2e                             2:
```

Fig. 16. The schedule after assigning node N_2 to P_2

```
Node        11:00                              11:30      Platform
 0:         N0s ———————————————————— N0e         1:

 1:         N1s———————————— N1e                   1:

2,3:        N2s ———N2e N3s ———————— N3e          2,1:
```

Fig. 17. The schedule after assigning node N_3 to P_1

```
Node        11:00                              11:30      Platform
 0:         N0s ———————————————————— N0e         1:

1,4:        N1s———————————— N1e  N4s — N4e       1,2:

2,3:        N2s ———N2e N3s ———————— N3e          2,1:
```

Fig. 18. The schedule after assigning node N_4 to P_2, which is the complete schedule

The remaining node, N_4 is delegated to platform P_2. The entire TST is now allocated. The complete schedule is shown in Figure 18.

The operator approves the allocation and starts the mission. An *accept-proposal* message is sent to P_1. P_1 recursively traverses the TST marking the nodes as ready for execution in depth-first order. Nodes allocated to another platform are marked by sending a *accept-proposal* to the platform. P_1 therefore sends *accept-proposal* messages to P_2 for node N_2 and N_4. The execution starts and the platforms scans the area creating the saliency map shown in Figure 19.

8.2 Leg II: The Supply Delivery Case Study

The supply delivery case study covers the second part of the emergency services assistance scenario. One approach to solving this type of logistics problems is to use a task planner to generate a sequence of actions that will transport each box to its destination. Each action must then be executed by a platform. We have previously shown how to generate pre-allocated plans and monitor their execution [21, 51]. In this paper we show how a plan without explicit allocations expressed as a TST can be cooperatively allocated to a set of unmanned aircraft platforms which where not known at the time of planning.

Fig. 19. The disaster area with platforms P_1–P_3, survivors S_1–S_5, and operators OP_1 and OP_2

In this particular scenario, shown in Figure 19, five survivors (S_1–S_5) are found in Leg I, and there are two platforms (P_1–P_2) and one carrier available. At the same time another operator OP_2 is performing a mission with the platforms P_3 and P_4 north of the area in Figure 19. P_3 is currently idle and OP_1 is therefore allowed to borrow it if necessary.

To start Leg II, the operator creates a TST, for example using a planner, that will achieve the goal of distributing relief packages to all survivor locations in the saliency map. The resulting TST is shown in Figure 20. The TST contains a sub-TST (N_1–N_{12}) for loading a carrier with four boxes (N_2–N_6), delivering the carrier (N_7), and unloading the packages from the carrier and delivering them to the survivors (N_8–N_{12}). A package must also be delivered to the survivor in the right uppermost part of the region, far away from where most of the survivors were found (N_{13}). The delivery of packages can be done concurrently to save time, while the loading, moving, and unloading of the carrier is a sequential operation.

To delegate the TST, the Delegation Agent of OP_1 searches for a platform that can achieve the TST. It starts by finding all platforms that have the capabilities for the top node N_0, which is both platforms. It then auctions out N_0 to both platforms to find the best initial choice. In this case, the marginal cost is the same for both platforms and the first platform, P_1 is chosen. The Delegation Agent of OP_1 then sends a *call-for-proposal* message with the TST to the winner, P_1. This invokes the Delegation Protocol on P_1.

P_1 is now responsible for N_0 and for recursively delegating the nodes in the TST that it is not able to do itself. The allocation algorithm traverses the TST in depth-first order. P_1 will first find a platform for node N_1. When the entire sub-TST rooted in N_1 is allocated then it will find an allocation for node N_{13}. Nodes N_1 and N_2 are composite action nodes which have the same marginal cost for all platforms. P_1 therefore allocates

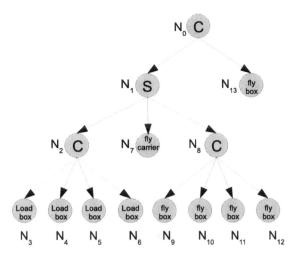

Fig. 20. The TST for the supply delivery case study

N_1 and N_2 to itself. The constraints from nodes N_0–N_2 are added to the constraint network of P_1. The network is consistent because the composite action nodes describe a schedule without any restrictions.

Below node N_2 are four elementary action nodes. Since P_1 is responsible for N_2, it tries to allocate them one at the time. For elementary action nodes, the choice of platform is the key to a successful allocation. This is because of each platform's unique state, constraint model for the action, and available resources. The candidates for node N_3 are platforms P_1 and P_2. P_1 is closest to the package depot and therefore gives the best bid for the node. P_1 is allocated to N_3. For node N_4, platform P_1 is still the best choice, and it is allocated to N_4. Given the new position of P_1 after being allocated N_3 and N_4, P_2 is now closest to the depot resulting in the lowest bid and is allocated to N_5 and N_6. The schedule initially defined by nodes N_0–N_2 is now also constrained by how long it takes for P_1 and P_2 to carry out action nodes N_3–N_6. The constraint network is distributed among platforms P_1 and P_2.

The next node to allocate for P_1 is node N_7, the carrier delivery node. P_1 is the only platform that has the capabilities for the fly carrier task and is allocated the node. Continuing with nodes N_8–N_{12}, the platform with the lowest bid for each node is platform P_1, since it is in the area after delivering the carrier. P_1, is therefore allocated all the nodes N_8–N_{12}.

The final node, N_{13}, is allocated to platform P_2 and the allocation is complete. The resulting schedule is shown in Figure 21.

The only non-local information used by P_1 was the capabilities of the available platforms which was gathered through a broadcast. Everything else is local. The bids are made by each platform based on local information and the consistency of the constraint network is checked through distributed constraint satisfaction techniques.

The total mission time is 58 minutes, which is much longer than the operator expected. Since the constraint problem defined by the allocation of the TST is distributed

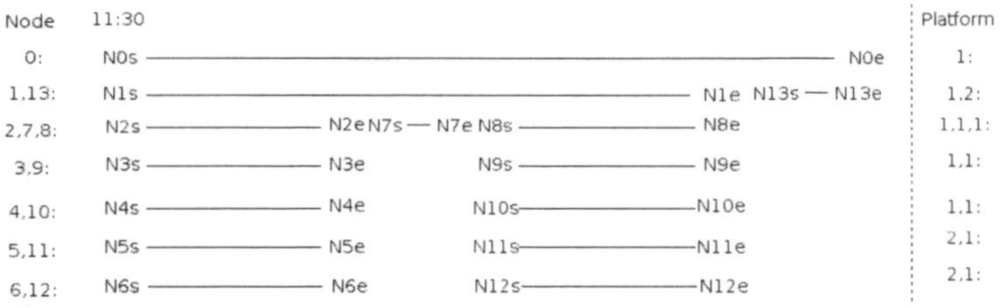

Node   11:30   Platform

0:      N0s ———————————————————————————————— N0e   1:

1,13:   N1s ——————————————————————— N1e N13s — N13e   1.2:

2,7,8: N2s ——————— N2e N7s — N7e N8s ——————— N8e   1.1.1:

3,9:   N3s ——————— N3e   N9s ——————— N9e   1.1:

4,10:   N4s ——————— N4e   N10s———————N10e   1.1:
                                                         2.1:
5,11:   N5s ——————— N5e   N11s———————N11e
                                                         2.1:
6,12:   N6s ——————— N6e   N12s———————N12e

Fig. 21. The complete schedule when using two platforms and no deadline

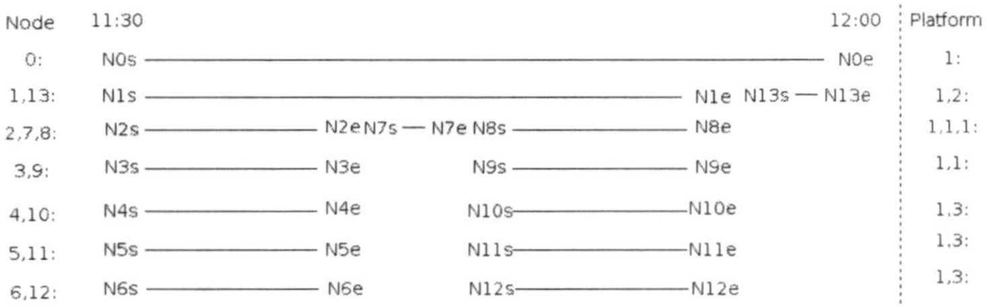

Node   11:30   12:00   Platform

0:      N0s ———————————————————————————————— N0e   1:

1,13:   N1s ——————————————————————— N1e N13s — N13e   1.2:

2,7,8: N2s ——————— N2e N7s — N7e N8s ——————— N8e   1.1.1:

3,9:   N3s ——————— N3e   N9s ——————— N9e   1.1:

4,10:   N4s ——————— N4e   N10s———————N10e   1.3:

5,11:   N5s ——————— N5e   N11s———————N11e   1.3:
                                                         1.3:
6,12:   N6s ——————— N6e   N12s———————N12e

Fig. 22. The resulting schedule after adding the new time constraint

between the platforms, it is possible for the operator to modify the constraint problem by adding more constraints, and in this way modify the resulting task allocation. The operator puts a time constraint on the mission, restricting the total time to 30 minutes.

To re-allocate the TST with the added constraint, operator OP_1 sends a *reject-proposal* to platform P_1. The added time constraint makes the current allocation inconsistent. The last allocated node must therefore be re-allocated. However, no platform for N_{13} can make the allocation consistent, not even the unused platform P_3. Backtracking starts. Platform P_1 is in charge, since it is responsible for allocating node N_{13}. The N_1 sub-network is disconnected. Trying different platforms for node N_{13}, P_1 discovers that N_{13} can be allocated to P_2. P_1 sends a *backjump-search* message to the platform in charge of the sub-TST with top-node N_1, which happens to be P_1. When receiving the message, P_1 continues the search for the backjump point. Since removing all constraints due to the allocation of node N_1 and its children made the problem consistent, the backjump point is in the sub-TST rooted in N_1. Removing the allocations for sub-tree N_8 does not make the problem consistent so further backjumping is necessary. Notice that with a single consistency check the algorithm could deduce that no possible allocation of N_8 and its children can lead to a consistent allocation of N_{13}. Removing the allocation for node N_7 does not make a difference either. However, removing the allocations for the sub-TST N_2 makes the problem consistent. When finding an allocation of N_{13} after removing the constraints from N_6 the allocation process continues from N_6 and tries the next platform for the node, P_1.

When the allocation reaches node N_{11} it is discovered that since P_1 has taken on nodes N_3–N_8, there is not enough time left for P_1 to unload the last two packages from the carrier. Instead P_3, even though it makes a higher bid for N_{11}–N_{12}, is allocated to both nodes. Finally platform P_2 is allocated to node N_{13}. It turns out that since platform P_2 helped P_1 loading the carrier, it has not enough time to deliver the final package. Instead, a new backjump point search starts, finding node N_5. The search continues from N_5. This time, nodes N_3–N_9 are allocated to platform P_1, platform P_3 is allocated to node N_{10}–N_{12}, and platform P_2 is allocated to node N_{13}. The allocation is consistent. The resulting schedule is shown in Figure 22. The allocation algorithm finishes on platform P_1, by sending a *propose* message back to the operator. The operator inspects the allocation and approves it, thereby confirming the delegation and starting the execution of the mission.

9 Related Work

Due to the multi-disciplinary nature of the work considered here, there is a vast amount of related work too numerous to mention. In addition to the work referenced in the article, we instead consider a number of representative references from the areas of autonomy, cooperative multi-robot systems, task allocation from a robotic perspective, and auctions.

The concept of autonomy has a long and active history in multi-agent systems [44, 47]. One early driving force was space missions that focused on the problem of interaction with autonomous agents and the adjustability of this autonomy [4, 26]. Later, Hexmoor and McLaughlan argue that reasoning about autonomy is an integral component of collaboration among computational units [45]. Hexmoor also argues that trust is essential for autonomy [46]. According to his definition, the autonomy of an agent A with respect to a task t is the degree of self-determination the agent possesses to perform the task. This is similar to the view on autonomy in our approach, where the level of autonomy for an agent is dependent on the strictness of the constraints on the tasks that are delegated to the agent.

Cooperative multi-robot systems have a long history in robotics, multi-agent systems and AI in general. One early study presented a generic scheme based on a distributed plan merging process [2], where robots share plans and coordinates their own plans to produce coordinated plans. In our approach, coordination is achieved by finding solutions to a distributed constraint problem representing the complex task, rather than by sharing and merging plans. Another early work is ALLIANCE [57], which is a behavior-based framework for instantaneous task assignment of loosely coupled subtasks with ordering dependencies. Each agent decides on its own what tasks to do based on its observations of the world and the other agents. Compared to our approach, this is a more reactive approach which does not consider what will happen in the future. M+ [3] integrates mission planning, task refinement and cooperative task allocation. It uses a task allocation protocol based on the Contract Net protocol with explicit, predefined capabilities and task costs. A major difference to our approach is that in M+ there is no temporally extended allocation. Instead, robots make incremental choices of tasks to perform from the set of executable tasks, which are tasks whose prerequisite tasks are achieved or underway. The M+CTA framework [1] is an extension of

M+, where a mission is decomposed into a partially ordered set of high-level tasks. Each task is defined as a set of goals to be achieved. The plan is distributed to each robot and task allocation is done incrementally like in M+. When a robot is allocated a task, it creates an individual plan for achieving the task's goals independently of the other agents. After the planning step, robots negotiate with each other to adapt their plans in the multi-robot context. Like most negotiation-based approaches, M+CTA first allocates the tasks and then negotiates to handle coordination. This is different from our approach which finds a valid allocation of all the tasks before committing to the allocation. ASyMTRe [58], uses a reconfigurable schema abstraction for collaborative task execution providing sensor sharing among robots, where connections among the schemas are dynamically formed at runtime. The properties of inputs and outputs of each schema is defined and by determining a valid information flow through a combination of schemas within, and across, robot team members a coalition for solving a particular task can be formed. Like ALLIANCE, this is basically a reactive approach which considers the current task, rather than a set of related tasks as in our approach. Other Contract-Net and auction-based systems similar to those described above are COMETS [53], MURDOCH system [39], Hoplites [49] and TAEMS [12].

Many task allocation algorithms are, as mentioned above, auction-based [13, 39, 49, 63, 71, 72]. There, tasks are auctioned out and allocated to the agent that makes the best bid. Bids are determined by a utility function. The auction concept decentralizes the task allocation process which is very useful especially in multi-robot systems, where centralized solutions are impractical. For tasks that have unrelated utilities, this approach has been very successful. The reason is that unrelated utilities guarantees that each task can be treated as an independent entity, and can be auctioned out without affecting other parts of the allocation. This means that a robot does not have to take other tasks into consideration when making a bid. More advanced auction protocols have been developed to handle dependencies between tasks. These are constructed to deal with complementarities. Examples are sequential single item auctions [50] and combinatorial auctions [64]. These auctions typically handle that different combinations of tasks have different bids, which can be compared to our model where different sets of allocations result in different restrictions to the constraint network between the platforms.

The sequential single item (SSI) auction [50] is of special interest since it is similar to our approach. In SSI auctions, like our task allocation approach, tasks are auctioned out in sequence, one at a time to make sure the new task fits with the previous allocations. The difference is what happens when there is no agent that can accept the next task. In SSI auctions common strategies are to return a task in exchange for the new task or to start exchanging tasks with other agents. This is basically a greedy approach which is incomplete. Our approach on the other hand uses backtracking which is a complete search procedure. Normally SSI auctions are applied to problems where it is easy to find a solution but it is hard to find a good solution. When allocating the tasks in a TST it is often hard to find any solution and SSI auctions are therefore not appropriate.

Combinatorial auctions deal with complementarities by bidding on bundles containing multiple items. Each bidder places bids on all the bundles that are of interest, which could be exponentially many. The auctioneer must then select the best set of bids, called the winner determination problem, which is NP-hard [64]. Since all agents have to bid on all bundles, in our case tasks, they could accept in one round it means that even in the best case there is a very high computational cost involved in using combinatorial auctions. Another weakness is that they do not easily lend themselves to a recursive process where tasks are recursively decomposed and allocated. Our approach, on the other hand, is suitable for recursive allocation and by using heuristic search will try the most likely allocations first which should result in much better average case performance.

10   Conclusions

Collaborative robotic systems have much to gain by leveraging results from the area of multi-agent systems and in particular agent-oriented software engineering. Agent-oriented software engineering has much to gain by using collaborative robotic systems as a testbed. We have proposed and specified a formally grounded generic collaborative system shell for robotic systems and human operated ground control systems. The software engineering approach is based on the FIPA Abstract Architecture and uses JADE to implement the system shell. The system shell is generic in the sense that it can be integrated with legacy robotic systems using a limited set of assumptions. Collaboration is formalized in terms of the concept of delegation and delegation is instantiated as a speech act. The formal characterization of the Speech act has a BDI flavor and KARO, which is an amalgam of dynamic logic and epistemic/doxastic logic, is used in the formal characterization. Tasks are central to the delegation process. Consequently, a flexible, specification language for tasks is introduced in the form of Task Specification Trees. Task Specification Trees provide a formal bridge between the abstract characterization of delegation as a speech act and its implementation in the collaborative system shell. Using this idea, the semantics of both delegation and tasks is grounded in the implementation in the form of a distributed constraint problem which when solved results in the allocation of tasks and resources to agents. We show the potential of this approach by targeting a real-life scenario consisting of UAV's and human resources in an emergency services application. The results described here should be considered a mature iteration of many ideas both formal and pragmatic which will continue to be pursued in additional iterations as future work.

References

1. Alami, R., Botelho, S.C.: Plan-based multi-robot cooperation. In: Advances in Plan-Based Control of Robotic Agents (2001)
2. Alami, R., Ingrand, F., Qutub, S.: A scheme for coordinating multirobot planning activities and plans execution. In: Proc. ECAI (1998)
3. Botelho, S., Alami, R.: M+: a scheme for multi-robot cooperation through negotiated task allocation and achievement. In: Proc. ICRA (1999)
4. Bradshaw, J., Sierhuis, M., Acquisti, A., Gawdiak, Y., Jeffers, R., Suri, N., Greaves, M.: Adjustable autonomy and teamwork for the personal satellite assistant. In: Proc. IJCAI Workshop on Autonomy, Delegation, and Control: Interacting with Autonomous Agents (2001)
5. Castelfranchi, C., Falcone, R.: Toward a theory of delegation for agent-based systems. Robotics and Autonomous Systems 24, 141–157 (1998)

6. Cohen, P., Levesque, H.: Intention is choice with commitment. Artificial Intelligence 42(3), 213–261 (1990)
7. Cohen, P., Levesque, H.: Teamwork. Nous, Special Issue on Cognitive Science and AI 25(4), 487–512 (1991)
8. Conte, G., Doherty, P.: Vision-based unmanned aerial vehicle navigation using georeferenced information. EURASIP Journal of Advances in Signal Processing (2009)
9. Conte, G., Hempel, M., Rudol, P., Lundström, D., Duranti, S., Wzorek, M., Doherty, P.: High accuracy ground target geo-location using autonomous micro aerial vehicle platforms. In: Proceedings of the AIAA 2008 Guidance, Navigation, and Control Conference (2008)
10. Dastani, M., Meyer, J.J.C.: A practical agent programming language. In: Dastani, M., Hindriks, K.V., Sterling, M.P.P.,, L. (eds.) Proc. of the AAMAS 2007 Workshop on Programming Multi-Agent Systems (ProMAS 2007), pp. 72–87 (2007)
11. Davis, E., Morgenstern, L.: A first-order theory of communication and multi-agent plans. Journal Logic and Computation 15(5), 701–749 (2005)
12. Decker, K.: TAEMS: A framework for environment centered analysis and design of coordination mechanisms. In: Foundations of Distributed Artificial Intelligence. Wiley Inter-Science, Chichester (1996)
13. Dias, M., Zlot, R., Kalra, N., Stentz, A.: Market-based multirobot coordination: a survey and analysis. Proc. of IEEE 94(1), 1257–1270 (2006)
14. Doherty, P.: Advanced research with autonomous unmanned aerial vehicles. In: Proceedings on the 9th International Conference on Principles of Knowledge Representation and Reasoning (2004), extended abstract for plenary talk
15. Doherty, P.: Knowledge representation and unmanned aerial vehicles. In: Proceedings of the IEEE Conference on Intelligent Agent Technolology, IAT 2005 (2005)
16. Doherty, P., Granlund, G., Kuchcinski, K., Sandewall, E., Nordberg, K., Skarman, E., Wiklund, J.: The WITAS unmanned aerial vehicle project. In: Proceedings of the 14th European Conference on Artificial Intelligence, pp. 747–755 (2000)
17. Doherty, P., Haslum, P., Heintz, F., Merz, T., Persson, T., Wingman, B.: A distributed architecture for intelligent unmanned aerial vehicle experimentation. In: Proceedings of the 7th International Symposium on Distributed Autonomous Robotic Systems (2004)
18. Doherty, P., Kvarnström, J.: TALplanner: A temporal logic based forward chaining planner. Annals of Mathematics and Artificial Intelligence 30, 119–169 (2001)
19. Doherty, P., Kvarnström, J.: TALplanner: A temporal logic based planner. Artificial Intelligence Magazine (Fall Issue 2001)
20. Doherty, P., Kvarnström, J.: Temporal action logics. In: Lifschitz, V., van Harmelen, F., Porter, F. (eds.) The Handbook of Knowledge Representation, ch. 18, pp. 709–757. Elsevier, Amsterdam (2008)
21. Doherty, P., Kvarnström, J., Heintz, F.: A temporal logic-based planning and execution monitoring framework for unmanned aircraft systems. Journal of Automated Agents and Multi-Agent Systems 19(3), 332–377 (2009)
22. Doherty, P., Landén, D., Heintz, F.: A distributed task specification language for mixed-initiative delegation. In: Proceedings of the 13th International Conference on Principles and Practice of Multi-Agent Systems, PRIMA (2010)
23. Doherty, P., Łukaszewicz, W., Szałas, A.: Approximative query techniques for agents with heterogenous ontologies and perceptual capabilities. In: Proceedings on the 7th International Conference on Information Fusion (2004)
24. Doherty, P., Łukaszewicz, W., Szałas, A.: Communication between agents with heterogeneous perceptual capabilities. Journal of Information Fusion 8(1), 56–69 (2007)
25. Doherty, P., Meyer, J.-J.C.: Towards a delegation framework for aerial robotic mission scenarios. In: Proceedings of the 11th International Workshop on Cooperative Information Agents (2007)

26. Dorais, G., Bonasso, R., Kortenkamp, D., Pell, B., Schreckenghost, D.: Adjustable autonomy for human-centered autonomous systems on mars. In: Proc. Mars Society Conference (1998)
27. Dunin-Keplicz, B., Verbrugge, R.: Teamwork in Multi-Agent Systems. Wiley, Chichester (2010)
28. Duranti, S., Conte, G., Lundström, D., Rudol, P., Wzorek, M., Doherty, P.: LinkMAV, a prototype rotary wing micro aerial vehicle. In: Proceedings of the 17th IFAC Symposium on Automatic Control in Aerospace (2007)
29. Bellifemine, F., Greenwood, G.C.: Developing Multi-Agent Systems with JADE. John Wiley and Sons, Ltd., Chichester (2007)
30. Bellifemine, F., Bergenti, F., Caire, G., Poggi, A.: JADE – a Java agent development framework. In: Bordini, R.H., Dastani, M., Dix, J., Seghrouchni, A. (eds.) Multi-Agent Programming - Languages, Platforms and Applications. Springer, Heidelberg (2005)
31. Falcone, R., Castelfranchi, C.: The human in the loop of a delegated agent: The theory of adjustable social autonomy. IEEE Transactions on Systems, Man and Cybernetics–Part A: Systems and Humans 31(5), 406–418 (2001)
32. Foundation for Intelligent Physical Agents: FIPA Abstract Architecture Specification, http://www.fipa.org
33. Foundation for Intelligent Physical Agents: FIPA Communicative Act Library Specification, http://www.fipa.org
34. Foundation for Intelligent Physical Agents: FIPA Contract Net Interaction Protocol Specification, http://www.fipa.org
35. Frisch, A., Grum, M., Jefferson, C., Hernández, B.M., Miguel, I.: The Design of ESSENCE: A Constraint Language for Specifying Combinatorial Problems. In: IJCAI, pp. 80–87 (2007)
36. Gent, I.P., Jefferson, C., Miguel, I.: Minion: A fast scalable constraint solver. In: Proceedings of ECAI 2006, Riva del Garda, pp. 98–102 (2006)
37. Gent, I.P., Miguel, I., Rendl, A.: Tailoring solver-independent constraint models: A case study with essence' and minion. In: Proceedings of the 7th International Conference on Abstraction, Reformulation, and Approximation (SARA 2007), pp. 184–199 (2007)
38. Gerkey, B.: On multi-robot task allocation. Ph.D. thesis (2003)
39. Gerkey, B., Mataric, M.: Sold!: Auction methods for multi-robot coordination. IEEE Transactions on Robotics and Automation (2001)
40. Heintz, F., Doherty, P.: DyKnow: A knowledge processing middleware framework and its relation to the JDL fusion model. Journal of Intelligent and Fuzzy Systems 17(4) (2006)
41. Heintz, F., Doherty, P.: DyKnow federations: Distributing and merging information among UAVs. In: Eleventh International Conference on Information Fusion, FUSION 2008 (2008)
42. Heintz, F., Kvarnström, J., Doherty, P.: A stream-based hierarchical anchoring framework. In: Proceedings of the International Conference on Intelligent Robots and Systems, IROS (2009)
43. Heintz, F., Kvarnström, J., Doherty, P.: Bridging the sense-reasoning gap: DyKnow - stream-based middleware for knowledge processing. Journal of Advanced Engineering Informatics 24(1), 14–25 (2010)
44. Hexmoor, H., Kortenkamp, D.: Autonomy control software. An Introductory Article and Special Issue of Journal of Experimental and Theoretical Artificial Intelligence (2000)
45. Hexmoor, H., McLaughlan, B.: Computationally adjustable autonomy. Journal of Scalable Computing: Practive and Experience 8(1), 41–48 (2007)
46. Hexmoor, H., Rahimi, S., Chandran, R.: Delegations guided by trust and autonomy. Web Intelligence and Agent Systems 6(2), 137–155 (2008)
47. Hexmoor, H., Castelfranchi, C., Falcone, R. (eds.): Agent Autonomy. Springer, Heidelberg (2003)

48. van der Hoek, W., van Linder, B., Meyer, J.-J.C.: An integrated modal approach to rational agents. In: Wooldridge, M., Rao, A. (eds.) Foundations of Foundations of Rational Agency. Applied Logic Series, vol. 14. An Integrated Modal Approach to Rational Agents (1998)
49. Kaldra, N., Ferguson, D., Stentz, A.: Hoplites: A market-based framework for planned tight coordination in multirobot teams. In: Proc. ICRA (2005)
50. Koenig, S., Keskinocak, P., Tovey, C.: Progress on agent coordination with cooperative auctions. In: Proc. AAAI (2010)
51. Kvarnström, J., Doherty, P.: Automated planning for collaborative systems. In: Proceedings of the International Conference on Control, Automation, Robotics and Vision, ICARCV (2010)
52. Landén, D., Heintz, F., Doherty, P.: Complex task allocation in mixed-initiative delegation: A UAV case study (early innovation). In: Proceedings of the 13th International Conference on Principles and Practice of Multi-Agent Systems, PRIMA (2010)
53. Lemaire, T., Alami, R., Lacroix, S.: A distributed tasks allocation scheme in multi-uav context. In: Proc. ICRA (2004)
54. Magnusson, M., Landen, D., Doherty, P.: Planning, executing, and monitoring communication in a logic-based multi-agent system. In: 18th European Conference on Artificial Intelligence, ECAI 2008 (2008)
55. Merz, T., Rudol, P., Wzorek, M.: Control System Framework for Autonomous Robots Based on Extended State Machines. In: Proceedings of the International Conference on Autonomic and Autonomous Systems (2006)
56. Modi, P., Shen, W.M., Tambe, M., Yokoo, M.: Adopt: Asynchronous distributed constraint optimization with quality guarantees. AI 161 (2006)
57. Parker, L.E.: Alliance: An architecture for fault tolerant multi-robot cooperation. IEEE Trans. Robot. Automat. 14(2), 220–240 (1998)
58. Parker, L.E., Tang, F.: Building multi-robot coalitions through automated task solution synthesis. Proceeding of the IEEE, Special Issue on Multi-Robot Systems (2006)
59. Rudol, P., Doherty, P.: Human body detection and geolocalization for UAV search and rescue missions using color and thermal imagery. In: Proc. of the IEEE Aerospace Conference (2008)
60. Rudol, P., Wzorek, M., Conte, G., Doherty, P.: Micro unmanned aerial vehicle visual servoing for cooperative indoor exploration. In: Proceedings of the IEEE Aerospace Conference (2008)
61. Smith, R.: The contract net protocol. IEEE Transactions on Computers C-29(12) (1980)
62. Telecom Italia Lab: The Java Agent Development Framework (JADE), http://jade.tilab.com
63. Viguria, A., Maza, I., Ollero, A.: Distributed service-based cooperation in aerial/ground robot teams applied to fire detection and extinguishing missions. Advanced Robotics 24, 1–23 (2010)
64. de Vries, S., Vohra, R.: Combinatorial auctions: A survey. Journal on Computing 15(3), 284–309 (2003)
65. Wallace, M.G., Schimpf, J., Novello, S.: A Platform for Constraint Logic Programming. ICL System Journal 12(1), 159–200 (1997)
66. Wzorek, M., Conte, G., Rudol, P., Merz, T., Duranti, S., Doherty, P.: From motion planning to control – a navigation framework for an unmanned aerial vehicle. In: Proceedings of the 21st Bristol International Conference on UAV Systems (2006)
67. Wzorek, M., Doherty, P.: Reconfigurable path planning for an autonomous unmanned aerial vehicle. In: Proceedings of the 16th International Conference on Automated Planning and Scheduling, pp. 438–441 (2006)

68. Wzorek, M., Kvarnström, J., Doherty, P.: Choosing path replanning strategies for unmanned aircraft systems. In: Proceedings of the International Conference on Automated Planning and Scheduling, ICAPS (2010)
69. Wzorek, M., Landen, D., Doherty, P.: GSM technology as a communication media for an autonomous unmanned aerial vehicle. In: Proceedings of the 21st Bristol International Conference on UAV Systems (2006)
70. Yokoo, M.: Asynchronous weak-commitment search for solving distributed constraint satisfaction problems. In: Montanari, U., Rossi, F. (eds.) CP 1995. LNCS, vol. 976. Springer, Heidelberg (1995)
71. Zlot, R.: An auction-based approach to complex task allocation for multirobot teams. Ph.D. thesis (2006)
72. Zlot, R., Stentz, A.: Complex task allocation for multiple robots. In: Proc. ICRA (2005)

Author Index